CONGRESS, THE CONSTITUTION, AND THE SUPREME COURT

CONGRESS,
THE CONSTITUTION,
AND
THE SUPREME COURT

BY

CHARLES WARREN

AUTHOR OF "A HISTORY OF THE AMERICAN BAR",
"THE SUPREME COURT IN UNITED STATES HISTORY", ETC.

BOSTON
LITTLE, BROWN, AND COMPANY
1925

342.73
W251c

Copyright, 1925,
BY LITTLE, BROWN, AND COMPANY.

All rights reserved

Published October, 1925

FEB 1 6 1926
213114
Pol. Sci.

PRINTED IN THE UNITED STATES OF AMERICA

PREFACE

THE story is told that, when Alexander Hamilton was killed in a duel, in 1804, a meeting of staunch Federalists gathered in Maryland to deplore the great national loss; whereat, one candid citizen exclaimed that, after listening to his friends' expressions of lament, he must state that his own grief was greater than theirs, "for, as long as Hamilton lived, he had never been put to the labor and trouble of investigating questions for himself, and now that Hamilton was dead, he, alas, would be forced to the dire necessity of thinking for himself."[1]

The function which the Supreme Court of the United States was intended to exercise and which it has exercised in relation to Acts of Congress is of vital concern to American citizens, men and women alike. In the present era of extension of Federal legislation, an accurate knowledge of this subject is of especial importance. This book is an effort to supply the facts, so that each American may "think for himself" or herself, and not rely on the say-so of politicians, labor-leaders, or social reformers, of whatever degree of eminence. It may serve as a check on those who (as Caesar A. Rodney long ago said in Congress) "hop and skip over truth, and perch upon assertion and call it truth." Declamation must bow before history and actual cases.

[1] See William Cost Johnson of Maryland, in the House, Oct. 12, 1837. 25th Cong., 1st Sess.

PREFACE

This book is intended to afford a clear idea of the Constitution as an American document embodying American ideas, and of the functions which the Court as an American invention was intended to exercise. Just as a written Constitution amendable only by the people was wholly an American idea, so the proposal of a Court with authority to determine when Congress had overstepped the bounds set by the Constitution and to curb attempts by Congress to amend or alter the Constitution was purely American; it was the result of a determination to escape from the English system of an omnipotent Parliament unrestricted by any Court; it was a rejection of the British plan.

The book contains a full statement of the historical origins of the power of the Court to disregard an Act of Congress when in conflict with the Constitution. It presents, for the first time, a detailed statement of the views of the early Congresses on the subject; for it was the men who composed the National Legislature in the early days who were primarily interested to see that the Court did not "usurp" any powers. The book presents, furthermore, an extended and detailed consideration of the practical operation of various proposals recently made to abolish or impair the power of the Court. All Americans should give careful thought to the probable effect of an adoption of either of these (though similar proposals have, several times in the past, been rejected by Congress). Especially should Americans realize the facts as to the slight extent of the alleged evils for which the proposals are suggested as a remedy, and hence the slight basis or need for the proposed changes in the powers of the Court. The book includes a brief description of every case in which the Court has held an Act of Congress unconstitutional, as well as a description of the cases decided by the Court, whether on constitutional grounds or otherwise, especially affecting Labor.

An attempt has been made to state all this in language that, while exact, may be easily understandable by every layman, as well as by lawyers, and to afford to them at least the facts, on which any conclusions at which they may arrive must be based.

"The Constitution has but two enemies, whether foreign or domestic, who are in the least to be feared. The first of these is ignorance — ignorance of its contents, ignorance of its meaning, ignorance of the great truths on which it is founded and of the great things that have been done in its name. And the second is indifference — the sort of indifference which leads many people, otherwise well enough behaved, to ignore both the rights and duties of citizenship."[1]

CHARLES WARREN.

WASHINGTON, D.C.

[1] *What does the Constitution mean to you?* by John W. Davis, *Amer. Bar Ass. Journal* (July, 1925), XI.

CONTENTS

CHAPTER		PAGE
	PREFACE	V
I.	THE CONSTITUTION AND AMERICAN IDEAS	3
II.	THE CONSTITUTION AND THE COURT	41
III.	THE BILL OF RIGHTS AND THE COURT	75
IV.	EARLY CONGRESSES AND THE COURT	95
V.	THE PROPOSAL TO MAKE CONGRESS THE SUPREME AND FINAL JUDGE OF ITS OWN POWERS	128
VI.	THE PROPOSAL TO VEST IN A MINORITY OF THE COURT THE POWER TO CONTROL ITS DECISIONS	178
VII.	LABOR AND THE SUPREME COURT	222
VIII.	THE INDEPENDENCE OF THE COURT	246
IX.	DECISIONS OF THE COURT HOLDING ACTS OF CONGRESS UNCONSTITUTIONAL	273
	INDEX	303

CONGRESS, THE CONSTITUTION, AND THE SUPREME COURT

"When I consider the amazing extent of this country, the immense population which is to fill it, the influence of the government we are to form will have, not only on the present generation of our people and their multiplied posterity, but on the whole globe — I am lost in the magnitude of the object." — JAMES WILSON, in the Federal Convention, June 25, 1787.

"We are providing for our posterity, for our children and our grandchildren, who would be as likely to be citizens of new Western States as of old States." — ROGER SHERMAN, in the Federal Convention, July 14, 1787.

"The Constitution is a written instrument. As such its meaning does not alter. That which it meant when adopted, it means now. Being a grant of powers to a government, its language is general, and as changes come in social and political life it embraces in its grasp all new conditions which are within the scope of the powers in terms conferred. . . . Those things which are within its grants of power, as those grants were understood when made, are still within them, and those things not within them remain still excluded. . . . It must also be remembered that the framers of the Constitution were not mere visionaries, toying with speculations or theories, but practical men, dealing with the facts of political life as they understood them, putting into form the government they were creating, and prescribing in language clear and intelligible the powers that government was to take. . . ." — BREWER, J., in *South Carolina* v. *United States* (1905), 199 U. S. 437, 448, 456.

"In bestowing the eulogies due to the particular and internal checks of power, it ought not the less to be remembered that they are neither the sole nor the chief palladium of constitutional liberty. The people who are authors of this blessing must also be its guardians. Their eyes must be ever ready to mark, their voice to pronounce, and their arms to repel or repair, aggressions on the authority of their Constitutions." — JAMES MADISON, in *National Gazette* (Phil.), February 6, 1792.

"It is our propitious fortune to exist under a Government that has, in the main, answered all the great ends for which governments are instituted — enjoyed, in fact, a system of regulated liberty more perfect in its past operations than any which has hitherto existed in the world. It is the part of wisdom to abstain from change, until the actual existence or threatened approach of danger is clearly and satisfactorily demonstrated." — GEORGE McDUFFIE of South Carolina, in the House, Feb. 15, 1826. *19th Cong., 1st Sess.*

CONGRESS, THE CONSTITUTION, AND THE SUPREME COURT

CHAPTER ONE

THE CONSTITUTION AND AMERICAN IDEAS

"The Constitution has laid down the fundamental and immutable laws of justice for our Government, and the majority that constitutes the Government should not violate these. The Constitution is made to control the Government, it has no other object." — WILLIAM HARPER of South Carolina, in the Senate, April 14, 1826. *19th Cong., 1st Sess.*

"It is not to the scrip of parchment on which the Constitution was originally enrolled, that we are to look for the people's rights. Instead of looking for the people's rights, it is there you (Congress) must search for *your* powers. It is in that instrument, the people have told you what they have given; and such powers as they have not there given, they have expressly retained." — MICAH TAIL of Kentucky, in the House, Jan. 20, 1817. *14th Cong., 2d Sess.*

"The framers of the Constitution took particular care, not only to define the power they intended to give, but the objects to which that power should be applied, and, therefore, but for these defined objects, Congress have no powers at all." — LABAN WHEATON of Massachusetts, in the House, Jan. 9, 1813. *12th Cong., 2d Sess.*

"Our government is a government of checks; the power given by the Constitution to the Legislature is not *general*, but special; it is not *omnipotent*, but *limited;* therefore, *necessarily* a check against it must exist somewhere." — AARON OGDEN of New Jersey, in the Senate, Feb. 2, 1802. *7th Cong., 1st Sess.*

"It is impossible to avoid error of construction, if the Constitution of the United States be regarded (as it most frequently is by American statesmen) as furnishing the whole fundamental law governing the action of the Federal Government. The Constitutions of the several States form as much a part of the great code of constitutional law as the Constitution of the United States. The latter is but an emanation of the former, and depends essentially for the character, extent and exercise of its powers, upon proper understanding of the powers reserved to the States." — JOHN MCKINLEY of Alabama, in the Senate, March 26, 1828. *20th Cong., 1st Sess.*

An American citizen will never understand the form of government under which he is living, unless he understands why we must have a Supreme Court. And he will never understand why we must have a Supreme Court, until he understands the form of government under which he is living. He must thoroughly grasp the fact that the existence of the American form of government — a federal republic with limited national powers — implies and requires for its preservation the existence of a Supreme Court. The retention of such a republic is inseparably bound up with the retention of a Court having authority to enforce the limitation of national powers. "No conviction is deeper, in my mind," said Daniel Webster, "than that the maintenance of the Judicial power is essential and indispensable to the very being of this Government. The Constitution, without it, would be no Constitution — the Government, no Government. . . . *By the absolute necessities of the case*, the members of the Supreme Court become judges of the extent of constitutional powers." [1]

[1] Daniel Webster, in the House, Jan. 25, 1826 (*19th Cong., 1st Sess.*), continued: "The Judicial power is the protecting power of the whole Government. Its position is upon the outer wall. From the very nature of things and the frame of the Constitution, it forms the point at which our different systems of Government meet in collision, when collision unhappily exists."

Webster said in the Senate, Jan. 26, 27, 1830 (*21st Cong., 1st Sess.*): "The people, then, sir, erected this government. They gave it a Constitution, and in that Constitution they have enumerated the powers which they bestow on it. They have made it a limited government. They have defined its authority. They have restrained it to the exercise of such powers as are granted; and all others, they declare, are reserved to the States or the people. But, sir, they have not stopped here. If they had, they would have accomplished

Suppress its functions and the Constitution ceases to be a supreme law capable of enforcement, and becomes whatever the Congress, from time to time, decides it shall be.

It is, of course, possible to have a republic without a Supreme Court; but it will be a republic with a consolidated and autocratic government, a government in which the States and the citizens will possess no right or power save such as Congress, in its absolute discretion, sees fit to leave to them. Americans can, of course, adopt such a form of government if they choose — but they should adopt it consciously and by express action; they should not change their present form unwittingly or by indirection; they should not destroy its fundamental features, without realizing that it is the foundation which they are destroying. It is because American citizens have not realized that attacks upon the Supreme Court are attacks upon the very form of government of the United States, that these attacks have hitherto been regarded with so little attention by the average man. It is because so many American citizens seem to have the belief that Congress has the power to do anything which it is not expressly forbidden to do by the Constitution, that they are inclined to be resentful whenever the Court fails to

---

but half their work. No definition can be so clear as to avoid possibility of doubt; no limitation so precise as to exclude all uncertainty. Who, then, shall construe this grant of the people? Who shall interpret their will, where it may be supposed they have left it doubtful? With whom do they repose this ultimate right of deciding on the powers of the government? . . . To whom lies the last appeal? This, sir, the Constitution itself decides also, by declaring: 'That the judicial power shall extend to all cases arising under the Constitution and laws of the United States.' These two provisions, sir, cover the whole ground. They are, in truth, the keystone of the arch. With these, it is a Constitution; without them, it is a Confederacy."

uphold Congress in the exercise of some particular power which these citizens may think desirable. They entirely overlook the fact that, under the Constitution, Congress only possesses those limited powers granted to it by that instrument, all other powers being reserved to the States; and that if it is desirable that Congress should possess any other powers, they must be vested, and can be vested, in that body, only by action of the peoples of three fourths of the States in adopting a Constitutional Amendment.[1]

One hundred and fifty years ago (in June, 1776) George Mason of Virginia, in writing the first Bill of Rights in this country, placed at its head this sentiment — that "no free government or the blessing of liberty can be preserved to any people but by . . . frequent recurrence to fundamental principles." Benjamin Franklin followed this, three months later (in September, 1776), in his Bill of Rights for Pennsylvania — that "a frequent recurrence to fundamental principles . . . is absolutely necessary to preserve the blessings of liberty and keep a government free." And four years later, John Adams, in

---

[1] "This Government is to be administered according to written law, applied to defined objects and situations. It was a Government of definition and not of trust and discretion." William Vans Murray of Maryland, in the House, April 12, 1792. *2d Cong., 1st Sess.*

"This is a Government constituted for particular purposes only; and the powers granted to carry it into effect are specifically enumerated and disposed among the various branches. If those powers are insufficient, or if they are improperly distributed, it is not *our* fault, or within *our* power to remedy. The People, who bestowed them, must grant further powers, organize those already granted, in a more perfect manner, or suffer from the defect. *We* can neither enlarge nor modify this. This was the ground on which the friends of government supported the Constitution. It was a safe ground; and I venture to say it could not have been supported on any other." Alexander White of Virginia, in the House, June 18, 1789. *1st Cong., 1st Sess.*

CONSTITUTION AND AMERICAN IDEAS 7

the Massachusetts Bill of Rights in 1780, amplified it — that "a frequent recurrence to the principles of the Constitution . . . is absolutely necessary to preserve the advantages of liberty and to maintain a free government. The people . . . have a right to require of their law-givers and magistrates an exact and constant observance of them." Fifteen years later, the same thought was expressed by a great Englishman, Edmund Burke, who wrote: "The spirit of change that is gone abroad; the total contempt which prevails with you and may come to prevail with us, of all ancient institutions, when set in opposition to a present sense of inconvenience or to the bent of a present inclination; all these considerations make it not unadvisable, in my opinion, to call back our attention to the true principles of our own domestick laws."

For a "recurrence to fundamental principles", for a knowledge of the "true principles of our domestick laws", we must resort to history. And to appreciate why the Supreme Court has the power which it exercises, we must know something not only of the history of that part of the Federal Constitution which deals with the Supreme Court in its relation to Acts of Congress, but also of the history of the State Constitutions from which sources the Federal Constitution was in a large part drawn.

During the four hot summer months of 1787, in Philadelphia, fifty-five men — delegates from twelve States — took part in framing a new form of government. The proceedings of that Federal Convention should particularly appeal to the young men and women of this country; for it was a meeting of comparatively young men. Six of the fifty-five were under thirty-two years of age; forty-one were under fifty years of age; and only three were over sixty. George Washington, the President of the Convention, was only fifty-five; Edmund Randolph, who introduced the Virginia Plan (which was a basis for the final Constitution), was thirty-four, and James Madison, who drafted it, was thirty-six; Charles Pinckney of South Carolina, from whose plan much of the Constitution was taken, was only twenty-nine; Gouverneur Morris, who took a leading part in preparing the wording of the final draft, was thirty-five; Alexander Hamilton, to whose efforts in *The Federalist* the ratification of the Constitution was largely due, was only thirty.[1] On the other hand, men to-day, who may be called upon to take part in the administration and improvement of their government, will do well to note that it was largely due to the tactful wisdom and long experience of an old man of eighty-one that the members of the Convention ever finally agreed on any Constitution. And the words of Benjamin Franklin, in the closing hour of the Convention, may well be imprinted on the minds of all legislators, as the foundation for every successful achievement in government.

[1] Credit for phrasing the final draft has been given to Gouverneur Morris by historians, partly on the basis of his own assertions; see *The Framing of the Constitution of the United States* (1913), by Max Farrand. An unpublished letter from Timothy Pickering to John Marshall, in the *Pickering Papers MSS* in the Massachusetts Historical Society Library, is believed by the present writer to make it doubtful whether credit is wholly due to Morris. Writing, March 10, 1828, Pickering said: "James Wilson once told me that after the Constitution had been finally settled, it was committed to him to be critically examined respecting its style, in order that the instrument might appear with the most perfect precision and accuracy of language." And to John Lowell, Pickering wrote, January 9, 1828, that Wilson told him that "its final revision in regard to correctness of style was committed to him."

I confess that there are several parts of this Constitution which I do not at present approve; but I am not sure I shall never approve them. For, having lived long, I have experienced many instances of being obliged, by better information, or fuller consideration, to change opinions even on important subjects, which I once thought right, but found to be otherwise. It is, therefore, that the older I grow, the more apt I am to doubt my own judgment, and to pay more respect to the judgment of others. . . . Thus, I consent, Sir, to this Constitution because I expect no better, and because I am not sure that it is not the best. . . . On the whole, Sir, I cannot help expressing a wish that every member of the Convention who may still have objections to it, would, with me, on this occasion doubt a little of his own infallibility, and to make manifest our unanimity, put his name to this instrument.

Fortunately, Franklin was not obliged to describe this Convention, as he had a previous movement in 1754: "Everybody cries, a Union is absolutely necessary; but when they come to the manner and form of the Union, their weak noddles are perfectly distracted."[1] On September 17, 1787, moved by a wise spirit of compromise in the interest of the common welfare, the thirty-nine then remaining in Philadelphia signed a draft of the Constitution; and George Washington went back to his house that

[1] *Writings of Benjamin Franklin* (A. H. Smyth, Ed. 1907), III, 242, letter to Peter Collinson, Dec. 29, 1754. Franklin said in the Convention, June 11, 1787: "We are sent here to consult, not to contend, with each other; and declarations of a fixed opinion and of a determined resolution never to change it, neither enlighten nor convince us"; and again, June 30: "When a broad table is to be made, and the edges of the planks do not fit, the artist takes a little from both and makes a good joint. In like manner here, both sides must part with some of their demands, in order that they may join in some accommodating proposition." See also Richard Henry Lee to M. Weare, Nov. 21, 1777: "In this great business, dear Sir, we must yield a little to each other and not rigidly insist on having everything correspondent to the partial views of each State. On such terms, we can never confederate." *Letters of Members of the Continental Congress*, II, 569.

night, and wrote in his Diary: "The business being thus closed, the members adjourned to the City Tavern, dined together, and took cordial leave of each other. After which, I returned to my lodgings, did some business with and received the papers from the Secretary of the Convention, and retired to meditate on the momentous work which had been executed."

Washington's words were indeed accurate. It was a "momentous work" which had been accomplished. But in emphasizing the wonderful character of the work, historians, orators, and statesmen have imparted to the American people an erroneous idea as to the method of formation of the Constitution; and it is largely because of this misleading view that the people have failed to perceive the necessary connection between the Supreme Court and their form of government.

Nothing has given greater impetus to this misunderstanding as to the contents of the Constitution, than the widely known and much-quoted remark of Gladstone, to the effect that the "American Constitution is the most wonderful work ever struck off, at a given time, by the brain and purpose of man." This phrase has given to many the idea that the members of the Federal Convention invented the Constitution; that during the eighty-six working days of the Convention, its members originated something entirely new. Such a conception is very far from the truth. As a matter of fact, the Anglo-Saxon peoples differ from other peoples in the making of social and governmental institutions. As James Russell Lowell said: "Wise statesmanship does not so much consist in the agreement of its forms with any abstract ideal, however perfect, as in its adaptation to the wants of the governed and its capacity of shaping itself to the demands of the time. . . . The Anglo-Saxon soundness of understanding has shown itself in nothing more clearly than in allowing institutions to be formulated gradually by custom, convenience or necessity." The Anglo-Saxon rarely develops anything by logical process, or by adopting a theory or a principle and then seeking to apply it; he develops a principle from previous experience and by expedients found desirable to meet changes of conditions. Human nature and human experience, not human theorizing, is the foundation of his action. And John Dickinson of Delaware sagely recognized this trait, when he said in the Federal Convention: "Experience must be our guide. Reason may mislead us. It was not reason that discovered the singular and admirable mechanism of the English Constitution. It was not reason that discovered, or ever could have discovered the odd, and in the eye of those that are governed by reason, the absurd mode of trial by jury. Accidents probably produced these discoveries, and experience has given a sanction to them." [1]

---

[1] *First Century of the Constitution*, by Alexander Johnston, *New Princeton Rev.* (1887), IV; *Lowell's Prose Works*, V, 217. *Debates in the Federal Convention of 1787* (1920), edited by Gaillard Hunt and James Brown Scott (hereinafter referred to as *Debates*), speech of Dickinson, Aug. 13, 1787; see also George Mason of Virginia, Aug. 2, 1787, who "was for preserving the ideas familiar to the people." So also James Madison wrote in *The Federalist*, No. 4: "Is it not the glory of the people of America, that whilst they have paid a decent respect to the opinions of former times and other nations, they have not suffered a blind veneration for antiquity, for custom, or for names, to overrule the suggestions of their own good sense, the knowledge of their own situation, and the lessons of their own experience?"

It is of the utmost importance, therefore, that we should recognize that the Constitution was framed in the form which it took, because its framers were familiar, from experience, with the principles of most of the provisions which they inserted in that document, or had encountered actual evils for which they sought governmental remedies. The permanence of that unique instrument of government has been largely due to the skill, the common sense, and the spirit of compromise with which the framers built on old foundations, and adapted, modified, and reconstructed old principles to meet new conditions. And it is precisely because most of the Constitution was *not* a bold experiment on entirely new lines that it has proven to be generally acceptable to Americans during one hundred and thirty-six years; for it was the product of experience and of traditions that had long been American in 1787, and remained so thereafter.

In the first place, the very word "Constitution", when used to signify a supreme law binding upon, and unalterable by, the Legislature was a purely American idea.[1] "Constitution" originally meant an edict of the nation's ruler. The "Constitutions of Clarendon", promulgated by Henry II of England, in 1164, are an example of this sense of the word. In the eighteenth century, it had come to mean a general system of laws and framework of government;

---

[1] "Constitutions themselves were things of recent date. Before the American Revolution the word itself was never fully understood. Lexicographers who attempted to define it never could agree. There was no practice whereupon to try its meaning. No power on earth had a Constitution before the American States." William Findley of Pennsylvania, in the House, Jan. 8, 1805. *8th Cong., 2d Sess.*

and Bolingbroke, writing in 1735, "On Parties", said that: "By Constitutions we mean, whenever we speak with propriety and exactness, that assemblage of laws, institutions and customs derived from certain fixed principles of reason . . . that compose the general system, according to which the community hath agreed to be governed." It was in this sense that men spoke of the British Constitution — which was an aggregation of rights, liberties, and methods of government, established by Parliament or governmental practice or wrested from the King. But such a Constitution as this was subject to alteration at any time by Act of Parliament. Substantially the only suggestion in England of a written Constitution limiting sovereign powers so that (as he said) government should be an "empire of laws and not of men", was made by James Harrington in 1656, in his *Oceana;* and it was from his work that the Americans of a century later imbibed many of their ideas.[1] The charters of the American colonies were often referred to as "Constitutions"; but most

[1] See *Harrington and his Influence upon American Political Institutions and Political Thought*, by Theodore W. Dwight, *Pol. Sci. Qu.* (1887), II. A striking phrase, undoubtedly later borrowed by Jefferson, is to be found in a petition to the House of Commons, drawn by Harrington in 1659, urging the adoption of a definite political Constitution for England, in which he said "that the exercise of all just authority over a free people ought (under God) to arise from their own consent." James Otis, in *The Rights of the British Colonies Asserted and Proved* (1764), spoke of a theory which "the great, the incomparable Harrington has most abundantly demonstrated in his *Oceana.*" See also *The Laws and Jurisprudence of England and America* (1895), by John F. Dillon: "The absolutely unique feature of the political and legal institutions of the American Republic is its written Constitutions which are organic limitations whereby the people by an act of unprecedented wisdom have . . . protected themselves against themselves." Paterson, J., in *Vanhorne* v. *Dorrance* (1795), 2 Dallas 308: "A Constitution is the form of government delineated by the mighty hand of the people in which certain first principles of fundamental law are established." Nelson, J., in *Kamper* v. *Hawkins* (1791), 1 Va. Cases 24: "A Constitution is that by which the powers of government are limited."

of them were alterable by the King or by Parliament.[1]

A radical difference between the English and the American idea of a Constitution began to emerge from 1761 to 1775. When British statesmen and writers talked of a statute or action as "unconstitutional", they meant that it was something impolitic or contrary to the spirit of the British Constitution, but *not* that it was something beyond the power of Parliament to enact; for Parliament was supreme. When, on the other hand, James Otis, John Adams, and Samuel Adams of Massachusetts, James Wilson of Pennsylvania, Richard Bland and Richard Henry Lee of Virginia, and other leading men of the Colonies began talking, in letters and addresses, of the Stamp Tax Law, the Tea Tax Law, the Billeting Law, and other Acts of Parliament as "unconstitutional", they were using the word in an entirely new and purely American sense, which profoundly shocked England. For the Americans meant by "unconstitutional", Acts absolutely illegal, Acts which Parliament had no power to pass and which were to be disregarded by the Courts and by the citizens

[1] Thus, Benjamin Franklin published in London in 1759 "An historical review of the Constitution and Government of Pennsylvania from its origin"; and in his *Autobiography*, Franklin wrote that Lord Granville said to him, in 1757: "You Americans have wrong ideas of the nature of your Constitution." Samuel Adams wrote to George Washington, Nov. 13, 1765, of the colonists "under their several Constitutions of subordinate civil government." Daniel Dulany of Maryland wrote in 1765: "By their Constitutions of government, the Colonies are empowered to impose internal taxes."

The closest resemblance to a Constitution in the modern meaning of the word is to be found in "The Fundamental Constitutions of Carolina", framed by John Locke, in 1669; the "Fundamental Articles" of East Jersey in 1680, and William Penn's so-called "Frame of Government" (or as the document itself read "Charter of Liberties") in 1662 and his "Charter of Privileges and Concession in 1701 in Pennsylvania"; for these documents contained guaranties of specific civil rights and a full framework of government.

CONSTITUTION AND AMERICAN IDEAS 15

of the Colonies. "An Act against the Constitution is void; an act against natural equity is void; and if an Act of Parliament should be made in the very words of this petition, it would be void. The Executive Courts must pass such an Act into disuse," said James Otis in 1761; and John Adams wrote in 1765, that "the Stamp Act ought to be waived by the Judges, as against natural equity and the Constitution." Rev. Jonathan Mayhew in Massachusetts in 1766 preached of Acts contrary to Magna Charta as "*ipso facto*, null and void." In 1768, the Massachusetts House of Representatives issued an Address stating that: "The Supreme Legislature, in every free State, derives its power from the Constitution, by the fundamental rules of which it is bounded and circumstanced." This voiced a purely American idea of a Constitution as a law which was above the Government and enforceable against it. Such a conception was abhorrent to and subversive of British theories of government.[1] It was a "Constitution", in this American sense of the word,

[1] See especially *Political Ideas of the American Revolution* (1922), by Randolph Greenfield Adams, V, VI; *Works of John Adams* (1856), II, 522; *Writings of Samuel Adams* (1904), I, 8, 17, 39, 45, 133, 169. The Answer of the Massachusetts House of Representatives to the Governor's Speech, Oct. 23, 1765, written by Samuel Adams, stated that "there are certain original inherent rights belonging to the people which Parliament itself cannot divest them of, consistent with their own Constitution; among these is the right of representation in the same body which exercises the power of taxation." See also Address of the Massachusetts House of Representatives to Dennys de Berdt, Jan. 12, 1768: "In all free States, the Constitution is fixed; it is from thence that the Supreme Legislative as well as the supreme Executive derives its authority. Neither can break through the fundamental rules of the Constitution without destroying their own foundation." In the Pennsylvania Provincial Convention of January, 1775, James Wilson proposed resolutions "that the Acts of the British Parliament for altering the charter and Constitution of the Colony of Massachusetts Bay . . . and for quartering troops on the inhabitants of the colonies are unconstitutional and void."

which reached its full height in the written frames of government adopted by the separate States, in 1776. It is sometimes loosely said that the difference between the American and the British Constitutions is that the former is a written document and the latter an unwritten body of law. But it is not this which constitutes the real difference. It is the fact that the American Constitutions are unalterable and unamendable by a majority of the Legislature itself. This was the new idea which the States introduced in 1776, distinguishing their Constitutions from mere statutes by prescribing that they could not be repealed or amended, except by conventions of the people or by passage through two Legislatures or by a vote greater than the votes required for ordinary statutes.[1] When this new idea of a Constitution which the Legislature should be powerless to amend was introduced, *ipso facto*, it became necessary that there should be power vested somewhere

[1] It is to be noted that the Constitutions of Delaware (1776), Maryland (1776), Pennsylvania (1776), Georgia (1777), Massachusetts (1780), and New Hampshire (1784) contained these provisions for amendment. The Constitutions of New Jersey (1776), New York (1777), North Carolina (1776), and Virginia (1776) contained no provision for amendment.

The Constitutions of South Carolina of 1776 and 1778, being enacted by the Legislature, were only statutory in their nature. Connecticut adopted, by statute, its royal charter of 1662 as its "Civil Constitution." Rhode Island also retained its charter as its only Constitution.

It may also be noted that the States adopted different titles for their fundamental law; thus Virginia, Maryland, and North Carolina termed it "The Constitution or Form of Government"; New Jersey, "A Set of Charter Rights and the Form of a Constitution"; Pennsylvania, "Plan or Frame of Government"; Delaware, "The Constitution or System of Government"; Georgia, "Rules and Regulations for the Future Government of the State."

Thomas Jefferson, in his *Notes on Virginia* (1782), said: "This [Virginia] Constitution was formed when we were new and unexperienced in the science of government. It was the first, too, which was formed in the whole United States." *Writings* (Ford's Ed.), IV, 17, 25. In its letter of April 13, 1787, to the States, Congress termed the Articles of Confederation "our national Constitution." *Secret Journals of Congress.*

CONSTITUTION AND AMERICAN IDEAS 17

to see that the Legislature did not succeed in attempts to amend the Constitution. This power, as will be seen, had, by 1787, been recognized by many States to rest in the Judiciary. And it was the State Constitutions, with this cardinal and distinctively American provision as to amendment, from which the members of the Federal Convention drew the idea and form of a Constitution for the United States.

In the Federal Constitution itself it may be said, broadly speaking, that there was only one fundamentally new invention — the dual system of government, the combining of States and a Nation in one working whole. Never before in the world's history had there been a federal form of a republic, in which the States should remain as sovereigns acting with limited powers upon their own citizens, but in which a central government of the States should have Executive, Legislative, and Judicial authority to enforce its own limited sovereign powers directly upon the citizens of the States.[1] That was

[1] This principle was pointed out in the Convention. Edmund Randolph said, June 16: "We must resort, therefore, to a national legislation over individuals." Rufus King said, July 14, 1787: "He considered the proposed Government as substantially and formally a General and National Government over the people of America. There never will be a case in which it will act as a federal Government on the States and not on the individual citizens." James Madison also, on July 14, 1787, "called for a single instance in which the General Government was not to operate on the people individually. The practice of making laws with coercive sanctions for the States as political bodies had been exploded on all hands."

John Lansing said in the New York State Convention: "I know not that history furnishes an example of a confederated republic coercing the States composing it, by the mild influence of laws operating on the individuals of those States. This, therefore, I suppose to be a new experiment in politics." *Elliot's Debates*, II, 219.

Madison wrote to Robert S. Garnett, Feb. 11, 1824: "Whether the Constitution in any of its stages, or as it now stands, be a National or a Federal one, is a question which ought to be premised by a definition of the terms; and then the answer must be that it is neither the one nor the other — but possessing

the cardinal principle placed in the Constitution which differentiated the new government from all previous governments. Yet even this cardinal principle was not actually invented in the Convention. It was largely the application, to the new republican conditions, of ideas of the federal relations of the English Government with the Colonial Governments, which American writers and public men had gradually evolved, in the ten years before the Revolution. And as early as 1775, John Adams, convinced that America must be independent, had suggested a form of central government for the American States with the division of powers contained in the final Constitution.[1]

attributes of both. It is a system of Government emphatically *sui generis*, for designating which there consequently was no appropriate term or denomination pre-existing." *Writings of James Madison*, IX, 176.

Thomas H. Benton of Missouri, in the Senate, Jan. 29, 1824, speaking of this compromise between "a simple Confederacy voting by States and a consolidated Republic deciding every question by the majority of members," said : "The arbitration was new and happy. No example in any previous Confederacy, nor any writer nor theory had furnished the hint. The world is indebted for it to the great men who formed the American Constitution." *18th Cong., 1st Sess.*

[1] *Warren-Adams Letters, Mass. Hist. Soc. Coll.*, John Adams to James Warren, July 24, 1775, writing from Philadelphia : "We are between hawk and buzzard. We ought to have had in our hands a month ago the whole Legislative, Executive, and Judicial of the Whole Continent, and have compleatly modelled the Constitution."

The germ of the federal principle may be seen in the Message of Gov. Thomas Hutchinson to the Massachusetts Provincial Legislature and the Answer of the Council, *Mass. State Papers* (1773) : "It is impossible there should be two independent Legislatures in the one and the same State," said Hutchinson; to which the Council replied : "As, in fact, the two powers are not incompatible and do subsist together, each restraining its acts to their constitutional objects, can we not from hence see how the supreme power may supervise, regulate and make general laws for the kingdom, without interfering with the privileges of the subordinate powers within it ?"

"The principle of federalism was recognized, formulated and legalized in the Constitution; the new government was given its distinct sphere of action, and was made the recipient of a body of powers carefully named and carefully deposited in their proper places; but in the selection and deposition little needed to be done but to follow the practices of the old British Colonial system. The Convention of 1787 had difficulty in seeing the whole complicated scheme as a

CONSTITUTION AND AMERICAN IDEAS 19

An outline of such a federal form of government had been suggested several times, in the six years prior to the Convention. William Barton and Pelatiah Webster, merchants and economists of Philadelphia, had, in 1781 and 1783, respectively, published pamphlets setting forth such plans of government. Noah Webster of Connecticut, in 1784, had proposed "a new system of government which should act, not on the States, but directly on individuals and vest in Congress full power to carry its laws into effect." Washington had written to John Jay, August 1, 1786: "I do not conceive we can exist long as a nation, without having lodged somewhere a power which will pervade the whole nation in as energetic a manner as the authority of the State Governments extends over the several States." As early as August 7, 1786, Charles Pinckney made a report to Congress containing many of the fundamental principles later embodied in the Constitution. Rufus King wrote, September 3, 1786, that in New York there was agitation for the following plan: "Let the State Governments be confined to concerns merely internal, and let there be a Federal Government, with a vigorous Executive, wise Legislative, and independent Judicial." Jefferson wrote to Madison, December 16, 1786: "To enable the federal head to

---

working mechanism; but how could the members possibly have imagined it all . . . without the aid of the historical forces and the old historical practices? . . . Their chief difficulty was again the old one — Colonial disobedience, which was now State willfulness; and this difficulty was surmounted, as we know, by firm adherence to the principle of distinction between local and general authority, and by recognizing that each governmental authority was competent and supreme within its own sphere and had the legal power to enforce its lawful acts on its own citizens." *The Background of American Federalism*, by Andrew C. McLaughlin, *Amer. Pol. Sci. Rev.* (1918), XII.

exercise the powers given to the best advantage, it should be organized as the particular ones are, into Legislative, Executive and Judiciary." Jay wrote to Washington, January 7, 1787: "Would the giving any further degree of power to Congress do the business? I am much inclined to think it would not. . . . I therefore promise myself nothing very desirable from any change which does not divide the sovereignty into its proper departments. Let Congress legislate; let others execute; let others judge;" and to John Adams, Jay wrote, February 21, 1787, advising "to distribute the federal sovereignty into its three proper departments of Executive, Legislative and Judicial; for that Congress should act in these different capacities was, I think, a great mistake in our policy." Madison wrote to Jefferson, March 19, 1787, that it would be expedient to lay the foundation of a new system "clearly paramount" to the State Legislatures, with "an augmentation of the federal power as will render it efficient, without the aid of the Legislatures." A month later, he wrote to Edmund Randolph, advising a plan "which will at once support a due supremacy of the national authority and leave in force the local authorities, so far as they can be subordinately useful. . . . Let the National Government be armed with a positive and complete authority in all cases where uniform measures are necessary . . . let this national supremacy be extended to the Judiciary Department." George Mason of Virginia wrote to Arthur Lee, May 21, 1787, that: "The most prevalent idea, I think, at present, is a great change of the federal system and instituting a great national council or parliament upon the principles of equal proportionate representation, consisting of two branches of the Legislature invested with full legislative powers upon the objects of the Union, and to make the State Legislatures subordinate to the National by giving the latter a negative upon all such laws as they judge contrary to the principles and interest of the Union; to establish a National Executive, and a Judiciary system with cognizance of all such matters as depend upon the law of Nations and such other objects as the local Courts of Justice may be inadequate to."[1]

Thus it will be seen that when the members of the Convention assembled in Philadelphia, many were

[1] See *Observations on the Nature and Use of Paper Credits* (1781), by William Barton; *A Political Dissertation on the Political Union and Constitution of the Thirteen United States of North America which is necessary to their Preservation and Happiness* (1783), by Pelatiah Webster; see also *The Origin and Growth of the American Constitution* (1911), by Hannis Taylor; *Sketches of American Policy* (1785), by Noah Webster. James Madison in his *Preface to Debates in the Convention*, written late in his life and first printed in 1840 as an introduction to the *Madison Papers*, edited by Henry D. Gilpin, wrongly attributed to Pelatiah Webster the Barton pamphlet; see *Pelatiah Webster and the Constitution*, by Gaillard Hunt, *Nation*, Dec. 28, 1911; *The Constitution of the United States* (1910), by David K. Watson, I, 80–109.

Sketch of Pinckney's Plan for a Constitution, in *Amer. Hist. Rev.* (1904), IX, 735; *Mass. Hist. Soc. Proc.* (1915), XLIX, King to Jonathan Jackson, Sept. 3, 1786; *Jefferson's Correspondence* (ed. by T. J. Randolph), II, 64; *The Correspondence and Papers of John Jay* (1891), III; *Life of George Mason* (1912), by Kate Mason Rowland, II, 100–102; *Writings of James Madison*, II, Madison to Jefferson, March 19, 1787; Madison to Randolph, April 8, 1787; Madison to Washington, April 16, 1787.

Madison wrote to Noah Webster, Oct. 12, 1804 : "The change in our government, like most other important improvements, ought to be ascribed rather to a series of causes than to any particular and sudden one, and to the participation of many rather than to the efforts of a single agent. It is certain that the general idea of revising and enlarging the scope of the federal authority so as to answer the necessary purposes of the Union, grew up in many minds and by natural degrees, during the experienced inefficacy of the old confederation. The discernment of Gen. Hamilton must have rendered him an early patron of the idea. That the public attention was called to it by yourself at an early period is well known." *Writings of James Madison*, VII, 162.

fully familiar with the proposed fundamental change in government which they later adopted.

Aside from this idea of a Union of States acting upon the individual citizen rather than through the individual States, practically all the other provisions of the Constitution were adopted from State Constitutions already existing and tested in the States, and from the Articles of Confederation under the Government by which the people had been living for six years. While it has been frequently said that the Constitution embodied English principles and institutions found in Magna Charta and in the Petition and in the Bill of Rights, this remark is really chiefly applicable to the first ten Amendments. The original Constitution was mostly derived from the history and from the experience of the American Colonies and States. While it is true that the meaning of many of the words and phrases used in the instrument are to be interpreted in the light of the old English common law, much of which had been adopted by the Colonies, it still remains also true that most of the actual provisions comprising that instrument are purely American in their origin.

What are the chief principles of the Constitution?

First, there is this division of the government into three branches — the Executive, the Legislative, and the Judicial, each to remain independent of the other.[1] This principle was very familiar to the statesmen of the Colonies, and, as already pointed

[1] The Massachusetts House of Representatives, in a letter to the Earl of Shelburne, drafted by Samuel Adams as early as Jan. 22, 1768, had referred to the "Legislative, Executive and Judiciary powers of the Government . . . in the opinion of the greatest writers, always to be kept separate." *Writings*

CONSTITUTION AND AMERICAN IDEAS 23

out, was a cardinal feature of all the plans suggested for the new Government, between 1781 and 1787.

Moreover, a specific provision for such a division of governmental departments was found by the members of the Convention to exist in the written Constitutions or Bills of Rights of six of the thirteen States (Georgia, Maryland, Massachusetts, New Hampshire, North Carolina, and Virginia). (The Constitutions or Bills of Rights of the following States did not contain such a provision: Delaware, New Jersey, New York, Pennsylvania, and South Carolina.) It is to be noted, incidentally, that the further provision (as in the Virginia Bill of Rights) that "the Legislative, Executive and Judicial powers of government *ought to be forever separate and distinct from each other*" is not to be taken too literally. "Separate and distinct" did not mean "independent and unchecked." As a matter of fact, in the original establishment of these three branches of government and distribution of these powers, both in the States and in the United States, no one branch was constituted as completely independent of the other. Each was provided with certain checks upon the other (as will be more fully illustrated in a later chapter of this book). Many

of *Samuel Adams* (1904), I, 166, 168. Montesquieu's *Esprit des Lois* was published in 1745.

Richard Henry Lee, writing to Arthur Lee, Dec. 20, 1766, referred to the failure of the Virginia Charter system of government to follow Montesquieu's maxim and said, "by this injudicious combination, all the Executive, two thirds of the Legislative and the whole Judicial power are in the same body of magistracy." *Letters of Richard Henry Lee* (1911), I, 18.

Debates, July 17, 1787, pp. 271, *et seq.*, speeches of McClurg and Madison of Virginia, July 19, pp. 285, *et seq.*, by Madison; King, July 20, p. 291; Madison, July 21, p. 298.

writers and statesmen have said that the framers of the Constitution adopted Montesquieu's theory as to the division of governmental powers; but such is not strictly the case. These framers were practical men, working on a practical problem. They were not constructing a government on any set of definite or logical theories. They had encountered evil or unfortunate conditions in the past, in their royal and State governments; and they planned now to avoid a renewal of those conditions, by adopting theories to fit the circumstances. So far from intending each of the three branches to be wholly coördinate, they decided to curb any excess of power in any one branch by balancing it with an effective power in another. Where they had experienced an evil in an omnipotent Legislature, they checked it; where they had actually felt the oppression of a too strong Executive, they checked him; where they believed a Court had been too independent, they checked it.[1]

[1] See *Kilbourn* v. *Thompson* (1880), 103 U. S. 168, 190; *Ex parte Grossman* (1925), 267 U. S. 87.

Fisher Ames said in the House, June 18, 1789 (*1st Cong.*, *1st Sess.*) : "I appeal to that maxim which has the sanction of experience, and is authorized by the decision of the wisest men: to prevent an abuse of power, it must be distributed into three branches who must be independent, to watch and check each other. The people are to watch them all. While these maxims are pursued our liberties will be preserved."

John C. Calhoun said in the House, Dec. 5, 1811 (*12th Cong.*, *1st Sess.*) : "It is the theory of our Government, and was the favorite idea of all our politicians at the time of its formation, that liberty can only exist in a division of the sovereign power, and that such division could only be permanent where each of the parts had within itself the means of protection. . . . The first (the Executive) has its qualified veto and its patronage; the Judiciary, its independence; and each House, a veto on the proceedings of the other."

But as James Madison wrote in *The Federalist:* "If we look into the Constitutions of the several States, we find that, notwithstanding the emphatical and in some instances the unqualified terms in which the maxim has been laid down therein, there is not a single instance in which the several departments

Second, the plan of representative government — election, by the people or "the freemen", of their representatives to their legislative body to act *for* the people, instead of direct action *by* the people. That was a principle or a system which had grown up in the early Colonies, in some instances without specific provision in their original charters or under no legal authority of the English Crown, but as the product of their own peculiar circumstances; and in no case did it follow the extremely restricted form of representation of the English people in Parliament.[1]

Third, the principle of local self-government. That was a genuinely American principle. A govern-

---

of power have been kept absolutely separate and distinct." For example, in Delaware, the Executive sat as a member of the Court of Appeals; in New Jersey, the highest branch of the Legislature, the Council, sat with the Governor as a Court of Appeal; in New York, the members of the Senate sat on the highest Court — the Court for the Trial of Impeachments and Correction of Errors. In South Carolina, the Lieutenant Governor sat in the Court of Chancery, with the Privy Council. In many of the States, the Legislature possessed the power of appointment of the Governor, of Judges, and of other officials. In New York, the Governor and the Judges had a veto on Acts of the Legislature.

[1] See *The First State Constitutions*, by William C. Morey, *Annals of Amer. Acad. of Pol. and Soc. Science* (1893), IV; *The Evolution of Representative Constitutional Government*, by Hampton L. Carson, *Amer. Bar Ass. Journal* (Oct. 1920), VI.

As was said by Chief Justice Lemuel Shaw, in *Commonwealth* v. *Roxbury*, 9 Gray (Mass.) 451, 478, referring to a statute of Massachusetts in 1634, providing for choice of representatives to a Legislature by the freemen: "Here, then, was the origin of a representative government, probably not contemplated by the Charter. . . . In 1644, ten years later, a still more decisive step was taken. . . . In this, we perceive the complete establishment of a representative government, with a distribution and balance of powers. Whether this was perfectly consistent with the Charter or not, it was acquiesced in, acted on, and afterwards confirmed by the Province Charter."

How far the English idea was from the American may be seen from Sir William Blackstone, who in his *Commentaries*, Book I, Chapter II, published in 1765, had explained representative government merely as the means by which "all such men of property in the kingdom as have not seats in the House of Lords" could have a voice in Parliament by their representatives, when summoned "to advise his Majesty."

ment by themselves, and not by a central and distant Parliament in England, had been struggled for by the Colonies for one hundred and fifty years, and its denial had been the fundamental cause of the Revolution.[1] Assertion of it as an American right was found in the State Constitutions of Massachusetts and New Hampshire, and more specifically in that of Maryland, which provided "that the people of this State ought to have the sole and exclusive right of regulating the internal government and police thereof", and in that of Pennsylvania "that the people of this State have the sole, exclusive and inherent right of governing and regulating the internal police of the same."[2] The preservation to the people of each State of this inherent right of

[1] Gouverneur Morris wrote to Penn, May 20, 1774: "Not that Great Britain should lay imports upon us for the support of the government for its defense, nor should she regulate our *internal police*. These things affect us only. To these things, we ourselves are competent." *American Archives*, by Peter Force, 4th Ser. I, 343. Madison wrote to John Adams, Aug. 7, 1818: "Our forefathers brought with them the germ of Independence, in the principle of self-taxation. Circumstances unfolded and perfected it." *Writings of James Madison* (1905), VIII, 413.

[2] Charles Pinckney said, June 25, 1787: "No principle appears to me more true than this; that the General Government cannot effectually exist without securing to the States the possession of their local rights." Madison wrote in *The Federalist*, No. 45, Jan. 29, 1788: "The powers reserved to the States will extend to all the objects which, in the ordinary course of affairs, concern the lives, liberties and properties of the people and the internal order, improvement and prosperity of the State."

It is to be noted that the powers to be possessed by the Congress as proposed in the Virginia Plan, May 29, 1787, were: "That the National Legislature ought to be impowered to enjoy the legislative rights vested in Congress by the Confederation" (which was at first adopted on July 16), and moreover "to legislate in all cases to which the individual States are incompetent or in which the harmony of the United States may be interrupted by the exercise of individual legislation." Roger Sherman of Connecticut proposed an amendment, July 17, 1787, embodying a reservation of the right of local self-government as follows: "to make laws binding on the people of the United States in all cases which may concern the common interests of the Union; but not to interfere with the government of the individual States *in any matters of internal police* which respect the government of such States only, and wherein the general welfare of the United

regulating "the internal government and police thereof" was, to the framers of the Constitution, of equal importance with the establishment of a National Government. It was with knowledge of the specific provisions of the State Constitutions as to matters of an internal nature, that the framers withheld from the new Federal Government control over such matters as could be adequately dealt with by the separate States. The framers knew from experience, and they intended to preserve the principle, that a local government is a responsible government — a government which can never long be conducted in defiance of the opinions, desires, or prejudices of the governed; they knew that a distant and centralized government had been and could be conducted otherwise; and they were not inclined to authorize such a central government to interfere with or administer their local affairs, unless absolutely necessary for the safety, welfare, and permanence of the Nation as a Nation.

Fourth, the division of the elective Legislature

States is not concerned." James Wilson of Pennsylvania favored this amendment. The amendment was defeated and, instead, a substitute proposed by Gunning Bedford, Jr., of Delaware was adopted temporarily, "to legislate in all cases for the general interests of the Union, *and also in those to which the States are separately incompetent.*" On August 22, 1787, John Rutledge reported from the Committee of Detail an amendment giving to Congress the power "to provide as may become necessary from time to time, for the well managing and securing the common property and general interests and welfare of the United States in such manner, as shall not interfere with the governments of individual States in matters *which respect only their internal police,* or for which their individual authorities may be competent." None of these provisions appeared in the final draft of the Constitution, but by the inclusion of specific grants of power to Congress, the balance of powers was impliedly left to the States. On Sept. 15, 1787, Roger Sherman of Connecticut proposed that Article V as to amendments should be so altered as to provide "that no State shall without its consent be affected *in its internal police* or deprived of its equal suffrage in the Senate." Only the latter part of his proposal was adopted.

into two branches, a Senate and House. That principle the framers took from the Constitutions of twelve of the then existing States, and they rejected the plan of a Legislature consisting of only one branch, which was then in vogue in the great State of Pennsylvania.

Fifth, the election of the Executive directly or indirectly by the people. That principle was found in the written Constitutions of the three States of Massachusetts, New Hampshire, and New York; and the framers adopted it by a modified scheme of popular election of President, after rejecting a proposal for an election of President by the Legislature, which was the system prevailing in the eight States of Delaware, Georgia, Maryland, New Jersey, North Carolina, Pennsylvania, South Carolina, and Virginia; while the plan for choice of President by electors was adapted from the provision of the Maryland Constitution as to election of State Senators.[1]

Sixth. The powers given to the President were largely the powers specifically vested by the State Constitutions in the Governors of the existing States, including the power of pardon, the power to act as Commander in Chief, the power to appoint civil officers of government.

Seventh, the appointment of the Judiciary by the Executive, by and with the advice of the Senate. That principle was taken from the State Constitu-

---

[1] See *Debates*, June 2, 4, 5, 20, 24, 25, 26, Aug. 24, Sept. 4, 5, 6, 7; July 17, 19, 1789. James Bowdoin said in the Massachusetts Convention of 1788 (*Elliot's Debates*, II, 128): "This method of choosing (the President) was probably taken from the manner of choosing Senators under the Constitution of Maryland."

tions of Massachusetts, Maryland, New Hampshire, and Pennsylvania; and the framers rejected the system of appointment of Judges by the Legislature then prevailing in Connecticut, Delaware, Georgia, New Jersey, North Carolina, South Carolina, and Virginia. It wisely rejected the system prevailing in New York and Connecticut, where the Legislative body acted on appeal as the Judiciary.[1]

Eighth, the jurisdiction given to the Judiciary over national matters. In one particular of this jurisdiction, the framers of the Constitution embodied a principle, new and untried in history. In the Supreme Court, they vested the power to summon sovereign States before it as parties litigant, to try controversies between sovereign States, to determine their respective rights, to enter judgment against such States, and to enforce such judgment against them. Never before had there existed a permanent judicial tribunal with such powers.[2] The remaining portions of jurisdiction granted to the Federal Judiciary were simply an extension of similar jurisdiction possessed by Courts under the Articles of Confederation as to such national matters as admiralty cases. Many of the subjects over which jurisdiction was granted by the Constitution had been

---

[1] See *Debates*, July 18, 21, 1789; and see Hamilton in *The Federalist*, No. 81, July 4, 8, 1789: "Applaud the wisdom of those States who have committed the judicial power, in the last resort, not to a part of the Legislature, but to distinct and independent bodies of men. . . . The plan of the Convention in this respect . . . is but a copy of the Constitutions of New Hampshire, Massachusetts, Pennsylvania, Delaware, Maryland, Virginia, North Carolina, South Carolina, and Georgia; and the preference which has been given to these models is highly to be commended."

[2] See *The Supreme Court and Sovereign States* (1924), by Charles Warren, Chapter I; *Sovereign States before Arbitral Tribunals and Courts of Justice* (1925), by James Brown Scott.

30 CONSTITUTION AND AMERICAN IDEAS

suggested in pamphlets and letters, for four years prior to the Convention.[1]

Ninth. The provisions regulating the methods of action by Houses of Congress, and the modes of election, were largely mere mechanism of government; they were not matters of fundamental principle; and most of this mechanism was also taken directly from the State Constitutions.

Any one who will lay the Federal Constitution side by side with the State Constitution of Massachusetts (adopted in 1780) and with the State Constitution of New York (adopted in 1777) will be

---

[1] See *Debates*, July 18, 1789. Pelatiah Webster, Feb. 16, 1783, had proposed a Federal Judiciary. Rufus King wrote to Jonathan Jackson, Sept. 3, 1786 (*Mass. Hist. Soc. Proc.*, 1915, XLIX), that: "Mr. Madison . . . does not discover or propose any other plan than that of investing Congress with full powers for the regulation of commerce, foreign and domestic. But this power will run deep into the authorities of the individual States, and can never be well exercised, without a Federal Judicial. The reform must necessarily be extensive."

Charles Pinckney's plan submitted to the Federal Convention, but probably devised as early as his report to Congress of August 7, 1786, provided for "a Federal Judicial Court to which an appeal shall be allowed from the Judicial Courts of the several States in all cases wherein questions shall arise on the construction of the law of Nations, or on the regulations of the United States concerning trade or revenue, or wherein the United States shall be a party" — Congress also to have the exclusive right of instituting in each State a Court of Admiralty. George Mason wrote to Arthur Lee: "The most prevalent idea, I think, at present, is . . . to establish a National Executive, and a Judiciary system with a cognizance of all such matters as depends upon the law of nations and such other objects as the local Courts of Justice may be inadequate to."

Madison wrote to Randolph, April 8, 1787: "It seems at least essential that an appeal should lie to some national tribunal in all cases which concern foreigners or inhabitants of other States. The admiralty jurisdiction may be fully submitted to the National Government"; and to Washington, April 16, 1787: "It seems at least necessary that . . . an appeal should lie to some National tribunals in all cases to which foreigners or inhabitants of other States may be parties. The admiralty jurisdiction seems to fall entirely within the purview of the National Government."

Jefferson wrote to Madison, June 20, 1787: "The negative proposed them [Congress] on all the acts of the several Legislatures is now for the first time suggested to my mind. *Prima facie*, I do not like it. . . . Would not an appeal from the State Judicatures to a federal Court . . . be as effectual a remedy?"

CONSTITUTION AND AMERICAN IDEAS 31

startled by the extent to which the members of the Federal Convention not only followed the principles, but used the exact phraseology of those State documents.[1] For instance, the Preamble of the Massachusetts Constitution began:

> We . . . the people of Massachusetts . . . do . . . ordain and establish the following . . . as the Constitution of the Commonwealth of Massachusetts.

Compare this with the Federal preamble:

> We, the people of the United States . . . do ordain and establish this Constitution for the United States of America.

Take the Massachusetts provision as to impeachment:

> Judgment shall not extend further than to removal from office and disqualification to hold or enjoy any place of honor, trust, or profit under this Commonwealth; but the party so convicted shall be, nevertheless, liable to indictment, trial, judgment and punishment, according to the laws of the land.

The Federal Constitution follows it word for word:

> Judgment . . . shall not extend further than to removal from office and disqualification to hold and enjoy any office of honor, trust or profit under the United States; but the party convicted shall, nevertheless, be liable and

[1] See *The Evolution of the Constitution* (1910), by Sydney George Fisher; *The Constitutional History of the United States* (1901), by Frederic N. Thorpe, I, 475 *et seq.*; *Law of the Federal and State Constitutions of the United States* (1908), by Frederic J. Stimson; *The Original and Derived Features of the Constitution*, by James Harvey Robinson, *Annals of the American Academy of Political and Social Science* (1890), I; *Comparative Study of the State Constitutions of the American Revolution*, by William C. Webster, *ibid.* (1897). John P. Van Ness said in the House of Representatives, Jan. 17, 1803 (*7th Cong., 2d Sess.*, p. 395): "The Constitution was only a digest of the most approved principles of the Constitutions of the several States, in which the spirit of those Constitutions was combined."

subject to indictment, trial, judgment and punishment according to law.

Massachusetts says:

The Senate shall be the final judge of the elections, returns and qualifications of its own members . . . determine its own rules of proceedings.

The Federal Constitution says:

Each House shall be the judge of the elections, returns and qualifications of its own members . . . determine the rules of its proceedings.

Massachusetts (as well as seven other States) says:[1]

All money bills shall originate in the House of Representatives; but the Senate may propose or concur with amendments as on other bills.

The Federal Constitution says:

All bills for raising revenue shall originate in the House of Representatives; but the Senate may propose or concur with amendments as on other bills.

The provisions of the Federal Constitution as to the President's veto, the choice of Speaker by the House, the Senate as the body to try all impeachments, the President as Commander in Chief of the army and navy, appointment of officers by the President "by and with the advice and consent of the Senate" are all taken almost *verbatim* from the Massachusetts document.

[1] See especially debates in the Federal Convention, July 6, Aug. 13, 15, Sept. 5, 8, 1787; see also historical sketch by Henry St. George Tucker in *68th Cong., 2d Sess.*, Feb. 3, 1925.

The New York Constitution said:

It shall be the duty of the Governor to inform the Legislature at every session, of the condition of the State . . . ; to recommend such matters to their consideration as shall appear to him to concern its good government, welfare and prosperity . . . to take care that the laws are faithfully executed.

The Federal Constitution said:

He shall from time to time give to the Congress information of the state of the Union, and recommend to their consideration such measures as he shall judge necessary and expedient. . . . He shall take care that the laws be faithfully executed.

The provision as to the duties of the President and as to the Vice-President as the president of the Senate, the provision authorizing the President "to convene both Houses or either of them" "on extraordinary occasions"; the provision as to adjournment of the branches of the Legislature, all came from the New York Constitution.

Clause three of Article Six of the Federal Constitution providing that: "No religious test shall ever be required as a qualification to any office or public trust under the United States," came word for word from the Maryland State Constitution of 1776; and the provision for a long term for Senators, as a means of increasing the stability of that body, was suggested by the Maryland Constitution.

As has already been stated, the provision that the Constitution should be unamendable except by reference to the peoples of the States was suggested by similar provisions in the State Constitutions, notably in those of Massachusetts and New Hampshire.[1]

Apart from the principles and the mechanism above referred to, the remainder of the Constitution is concerned solely with grants and prohibitions of power to the Federal Government and with prohibitions of power to the State Governments.

It is a notable fact that, while there are *twenty*

---

[1] The Virginia Plan, introduced by Edmund Randolph at the outset of the Convention contained a clause "that provision ought to be made for hereafter amending the system now to be established, without requiring the assent of the National Legislature." Elbridge Gerry of Massachusetts, arguing in its favor, said that "the novelty and difficulty of the experiment requires periodical revision. The prospect of such a revision would also give intermediate stability to the Government." On June 5, 1787, further consideration was postponed. On July 23, it was voted that "provision ought to be made for future amendments of the Articles of Union"; and in the draft submitted by John Rutledge for the Committee of Detail, of which Nathaniel Gorham of Massachusetts was a member, August 6, it was provided that "on the application of the Legislatures of two thirds of the States in the Union for an amendment of this Constitution, the Legislature of the United States shall call a Convention for that purpose." On August 30, it was voted, on motion of Gouverneur Morris, that the Congress "should be left at liberty to call a Convention whenever they please." Finally, in the closing days of the Convention on September 10 and 15, the provision regarding amendments as it now appears in the Constitution, and based on a draft offered by James Madison, was adopted.

The conception of the Virginia Plan was explained by James Madison as follows, in a letter to John Tyler, in 1833: "The resolutions proposed by him [Edmund Randolph] were the result of a consultation among the deputies, the whole number, seven, being present. The part which Virginia has borne in bringing about the Convention suggested the idea that some such initiative step might be expected from their deputation; and Mr. Randolph was designated for that task. It was perfectly understood that the propositions committed no one to their precise tenor or form; and that the members of the deputation would be as free in discussing and shaping them as the other members of the Convention. Mr. R. was made the organ on the occasion, being then the Governor of the State, of distinguished talents, and in the habit of public speaking. General Washington, though at the head of the list, was, for obvious reasons, disinclined to take the lead. It was foreseen that he would be immediately called to the presiding station. That the Convention understood the entire Resolutions of Mr. R. to be a mere sketch, in which omitted details were to be supplied and the general terms and phrases to be reduced to their proper details, is demonstrated by the use made of them in the Convention." *Writings of James Madison*, IX, 502; see also Madison to Noah Webster, Oct. 12, 1804, *ibid.*, VII, 162.

grants of power in the Constitution, there are *thirty-one* prohibitions and restrictions.

Of the grants of power to Congress, and of the prohibitions on Congress, many were taken *verbatim* from the old Articles of Confederation, such as the power to borrow money on the credit of the United States, regulating trade with the Indians, to coin money and fix the standard of weights and measures, to establish post offices, to try piracies and felonies committed on the high seas, declare war, grant letters of marque and reprisal, make rules concerning captures on land and water, provide a navy, make rules for the government and regulation of the land and naval forces, and the prohibition of grant of titles of nobility, etc. And so far as entirely new powers were granted to Congress by the Constitution, they were not the invention of the members of the Convention. The necessity for the grant of such powers as that to regulate commerce between the States, and that to lay and collect taxes and borrow money, had been the subject of debate throughout the States for over five years.

So, too, with respect to the prohibitions and restrictions on the States, many were taken *verbatim* from the Articles of Confederation, such as the requirements for interstate extradition; for full faith and credit to judicial acts and records by each State; that "the free inhabitants of each of these States . . . shall be entitled to all privileges and immunities of free citizens in the several States"; the prohibitions on the States to enter into alliances or treaties with foreign powers, to grant titles of nobility, to enter into agreements with each other without the consent of Congress, to lay imports or duties interfering with treaties, to maintain land or sea forces except as deemed necessary by Congress for defense; to engage in war without the consent of Congress, to commission vessels of war or issue letters of marque or reprisal except on declaration of war by Congress. And the new prohibitions on the States were not novel ideas of the Convention. The necessity for the chief restrictions on the power of the States, such as forbidding the States to levy export or import taxes, to issue bills of credit, to pass tender laws or laws impairing the obligation of contract, had been made plain by many years' experience of actual evils in the States; and they had been suggested and long discussed by many public men in most of the States.

Moreover, there was nothing new in the idea of inserting in a written Constitution written limitations on the power of Legislative bodies, either Federal or State. The people of practically every State had, since 1776, embodied such limitations on their State Legislature in their State Constitutions.

Written Bills of Rights, setting forth the inalienable privileges of all citizens, existed in eight States — Delaware, Maryland, Massachusetts, New Hampshire, North Carolina, Pennsylvania, South Carolina, Virginia.[1] Moreover, the people of these States,

---

[1] *The Federal and State Constitutions* (1909), by Frederic N. Thorpe; *The Delaware Bill of Rights*, by Max Farrand, *Amer. Hist. Rev.* (1898), III. Connecticut, in a statute passed by its Legislature in 1776, adopting its royal charter of 1662 as its "civil Constitution" provided for guarantees of due process, enjoyment of local justice and law by all free inhabitants of any other States and by foreigners, trial by law and liberty of bail. *The Federal and State Constitutions, Colonial Charters and Other Organic Laws of the United States* (1877), by Ben. Perley Poore.

together also with States which had no Bill of Rights like New York, New Jersey, and Georgia, had inserted in their State Constitutions, between 1776 and 1787, many other and further restrictions on their Legislatures. Thus, Delaware had provided against slavery and against preference of any religious sect; Georgia had provided for freedom of religion, habeas corpus, freedom of the press, trial by jury, and moderate bail; Massachusetts, New Hampshire, and North Carolina had provided against withholding of habeas corpus; New Jersey and New York had provided against impairment of freedom of religion, bills of attainder, and refusal of jury trial; North Carolina, Pennsylvania, and South Carolina had provided against imprisonment for debt and against refusal of bail; South Carolina had provided against depriving a citizen of life, liberty, or property without due process of law; Pennsylvania had provided for jury trial and moderate bail. And three States (Delaware, North Carolina, and Pennsylvania) had enforced their Declarations of a Bill of Rights by specific provision in their State Constitutions, to the effect that no article of such Bill of Rights "ought ever to be violated on any pretence whatever."

Moreover, experience had shown that there was need of even further curbs on the Legislative bodies, in order to prevent gross violations by them of the citizens' rights of liberty and property. In fact, it was because (as an eminent New Hampshire man, Jeremy Belknap, wrote) "the present Constitution strikes at the root of such evils as we have suffered by the madness of sovereign State Assemblies", that it commended itself to many.[1] James Madison said in the Convention: "Experience had proved a tendency in our governments to throw all power into the Legislative vortex. The Executives of the States are, in general, little more than ciphers; the Legislature omnipotent. If no effectual check be devised for restraining the instability and encroachments of the latter, a revolution of some kind or other would be inevitable."[2]

It has been well pointed out that "the task before the Convention arose by no means exclusively from the inadequacies of the Articles of Confederation for the 'exigencies of the Union.' Of at least equal urgency were the questions which were thrust upon its attention by the shortcomings of the State governments for their purpose."[3] State Legislative omnipotence or despotism, which had been favored at the time of the Revolution as a reaction against Royal or Parliamentary power, was felt by many, in 1787, to be a real danger in the States. To the members of the Convention, Federal Legislative

---

[1] Jeremy Belknap to Ebenezer Hazard, Dec. 8, 1787, *Belknap Papers*, Part III, *Mass. Hist. Soc. Coll.*, *4th Series*. See also speech of Gouverneur Morris, July 21, 1787, p. 297: "He concurred in thinking the public liberty in greater danger from Legislative usurpation than from any other source."

[2] *Debates*, July 17, 1787, p. 273. Madison also said, Sept. 12, 1787, p. 556: "The experience of the States had demonstrated that their checks are insufficient;" and in *The Federalist*, No. 48, Feb. 1, 1788, Madison wrote: "The Legislative department is everywhere extending the sphere of its activity and draining all power into its impetuous vortex. . . . I have appealed to experience for the truth of what I advanced on this subject." James Wilson said, June 16, 1787: "If the legislative authority be not restrained, there can be neither liberty nor stability."

[3] *The Progress of Constitutional Theory between the Declaration of Independence and the Meeting of the Philadelphia Convention*, by Edward S. Corwin, *Amer. Hist. Rev.* (1925), XXX; see *Notes on Virginia*, in *Writings of Jefferson* (Ford's Ed.), II, 163–164; *Vices of the Political System of the United States* (April, 1787), in *Writings of James Madison* (Hunt's Ed.), III, 361.

CONSTITUTION AND AMERICAN IDEAS 39

omnipotence appeared equally a danger. How was it to be avoided or prevented? That was a matter of grave concern to them.

How was Congress to be prevented from amending the Constitution by assuming to exercise powers not granted to it?

Modern writers upon the Constitution, in describing the conflicts in the Convention, have been apt to lay their chief stress upon the compromises of the Constitution [1] — that through which the small States secured equal representation in the Senate, and the large States proportional representation and origination of revenue bills in the House; that through which the Northern States secured Federal regulation of commerce, and the Southern, prohibition of Federal interference with importation of slaves for twenty years, and representation of three fifths of their slaves in elections to the House.

While these compromises were essential in obtaining the signatures of delegates from all the States represented, it must not be forgotten that there were other matters which the framers regarded as fully as essential to their acceptance of the Constitution; and chief of these was their insistence on the limitation of the authority and term of office of the Executive — the President; [2] on the restraint

---

[1] Charles Pinckney of South Carolina said, in the House, Feb. 13, 1821 (*10th Cong., 2d Sess.*): "This Constitution of the United States itself was the work of compromise . . . and this Constitution of compromise was formed by a body of men, at least as well-informed and disinterested and as much lovers of freedom and humanity as may probably ever again be assembled in this country."

[2] Benjamin Huger of South Carolina said, in the House, Dec. 19, 1816 (*19th Cong., 2d Sess.*): "All those who were at all versed in the history of the times or had ever heard anything of the proceedings in the Convention which formed the Constitution well knew that by far the greatest difficulty experi-

and precise definition of the powers of the Legislative — the Congress; and on the curbs upon the States in the matter of tender laws, paper money, export duties, and the like.

enced in adjusting the provisions of it, was with regard to the Executive branch of the Government, and in particular as to the mode of selecting or electing the Chief Magistrate. . . . He had understood from all those of the original members of the Convention whom he had ever enjoyed the advantage of hearing converse on the subject, that this had been found the great Herculean task in the Convention, that this point had been longer and more frequently agitated, and that more projects and contrivances had been submitted to their consideration in regard to it, than perhaps all the other provisions of the Constitution taken together."

CHAPTER TWO

THE CONSTITUTION AND THE COURT

"The interpretation of the laws is the proper and peculiar province of the Courts. A Constitution is, in fact, and must be regarded, as a fundamental law. It must, therefore, belong to them to ascertain its meaning, as well as the meaning of any particular Act proceeding from the Legislative body. If there should happen to be an irreconcilable variance between the two, that which has the superior obligation and validity ought, of course, to be preferred. . . . Nor does the conclusion, by any means, imply a superiority of the Judicial to the Legislative power. It only supposes that the power of the people is superior to both, and that where the will of the Legislature declared in its statutes, stands in opposition to that of the people, declared in the Constitution, the Judges ought to be governed by the latter, rather than the former." — ALEXANDER HAMILTON, in *The Federalist*, No. 78, July 17–20, 1788.

"The framers of the Constitution, aware of the impossibility so to convey their meaning by any language which they could use, as to prevent different conclusions being drawn from it, were fully impressed with the necessity of devising some arbiter to prevent the distracting consequences which these conflicting conclusions would unavoidably produce. Had they devolved upon Congress the right of deciding these controversies, they would have exonerated the Federal Legislature from the limitations which had been imposed upon it, and converted it into a despotic assembly, uncontrolled excepting by its discretion. Had they vested this right in the parties differing, they would have organized a system of confusion and anarchy, which would soon have resolved society into its original elements. To avoid, therefore, the evils of despotism and anarchy, they established a Federal Judiciary, constituting it a separate and independent department of the Government. . . . If, they, the Federal Judiciary, decide that an Act of Congress is unconstitutional, it becomes inoperative and void." — WILLIAM DRAYTON of South Carolina, in the House, June 5, 1832. *22d Cong., 1st Sess.*

American citizens may see, from what has been said in the preceding chapter, that in those portions of the Federal Constitution devoted to grants of Legislative power and to prohibitions on the exercise by Congress of certain specific forms of Legislative power, the framers of the Constitution simply proceeded along very familiar lines of experience in their various States, and embodied in their new Constitution such provisions as had already been found in the Articles of Confederation or in the State Constitutions, together with such added restrictions on the power of the Legislatures, both Federal and State, as actual experience of evils in the past had shown to be necessary.

Now what was the purpose of setting forth categorically these restrictions and limitations of power in the new Constitution? What was the purpose of the thirty-one prohibitions? Did the framers mean them to be merely pleasant, political apothegms, expressions of aspiration, declarations of sentiment? Clearly not. The prohibitions were intended to prohibit. They were intended to be absolute legal safeguards to the citizens and to the States, strictly binding upon every agency of the new Government. They were intended to effectually prevent Congress, and the Executive himself, from going beyond the limits prescribed by the Constitution. In other words, they were declarations which were intended to be enforceable and to be enforced. "How vain is a paper restriction if it confers neither power nor right," exclaimed James A. Bayard, a few years later. "Of what importance is it to say, Congress are prohibited from doing certain acts, if no legitimate authority exists in the country to decide whether an act done *is* a prohibited act? Do gentlemen perceive the consequences which would follow from establishing the principle that Congress have the exclusive right to decide upon their own powers? This principle admitted, does any Constitution remain? Does not the power of the Legislature become absolute and omnipotent? Can you talk to them of transgressing their powers, when no one has a right to judge of those powers but themselves?"

But the only known method of enforcement of a law, other than force itself, is judicial action. This was perfectly well known to the framers of the Constitution and known not only in theory, but in practice. Limitations of this kind (*i.e.*, to the Legislative authority), wrote Alexander Hamilton in 1788, "can be preserved, in practice, in no other way than through the medium of Courts of Justice, whose duty it must be to declare all Acts contrary to the manifest tenor of the Constitution void. Without this, all the reservation of particular rights or privileges would amount to nothing."[1]

The framers knew that their State Courts had asserted the power of enforcing the State Constitutions, and that, too, without any specific provisions in those Constitutions for such action. And there was a very particular reason why the framers should desire and contemplate similar action on the part of the Federal Judiciary which they were establishing in the new Constitution. It was agreed by all that

---

[1] James A. Bayard of Delaware, in the House, Feb. 20, 1802. *7th Cong., 1st Sess.* William Smith of South Carolina said in the House, June 16, 1789: "A great deal of mischief has arisen in the several States by the Legislatures undertaking to decide constitutional questions. Sir, it is the duty of the Legislature to make laws. Your Judges are to expound them." *1st Cong., 1st Sess.* See also *The Federalist*, No. 78, June 17–20, 1788; No. 81, July 4–8, 1788.

one clause in this Constitution was absolutely essential, namely, that which guaranteed that "the trial of all crimes, except in cases of impeachment, shall be by jury." (Article III, section 2.) But it was precisely this provision, found in the Constitutions of all of the States, which had been grossly infringed by the Legislatures of at least five States. In Pennsylvania itself, a Committee of the Council of Censors, reporting in 1784 on breaches of the State Constitution, had recorded many "flagrant" and "wanton" violations of the "sacred rights of a citizen to trial by jury."[1] The Legislatures of four other States, prior to the Federal Constitution, had sought to deprive citizens of the right to jury trial; and in each State, a State Court had decided the State statute to be invalid. Now it is a curious fact that each of those judicial decisions was brought particularly to the attention of framers of the Constitution, during the sitting of the Convention in that summer of 1787. One case was the famous one of *Trevett* v. *Weeden*, in Rhode Island in 1786, in which the State Court had held invalid a State law providing for the issue of paper money as a legal tender; the pamphlet containing the full report of that case had just been published, and was elaborately advertised in the Philadelphia daily papers just at the time when the Convention was sitting.[2] Another case, that of *Holmes* v. *Walton*,

[1] *Report of the Committee published by Order of the Council of Censors*, dated *Sept. 1, 1784.* See *Respublica* v. *Chapman* (1781), 1 Dallas 52, and *Respublica* v. *Doan* (1785), 1 Dallas 86, 495, in both of which cases questions were raised as to the constitutionality of certain attainder statutes of Pennsylvania.

[2] See *Pennsylvania Packet*, April 25, May 2, 9, 16, 23, 1787. "Just come to hand and to be had of J. Dodson, Bookseller, Second Street, and J. Cruikshank, Market Street, Price 2sh. 6d. *The Case*, Trevett against Weeden on informa-

THE CONSTITUTION AND THE COURT

in New Jersey, in which a State Court held invalid a law relative to trial of persons possessing enemy goods, was known to one of the New Jersey delegates in the Convention, David Brearly, because he had sat as one of the Judges in the case; it was known to another New Jersey delegate, William Livingston, as he was Governor at the time of the decision, and to a third, William Paterson, as he was Attorney-General; and the case had been referred to by Gouverneur Morris, a delegate from Pennsylvania, in an argument and pamphlet written by him in 1785.[1] A third case was that of *Bayard* v. *Singleton* in North Carolina, in which the State Court held invalid a law relative to loyalist property; this case was decided on May 29, 1787, just while the Convention was sitting; and not only was a report of this decision holding the State statute invalid published in the Philadelphia papers in June, but the full opinion of the Judges was published in the Maryland and Virginia papers in July and sent

---

tion and complaint for refusing paper bills in payment for butcher's meat, etc. Tried before the honorable Superior Court in the County of Newport, Rhode Island. Also The Case of the Judges of said Court before the General Assembly, on citation for dismissing said complaint. By James M. Varnum, Esq., Counsellor at Law, etc."

The *Independent Gazetteer* (Phil.), June 26, 1787, also published "a letter from a gentleman in Virginia to his friend in this City", in which it was said: "The majority of the House of Delegates in Rhode Island have lost all character and even shame itself. Yet you see there are honest men in that State. The Judges behaved handsomely in the affair of the Tender Law."

James Madison in the Federal Convention, July 17, 1787, referred specifically to this Rhode Island case. See also *Trevett* v. *Weeden*, Thayer's *Cases on Constitutional Law*, I, 73–74; Chandler's *Criminal Trials*, II, 269–350.

[1] See specific reference to this case by Gouverneur Morris in *Life of Gouverneur Morris*, by Jared Sparks, III, 438; see also *Earliest Cases of Judicial Review of State Legislation by Federal Courts*, by Charles Warren, *Yale Law Journal* (1922); see also reference to *Holmes* v. *Walton*, in *State* v. *Parkhurst* (1804), 4 Halsted (N. J.) 433, 444; *Holmes* v. *Walton*, by Austin Scott, *Amer. Hist. Rev.* (1889).

on to Philadelphia; moreover, the lawyers on both sides of this case, William R. Davie and Richard D. Spaight, were members of the Convention.[1] A fourth case has been little referred to by historians; but it appears that inferior Courts of New Hampshire, in 1787, held invalid a law of that State depriving citizens of jury trial; and the news of this decision reached New York and Philadelphia and was published in the daily papers while the Federal Convention was sitting, and just at the time when the New Hampshire delegates arrived in the Convention; moreover, just before these delegates left the State, its leading newspaper had referred to the Judges' action "declaring that said Act of Legislature was unconstitutional, and therefore not binding on them, and have openly, manly and firmly refused to admit it as law."[2] Finally, just at the time when

[1] *Pennsylvania Packet*, June 27, 1787. "Newbern, N. C., May 30: Yesterday was agitated the celebrated question whether the suits brought for the recovery of confiscated property should be dismissed, according to the Act of Assembly commonly called the Quieting Act, when the Court gave their opinion in the negative." See also *Maryland Gazette*, July 3, 1787. In the previous year, the *Pennsylvania Packet*, July 1, Aug. 25, 1786, carried news items as to this case.

The *Virginia Independent Chronicle*, July 4, 1787, contained a full report of the case, beginning: "Newbern, June 7. On Saturday last, the term of the Superior Court of law and equity for the district was closed. . . . In the course of which term likewise was argued and determined that great constitutional point whether a citizen can be deprived of the right of a trial by jury, by an Act of Assembly made in opposition to the principles and express words of the Constitution, the fundamental law of the land, in a matter of controversy wherein his property is legally brought in question before the judicial power of the State. . . . The Court then, after every reasonable endeavor had been used in vain for avoiding a disagreeable difference between the Legislature and the judicial powers of the State, at length, with much apparent reluctance but with great deliberation and firmness, gave their opinions separately but unanimously, overruling the aforesaid motions for dismission of the suit. . . . 'The Constitution . . . standing in full force as the fundamental law of the land, notwithstanding the Act on which the present motion was granted, the Act must of course in that instance stand as abrogated and without effect.'"

[2] *Independent Gazetteer* (Phil.), July 18, 1787; *Pennsylvania Packet*, July 19; *New York Journal*, July 19, 1787. "Portsmouth, July 3. The General Court,

THE CONSTITUTION AND THE COURT 47

the Convention was sitting, the Philadelphia newspapers published reports of a case then argued which caused much local excitement — a petition for habeas corpus by one of the leaders of the radical party, Timothy Matlack, in which he claimed that a Pennsylvania statute unlawfully deprived him of trial by jury, and in which counsel argued:[1]

> The Constitution, having thus fixed this great right, no power of earth, not even the Legislature, can deprive a citizen of it. . . . Acts of Assembly contrary to the Constitution, being in themselves void, the Courts have a power of determining, as though such Act which is no law did not exist. . . . Such a power is the necessary consequence of their appointment to expound the law.

Nor were these cases the only examples of a readiness on the part of the State Courts to disregard statutes conflicting with a supreme law. In New York in 1784, in Connecticut in 1785, and in Massachusetts in 1786, the Courts had evinced a disposition in this direction.

In Virginia, in 1782, Judges had announced their power and intention to hold void statutes in contravention of the State Constitution; and two of these same Judges, George Wythe and John Blair,

during their late session, repealed the Ten Pound Act, and thereby justified the conduct of the justices of the Inferior Court who have uniformly opposed it as unconstitutional and unjust."
See also letter of "Watchmen" in *New Hampshire Spy*, June 30, 1787. See also *Amer. Hist. Rev.*, XII, 348; *Life of William Plumer* (1857), by William Plumer, Jr., 59; *The Relation of the Judiciary to the Constitution* (1919), by William M. Meigs, 73–74.

[1] See full account of the case and argument in *Pennsylvania Packet*, May 26, 1787. See also *Independent Gazetteer*, June 30, 1787, for a letter attacking the recent statute of Pennsylvania of March 28, 1787, appointing Commissioners to examine and pass on claims of Pennsylvania and Connecticut settlers in Luzerne County, on the ground that the statute granted away property without judge or jury, and thus deprived citizens of their right to trial by jury.

were members of this Convention. In Pennsylvania, in 1781, counsel had argued to the Court that a certain attainder statute should be disregarded as "contrary to the words and spirit of the Constitution"; but the Court held the defendant was not in a position to controvert the Act.[1]

Moreover, the Congress itself, under the Articles of Confederation, had, within two months before the sitting of the Federal Convention, adopted resolutions, drafted by John Jay, in which it was declared that when a treaty was made and ratified

---

[1] *Symsbury Case*, Kirby (Conn.) 444, 441; *History of the Foundation of the Constitution* (1882), by George Bancroft, II, 472; *Harv. Law Rev.* (1894), VII, 415; *Rutgers* v. *Waddington*, Thayer's *Cases on Constitutional Law*, I, 63, 68-72; *Com.* v. *Caton*, 4 Call (Va.) 5, 8, 16-20; see also *The Case of Josiah Phillips*, by W. P. Trent, *Amer. Hist. Rev.* (1898), I, and *Tucker's Blackstone*, I, App. 893; *Respublica* v. *Chapman* (1781), 1 Dallas 521. See in general *The Doctrine of Judicial Review* (1914), by Edward S. Corwin; *The Courts, the Constitution and Parties* (1912), by Andrew C. McLaughlin.

J. B. Cutting wrote to Thomas Jefferson, July 11, 1788: "I have also enclosed . . . the manly proceeding of a Virginia Court of Appeals. Without knowing the particular merits of the cause, I may venture to applaud the integrity of the Judges who thus fulfill their oaths and their duties. I am proud of such characters. They exalt themselves and their country, while they maintain the principles of the Constitution of Virginia and manifest the unspotted probity of its Judiciary Department. I hope you will not think me too local or statically envious when I mention that a similar instance has occurred in Massachusetts where the Legislature unintentionally trespassed upon a barrier of the Constitution, the Judges of the Supreme Court solemnly determined that the particular statute was unconstitutional. In the very next session, there was a formal and unanimous repeal of the law, which, perhaps, was unnecessary."

It is but fair to say that opponents of judicial review like Jackson H. Ralston, who as counsel for the American Federation of Labor submitted to it a *Study and Report* in 1922, have expressed the opinion that the New York case of *Rutgers* v. *Waddington* "instead of being an authority for, was one against the power of judicial review"; that the Connecticut case of *Symsbury* "may not be considered so much a precedent in favor of the judicial power as a judicial interpretation of a legislative Act"; and that the Massachusetts case referred to by Cutting, "was probably one in which the Court had ruled the Act of the Legislature involved to be repugnant to the treaty of 1783 with Great Britain." Whatever was the exact decision in those cases, however, there can be no doubt that in them there was recognized a power of the Courts to disregard State statutes.

by authority of those Articles, it became "part of the law of the land, and not only independent of the will and power of the (State) Legislatures, but also binding and obligatory on them"; that all existing State laws repugnant to the treaty ought to be forthwith repealed "to avoid the disagreeable necessity there might otherwise be of raising and discussing questions touching their validity and obligation"; and further that the States ought to provide that their Courts should decide all cases according to the intent of the treaty "anything in the Acts . . . to the contrary notwithstanding." These resolutions were not explicit in their recognition of the right of the State Courts to disregard State statutes without express authority from the States; but they contained a clear intimation that the Congress expected that the State Courts would take such action; and it is to be noted that arguments in behalf of such action were at once made in cases in such Courts.[1] From this recognition of a treaty made by Congress as a supreme law which, in behalf of individuals injured, the State Courts must enforce, even in the face of a conflicting State statute, it was but a step to the position that the new Federal Courts must have the power to enforce

[1] *Secret Journals of Congress, Foreign Affairs*, March 21, 1787; see also letters of Congress to the States, April 13, 1787. While the Federal Convention was still sitting, a case was argued in the Supreme Court of Pennsylvania at the September term of 1787, *Doane's Adm'rs* v. *Penhallow*, 1 Dallas 218, in which counsel argued that a law enacted by the Continental Congress, prior to the Articles of Confederation, was without authority, and that actions taken under such law were null and void. The President of the Court stated that the point involved in it, "the sovereignty of the separate States on the one hand and the supreme power of the United States in Congress assembled on the other, and is indeed, a momentous question"; but the case was decided on another point; see also *Respublica* v. *Gordon* (1788), 1 Dallas 233.

a Federal supreme law having the form of a Constitution, in the face of a conflicting Federal statute.[1]

With such practical illustrations of State Court actions and of the views of the Congress of the Confederation in their minds and before their very eyes in the newspapers, while they were sitting in Convention, the framers of the Constitution (several of whom were also Members of Congress) had no doubt as to what powers their new Federal Courts were to, and should, possess and exercise; nor did they omit to express their views on the floor of the Convention. Thus, Elbridge Gerry of Massachusetts spoke of the Judges' exposition of the laws, which "involved a power of deciding on the constitutionality", and said he: "In some States, the Judges had actually set aside laws as being against the Constitution. This was done too with general approbation." Luther Martin of Maryland said: "As to the constitutionality of laws, that point will come before the Judges in their proper official character." James Madison of Virginia said: "A law violating a Constitution established by the people themselves would be considered by the Judges as null and void." Gouverneur Morris and James Wilson of Pennsylvania, Caleb Strong of Massachusetts, George Mason of Virginia, Rufus King of Massachusetts, Hugh Williamson of North Carolina, and John Rutledge of South Carolina recognized and admitted the

---

[1] See *The Progress of Constitutional Theory*, etc., by Edward S. Corwin, *Amer. Hist. Rev.* (1925), XXX; *The Courts, the Constitution and Parties* (1912), by Andrew C. McLaughlin; *Writings of Jefferson* (Ford's Ed.), VII, Jefferson to George Hammond, May 29, 1792; *National Supremacy* (1913), by Edward S. Corwin, Ch. 3; *The Judicial Bulwark of the Constitution*, by Frank E. Melvin, *Amer. Pol. Soc. Rev.* (1919), VIII.

THE CONSTITUTION AND THE COURT 51

Judges' power over Acts of Congress, and Roger Sherman of Connecticut referred to the power of State Courts to set aside State statutes if violative of the Federal Constitution.

To these eleven men, there should be added at least the following — William Livingston, William Paterson, David Brearly, and Jonathan Dayton of New Jersey; William R. Davie of North Carolina; Abraham Baldwin of Georgia; John Blair, George Wythe, and Edmund Randolph of Virginia; Alexander Hamilton of New York; Oliver Ellsworth of Connecticut; Thomas Fitzsimmons of Pennsylvania; Charles C. Pinckney of South Carolina — each of whom, within a few years after the Convention, explicitly favored the judicial power. Only four members of the Convention announced themselves as opposed.

Any man who has ever taken part in a Convention, whether political, commercial, or religious, knows from common experience and common sense that when a constitution or by-law is discussed and the existence of a power under it is specifically stated and argued, amendments challenging the power are certain to be proposed if there is any considerable body of men opposed to its existence. No such motion was ever made in the Federal Convention.[1]

---

[1] For those who wish the details as to the evidence, the best works to be consulted are *The Supreme Court and the Constitution* (1912), by Charles A. Beard, and *The Judicial Bulwark of the Constitution*, by Frank E. Melvin, *Amer. Pol. Sci. Rev.* (1914), VIII, and the books and articles cited in the latter; see also *The American Doctrine of Judicial Supremacy* (1914), by Charles G. Haines. Beard lists 19 members of the Convention as showing definitely that they comprehended the doctrine of judicial control and others frankly approved it, or at least acquiesced in it, and 6 others who were favorable to it. Melvin says that 7 others "should surely be added" to Beard's list, and says that the evidence would indicate that 32 to 40 "upheld or accepted the right of the Courts

52   THE CONSTITUTION AND THE COURT

Some who now oppose the Court emphasize the fact that the Convention of 1787 rejected four times (by votes of June 4, 6, July 21, and August 15) a proposition urged strongly by Madison and others, that the Supreme Court should have a power of veto (with the President) of a bill after its passage.[1]

to disregard as law any unconstitutional legislation." See also *Debates*, June 4, 6, July 17, 23, Aug. 15, 22, 23, 28, 1787; and see a speech of Rufus King of Massachusetts, not reported in *Madison's Notes of Debates*, but given in *William Pierce's Notes, Amer. Hist. Rev.* (1898), III, 322–323.

Of the three members of the Convention expressing the contrary view, John F. Mercer of Maryland said, Aug. 15: "He disapproved the doctrine that the Judges as expositors of the Constitution should have authority to declare a law void. He thought laws ought to be well and cautiously made and then to be uncontrollable." Gunning Bedford, Jr., of Delaware said, June 4, he "was opposed to every check on the Legislature, even the Council of Revision first proposed. He thought it would be sufficient to mark out in the Constitution the boundaries to the Legislative authority. . . ." John Dickinson of Delaware said he was "strongly impressed with the remark of Mr. Mercer that as to the power of the Judges to set aside the law. He thought no such power ought to exist. He was at the same time at a loss what expedient to substitute." It is to be noted that later Dickinson changed his view; for in one of the "Fabius" letters written in 1788 by him in advocacy of the Constitution, he said, "In the President and the Federal independent Judges, so much concerned in the execution of the laws and in the determination of their constitutionality, the sovereignties of the several States, the people of the whole Union may be considered as conjointly represented." *Pamphlets on the Constitution* (1888), by Paul Leicester Ford, 184. One other, Richard D. Spaight of North Carolina, was opposed to the Court's power, but his views do not appear in the reports of the debates. To this, it may be fair to add that Robert Yates of New York in 1788 opposed the power but recognized its existence in the Constitution; Melvin thinks that John Lansing of New York was probably opposed; Charles Pinckney of South Carolina was not opposed in 1787, but changed his mind in 1799; and it is said by some that Abraham Baldwin of Georgia changed his mind in 1800 (see *infra*, p. 123, note 1). No historical writer has ever been able to find, at the utmost, any express statement of opposition by any other member of the Convention than the above eight.

For an unconvincing argument to the effect that most of the members of the Convention who voted for the Judiciary Act in 1789 in Congress, should be counted as opposed to the power of judicial review, see *Annulment of Legislation by the Supreme Court*, by Horace A. Davis, *Amer. Pol. Sci. Rev.* (1913), VII, embodied in his book *The Judicial Veto* (1914), and for a strong answer to this see *The Judicial Bulwark of the Constitution*, by Frank E. Melvin, *supra*.

[1] *Back to the Constitution*, by Walter Clark, *Amer. Law Rev.* (1916), L; *Withdrawing Power from Federal Courts to Declare Acts of Congress Void*, by Robert L. Owen, Jan. 27, 1917, *64th Cong., 2d Sess., Senate Doc. 737*.

THE CONSTITUTION AND THE COURT 53

But this proposition to make the Court part of the law-making body was a very different proposition from the power of judicial review which the Convention acknowledged the Court possessed. Judicial review can only be exercised if and when the statute is involved in a particular case between two parties; but a veto by the Judiciary could be exercised over any and every statute as soon as passed. Judicial review is only exercised after full argument of the case by counsel; but a veto is made without argument. The chief distinction between a veto and the power of judicial review, however, is more serious. James Wilson argued in favor of a veto, that "laws may be unjust, may be unwise, may be dangerous, may be destructive, and yet may not be so unconstitutional as to justify the Judges in refusing to give them effect"; and he urged that the Judges, with the President, should have the power to veto a law immediately upon its passage, simply because it was unwise and dangerous. It was the grave opposition to such an extreme proposition as this which brought about the defeat of the proposal for a judicial veto, on July 21, 1787. It was clearly seen that the Judges should not be allowed to concern themselves with the merits or demerits of a statute, for their functions only related to the legality and constitutionality of a statute; and this function could only properly be exercised in the decision of an actual lawsuit, after argument. Others were strongly opposed to the Judges having any power in the making of a statute which might come later before them for judicial decision. There was a general admission by the members of the Convention that the Court would have power, eventually, to pass on the validity of the Acts of Congress; and therefore, many did not believe it right that the Court should have a double chance. It will be seen, therefore, that the defeat of the proposal for a veto by the Court did not imply that the Convention was opposed to power of judicial review; but rather the contrary. It was because the Convention wished to confine the Court to its proper legal functions that it refused to grant to it broader, and really legislative, powers having no proper connection with judicial functions.

With such views and understanding as to what the new Federal Courts would do, and with such knowledge and experience as to what the State Court had done, the framers of the Constitution planned their Judiciary Article. And, just as they had embodied in the Constitution many provisions of their State Constitutions relating to the methods of action, powers, and rights of the State Legislature, and of the State Executive, so now, in planning for the enforcement of the Constitution, the framers undoubtedly determined to place this responsibility on the same branch of the government which was assuming that duty in the States — namely, the Judiciary. Accordingly, the framers provided in Article Three of the Constitution that: "The judicial power of the United States shall be vested in one Supreme Court and in such inferior Courts as the Congress may from time to time ordain and establish." They did not define, nor did they need to define, what power a Court should possess as a judicial body. The Court they were erecting was to possess all the powers which were exercised by Courts

THE CONSTITUTION AND THE COURT 55

as Courts in the States. The judicial power to determine that "wherever there is an evident opposition, the laws ought to give place to the Constitution" was a power which, in the States, had been found to be the necessary accompaniment to the effective existence of State Constitutions. As Hamilton wrote: "This doctrine is not deducible from any circumstance peculiar to the plan of the Convention; but from the general theory of a limited Constitution, and as far as it is true, is equally applicable to most, if not to all, the State Governments. There can be no objection, therefore, on this account to the Federal Judicature, which will not lie against the local Judicatures in general and which will not serve to condemn every Constitution that attempts to set bounds to Legislative discretion."

Many modern opponents of the Supreme Court seem to believe that they have an unanswerable question when they triumphantly cry out, "If the framers intended that the Court should have the power to hold Acts of Congress invalid, why did they not expressly so provide in the Constitution?"

There is a complete answer to that question. The framers did not make express provisions for the exercise of *this* power by that Court, because they made no express provision for the exercise of *any other* power by the Court. They did establish and define the jurisdiction, *i.e.*, the subject matters over and to which the judicial power of the Court should "extend"; but jurisdiction and judicial power are very separate things, though often confused. Judicial power comprises the functions exercised by a Court *after* it has obtained jurisdiction. Now it will be noticed that while the Constitution specifically states and limits the extent of the *jurisdiction* of the Federal Courts, it nowhere limits or even defines the *judicial power* of those Courts. Note the difference in language between Article One and Article Three of the Constitution. Article One reads: "All legislative powers *herein granted* shall be vested in a Congress of the United States." Article Three, however, reads: "*The* judicial power of the United States shall be vested in one Supreme Court and in such inferior Courts as the Congress may from time to time ordain and establish." It does *not* say: "All judicial powers *herein granted*." As to Congress, the legislative power is restricted to the specific grants of power contained in the Constitution. As to the Courts, the judicial power is not restricted, but includes all power which Courts at common law in the States had heretofore possessed and exercised as Courts. If the argument is raised that the Supreme Court did not possess the power of judicial review because it is not granted in specific terms by the Constitution, then the same argument can be raised against its possession of *any* judicial power, for the Constitution does not grant to the Court power to enter judgment, to issue execution, to enjoin, to commit for contempt, or to do any of the other things which the Court performs as a judicial body.[1] If lack of express grant of one power implies

---

[1] A far-fetched contention has been sometimes made that an express grant of power of judicial review was deliberately and intentionally omitted from the Constitution, the contention being based on a statement in a letter by Gouverneur Morris, in 1814, as to his part in writing the final draft of the Constitution, as follows: "Having rejected redundant and equivocal terms, I believed it to be as clear as our language would permit, excepting, nevertheless, a part of what relates to the Judiciary. On that subject, conflicting opinions had been main-

THE CONSTITUTION AND THE COURT

that the Court does not possess that power, then the lack of express grant of *any* powers at all must imply that the Court does not possess any powers — a ridiculous conclusion.

Now one of the judicial powers which a Court must possess, and inherent in it as a Court, is to decide, in a case brought before it, which of two conflicting laws apparently applying to the case must prevail — in other words, to say what the law is; and if these two apparently conflicting laws are a written Constitution and a statute, then in deciding what the law is, it must necessarily decide that a Constitution is *the* law, since being made by all the people, it must be superior to the conflicting enactment of a Congress acting as a mere agent of the people.[1] A Virginia Judge, who was an ardent

---

tained with so much professional astuteness, that it became necessary to select phrases which, expressing my own notions, would not alarm others nor shock their self love; and to the best of my recollection, this was the only part that passed without cavil." *Elliot's Debates*, I, 506. Morris' statement as to his selection of non-alarming phrases could not possibly refer to any grant or omission of grant of *powers* to the Court. The Constitution contains no grant of powers whatever; it concerns itself with grants of jurisdiction, *i.e.*, of subjects to which the judicial power should extend; and it actually did contain certain ambiguities as to jurisdiction, notably in the clause relative to jurisdiction over suits against States — an ambiguity which gave rise to the decision in the famous case of *Chisholm v. Georgia*, and to the 11th Amendment adopted to cure that decision. It was these jurisdictional ambiguities to which Morris was undoubtedly referring, and not to any omission of a grant of power of judicial review.

[1] Marshall, C. J., in *Marbury* v. *Madison* (1803), 1 Cranch 137. See also Sutherland, J., in *Adkins* v. *Children's Hospital* (1923), 261 U. S. 525, 544: "The Constitution, by its own terms, is the supreme law of the land, emanating from the people, the repository of ultimate sovereignty under our form of government. A Congressional statute, on the other hand, is the act of an agency of this sovereign authority, and, if it conflict with the Constitution, must fall; for that which is not supreme must yield to that which is. To hold it invalid (if it be invalid) is a plain exercise of the judicial power — that power vested in Courts to enable them to administer justice according to law. From the authority to ascertain and determine the law in a given case there necessarily results, in case of conflict, the duty to declare and enforce the rule of the supreme

strict-constructionist of the Constitution and a leading supporter of Jefferson, Spencer Roane, in a case in 1793, set forth a Court's necessary power as follows: "It is the province of the Judiciary to expound the laws. . . . The Judiciary may clearly say that a subsequent statute had not changed a former for want of sufficient words, though it was perhaps intended it should do so; it may say, too, that an Act of Assembly has not changed the Constitution, though its words are expressly to that effect, because a Legislature must have both the power and the will . . . to change the law. . . . In expounding laws, the Judiciary considers every law which relates to the subject. Would you have them shut their eyes against that law which is of the highest authority of any, or against a part of that law which either by its words or by its spirit denies to any but the people the power to change it?" In fact, it may almost be said that this function of the Court is a judicial *duty* rather than a *power* — a duty to apply the law, in litigated cases which come before the Court for decision. In such a case, if one party relies on an Act of Congress and the other party contends that the Act of Congress violates the Constitution, the Court has to decide which law governs. "From the nature of our Government, and the very terms of the Constitution itself, by which that instrument is declared to be the supreme

law and reject that of an inferior act of legislation which, transcending the Constitution, is of no effect, and binding on no one." See also *Kamper* v. *Hawkins* (1793), 1 Va. Cases 21. The opinions in this case upholding the power of judicial review are better worthy of study than any other case, especially since two of the opinions were rendered by violent Anti-Federalists and strict-constructionists — John Tyler and Spencer Roane.

law of the land, the Judges not only ought to exercise that power but they cannot avoid its exercise," said James Elliot of Vermont, in one of the very early Congresses. "The exercise of this negative power by the Court results from necessity, in the discharge of their judicial functions," said John Pope of Kentucky, in another early Congress. "A Court of justice ought to decide every case according to the right, whether that right be deduced from an Act of Congress or the Constitution." [1]

And then, Pope continued with a statement which constitutes almost contemporary evidence as to the possession of power by the Court. "I believe it was generally understood," he said, "when the Constitution was adopted that the Judiciary would, when necessary and proper, exercise this negative power. The different departments were expected to check and restrain each other from exceeding the proper limits. This negative power ... has been exercised by the Courts of the United States and of most of the States, ever since the commencement of the Government, without producing any serious inconvenience." And another almost contemporary Congressman well explained the reasons, saying:

The Convention of 1787, when devising a frame of Government for a free people, well understood the commotion that frequently agitated societies of men claiming the right to speak and act as they pleased. That sagacious body possessed perfect knowledge, from history, of the proscriptions and attainders which an overbearing ma-

[1] *8th Cong., 2d Sess.*, James Elliot, in the House, Jan. 30, 1805; *.10th Cong., 1st Sess.*, John Pope, in the House, Feb. 24, 1808; *10th Cong., 1st Sess.*, Samuel L. Mitchell of New York, in the House, Dec. 31, 1807.

jority were too prone to pass upon those who differed from them in their preference of one man or measure to another, or who thwarted their views of interest or ambition or resentment or power. They, therefore, provided a salutary check upon the will of the Congress itself, thereby guarding against that heat and violence which the collisions of party have been often observed to produce. This was a security enjoyed by the minority of the two Houses and of their adherents and supporters throughout the nation, against the exterminating spirit which the majority might feel and in an evil hour be tempted to exert.

Let us put the practical issue. Suppose that Congress should pass an Act granting to John Doe property already granted to Richard Roe (as, in fact Congress actually did attempt to do in 1908).[1] Such legislative transfer of Roe's property would unquestionably deprive him without the due process of law guaranteed by the Constitution. He sues Doe. What shall the Court do in deciding the rights of the parties? It cannot apply both the Act and the Constitution, for the application of the one would result in a different decision from the application of the other. How would any intelligent layman answer that question? Is it not clear, that though he might know nothing about distribution of federal powers between the branches of the government or between the Union and the States, though he might know nothing about theories of legislative omnipotence or judicial control, yet he would know that, having taken an oath to support the Constitution as the supreme law of the land, he could not,

---

[1] See *Choate* v. *Trapp* (1912), 224 U. S. 665, holding invalid section 4 of the Act of Congress of May 27, 1908 (35 Stat. 313).

without violating that oath, enforce and apply, in deciding a case, any Act of Congress which violated that Constitution. As that is the moral and practical view which a layman would take, so that is the legal view which a Judge must take.[1]

When, on August 23, 1787, three weeks before the end of the session, the members of the Convention proceeded to adopt Article Six of the Constitution, which specifically provided that "the Constitution and the laws of the United States which shall be made in pursuance thereof . . . shall be the supreme law of the land", they made their intent as to the power of the Judiciary even more clear. For this clause meant, as was later explained by Governor Johnston in the North Carolina Convention, that: "Every law consistent with the Constitution will have been made in pursuance of the powers granted by it. Every usurpation or law repugnant to it cannot have been made *in pursuance of its powers.* The latter will be nugatory and void."[2] And finally, when the framers, on August 27, inserted the provision that "the judicial power shall extend to all cases . . . arising under this Constitution", as well as under the laws and treaties of the United States, they left no possible room for any misunderstanding; for by this clause they meant that whenever a case should be presented to the Court in which one party claimed a right or a defense based on the provisions of the Constitution, and another party claimed a defense or a right based on something else (whether that something else was an Act of Congress, a State

---

[1] *The American Judiciary* by Joseph W. Bailey, *Amer. Bar Ass. Report* (1915).
[2] *Elliot's Debates*, IV, 187–188.

statute, or an order of the President), the Court should have jurisdiction to hear the case, and, necessarily, should have power to determine which right so asserted by the parties should lawfully prevail. It is to be especially noted that the Court does not decide *questions* in general; it only decides *cases*.[1]

It determines which of two opposing parties in an actual lawsuit shall prevail, according to the principles of law. It does not "nullify" Acts of Congress; but it simply declines to execute an Act of Congress in any suit of which it has jurisdiction, and in which it finds that the Act would operate to deprive one of the parties to the suit of rights claimed by him under the Constitution.[2] In other words, the Court does not claim nor does it possess a substantive

---

[1] John Marshall of Virginia said, in the House, in the debate on Jonathan Robbins, March 7, 1800: "A case in law or equity was a term well understood, and of limited signification. It was a controversy between parties, which had taken a shape for judicial decision. If the judicial power extended to every question under the Constitution it would involve almost every subject proper for Legislative discussion and decision; if to every question under the laws and treaties of the United States, it would involve almost every subject on which the Executive could act. . . . By extending the Judicial power to all cases in law or equity, the Constitution had never been understood to confer on that department any political power whatever. To come within this description, a question must assume a legal form for forensic litigation and judicial decision. There must be parties to come into Court, who can be reached by its process, and bound by its power; whose rights admit of ultimate decision by a tribunal to which they are bound to submit." *6th Cong., 1st Sess.*

[2] This distinction was early recognized in the famous debate over the repeal of the Circuit Court Act of 1801, when Thomas T. Davis of Kentucky, in the House, Feb. 17, 1802, said: "Never can I believe the Judiciary paramount to both branches of the Legislature. . . . I am willing to admit the Judiciary to be coördinate with the Legislature in this respect, to wit, that Judges thinking a law unconstitutional are not bound to execute it; but not to declare it null and void." *7th Cong., 1st Sess.* And it was strikingly stated by a strong State-rights Senator, who violently opposed most of the decisions of the Court, John Rowan of Kentucky, in the Senate, Feb. 8, 1830: "I deny that the power to declare a law of Congress or of any of the States unconstitutional was ever conferred, or intended to be conferred upon the Judiciary of the States or of

THE CONSTITUTION AND THE COURT 63

power of holding Acts of Congress unconstitutional. The exercise of such a power is simply incidental to exercise of general judicial power conferred upon it by the Constitution. Except as an Act of Congress is involved in a suit between two parties over which the Court is given jurisdiction by the Constitution, the Court has no power to determine for Congress, the President, or any one else the validity or invalidity of such an Act. It is unfortunate that Courts and writers have used the phrases "invalidating statutes", "nullifying statutes", and the like, for such expressions give a wrong idea of the Court's action. Those persons who oppose the Court's power because it appears to them to render the Court "superior to Congress" fail to note that the Court itself asserts no such superiority; it only asserts its duty under the Constitution to establish for parties in a lawsuit the rights which that document guarantees to them, viz., that it shall be regarded as the "supreme law of the land." [1]

With such express provisions contained in it, the

the General Government as a direct substantive power. The exercise of this power is incidental to the exercise of the mere judicial power which was conferred. The validity of a law involved by a case may be incidentally decided in deciding the law and justice of the case. But the decision must be made with an eye to the law and justice of the case, and not in reference to the just or unjust exercise of the Legislative power which was exerted in making the law, not in the view to check, control or restrain the Legislative power. It must be given in the exercise of merely a judicial and not of political power." *21st Cong., 1st Sess.*

[1] See Sutherland, J., in *Adkins* v. *Children's Hospital* (1923), 261 U. S. 525, 544: "From the authority to ascertain and determine the law in a given case, there necessarily results in cases of conflict, the duty to declare and enforce the rule of the supreme law and reject that of an inferior act of legislation which, transcending the Constitution, is of no effect, and binding on no one. *This is not the exercise of a substantive power to review and nullify Acts of Congress, for no such substantive power exists.* It is simply a necessary concomitant of the power to hear and dispose of a case or controversy properly before the Court, to the determination of which must be brought the test and measure of the law,"

Constitution was signed on September 17, 1787. Thereafter, all men at that time knew that if any case arose in the Supreme Court in which the provisions of an Act of Congress conflicted with the provisions of the Constitution, the Court would have but one duty — namely, to declare that the Constitution must prevail, as "the supreme law of the land."[1] And this duty and power of the Court was no new thing, but the embodiment in the Constitution, by its framers, of the well-known and necessary power of their own State Courts with reference to their own State Constitutions — a power without which a written Constitution, whether of the State or of the Nation, was unenforceable and useless, as a protection either to the citizens or to the States.

Not only did the framers of the Constitution

[1] The views of the ardent advocates of the Constitution respecting the Judiciary as a curb upon infringement of the Constitution by Congress were powerfully set forth by Alexander Hamilton in his essays (numbers 78 to 83) in the *New York Gazette*, published from June 17 to July 25, 1788. While these essays were not contained in the first two editions of *The Federalist* (published in March and in May, 1788), they received considerable newspaper circulation.

Madison, who was a co-author with Hamilton and Jay of this work, wrote to Jefferson, as to it, Feb. 8, 1825: "*The Federalist* may fairly enough be regarded as the most authentic exposition of the text of the Federal Constitution, as understood by the Body which prepared and the authority which accepted it. Yet it did not foresee all the misconstructions which have occurred; nor prevent some that it did foresee. And what equally deserves remark, neither of the great rival parties have acquiesced in all its comments." *Writings of James Madison*, IX, 218; see also Madison to Spencer Roane, May 6, 1821, *ibid.*, IX, 55.

For early views of *The Federalist* in Congress, see Elbridge Gerry, Feb. 7, 1791, *1st Cong., 3d Sess.*; Philip Barton Key, Nov. 13, 1807, *10th Cong., 1st Sess.*; and William Lowndes, March 10, 1818, who said: "*The Federalist* was written by men yet warm from debates, in which all their ingenuity and talent for refinement had been employed to prove that the powers which the Constitution gave were not great enough to be dangerous. That, with such powerful disturbing causes, the judgment of these distinguished men should so often have led to the same construction of the Constitution which cool examination has since confirmed, is a rare testimony of their merit." *15th Cong., 1st Sess.*

THE CONSTITUTION AND THE COURT 65

thoroughly understand the part which the Court was to play in its maintenance, but the general public had the same understanding, as shown by the newspapers of the time. Of these, the following, in 1788, are especially strong examples, since they were written by men opposed to the Constitution. Thus, George Bryan of Pennsylvania (under the name of "Centinel") wrote: "Should Congress be disposed to violate the fundamental articles of the Constitution . . . still it would be of no avail, as there is a further barrier opposed . . . namely, the Supreme Court of the Union, whose province it would be to determine the constitutionality of any law that may be controverted. . . . It would be their sworn duty to refuse their sanction to laws made in the force and contrary to the letter of the Constitution." And "Brutus" (Robert Yates), writing in the *New York Journal,* objected to the Constitution because of the power vested in the Court, since, he said, it "is in many cases superior to that of the Legislature, I have showed in a former paper that this Court will be authorized to decide upon the meaning of the Constitution. . . . In the exercise of this power they will not be subordinate to but above the Legislature. . . . The Supreme Court then have a right independent of the Legislature to give a construction to the Constitution and every part of it and there is no power provided in this system to correct their construction or do it away. If, therefore, the Legislature pass any laws inconsistent with the sense the Judges put upon the Constitution, they will declare it void, and, therefore, in this respect, their power is superior to that of the

Legislature." [1] As early as June, 1789, the leading paper in New York published a series of articles on the new Government, which spoke of the distribution of powers as forming the best security against encroachments or abuse of power by either, and said that "perhaps in no case can abstract and uncontrolled power be lodged with more security to liberty and the rights of the people", than in the Judiciary and that for "an impartial and able interpretation of the laws . . . necessary to secure the life, liberty and property of the subject. . . ." The Constitution had wisely provided for a National Judiciary "independent of the other branches of the Government." A New York correspondent of a London newspaper, in October, 1789, wrote specifically that the Court was to exercise a right of judicial review of Acts of Congress as follows: "The judicial power is established for the benefit of foreigners, and will be a check on any encroachment for the State or the United States on the Constitution. They have the power of declaring void any law infringing it." [2]

[1] *Independent Gazetteer* (Phil.), Feb. 26, 1788; *American Herald* (Boston), April 14, 1788, *New York Journal*, March 20, 1788; *Providence Gazette*, Aug. 9, 1788; see also "Solon, Jr.", in *Providence Gazette*, Aug. 9, 1788, who after discussing *Trevett* v. *Weeden* said: "Had that privilege (trial by jury) been ever so safe on paper and a phrenzy seized the Administration, similar to that under which this State at a certain time laboured, could not a penal law have passed Congress and been enforced by a federal Court — or a federal army — unless indeed they should have found the unconquerable spirit of an Adams in that Court to humble the pride of usurped power?" See also "Alfred" in *Independent Chronicle* (Boston), Oct. 23, 1788: "Congress are to appoint a Supreme Judicial to decide upon all matters which are within the legislative powers of the General Government."

[2] *New York Gazette*, June 3 to July 17, 1789. See *A Sketch of the Political State of America*, by "Americanus", in *Gazette of the United States*, May 13, June 10, 1789. For recognition of the Judiciary, both State and Federal, as "the only bulwark the faithful lieges have to depend on against lawless power and usurpation", see series of letters by "Aratus", in *State Gazette of North Carolina*, April 9, May 14, June 3, July 2, 23, 30, 1789. See also "Aristides" (Alexander

THE CONSTITUTION AND THE COURT 67

Finally, it must not be forgotten that in considering the effect of a written instrument, the views of those who voted to adopt it are even more important than the views of those who framed it.[1] James Madison himself wrote that if a key to the meaning of the Constitution was to be "sought elsewhere" than in the text itself, "it must not be in the opinion or intentions of the body which planned and proposed the Constitution, but in the sense attached to it by

Contee Hanson of Maryland), in *Pamphlets on the Constitution* (1888), by Paul Leicester Ford: "They may reflect, however, that every Judge in the Union, whether of Federal or of State appointment (and some persons would say, every jury), will have a right to reject any Act, handed to him as a law, which he may conceive to be repugnant to the Constitution." See also *London Public Advertiser*, Oct. 8, 1789, quoted in the *La Follette Veto*, by Noel Sargent in the *Forum* (1922), LXVIII.

[1] *Writings of James Madison*, IX, 71, Madison to Thomas Ritchie, Sept. 15, 1821. This letter stated as to Madison's Notes on the Federal Convention: "as a guide in explaining and applying the provisions of the Constitution, the debates and incidental decisions of the Convention can have no authoritative character. However desirable it be that they should be preserved as a gratification to the laudable curiosity felt by every people to trace the origin and progress of their political institutions, and as a source perhaps of some lights on the science of government, the legitimate meaning must be derived from the text itself." See also Madison to M. L. Hurlbert, May, 1830, *ibid.*, IX, 370; and see especially speech of Madison, in the House, March 30, 1796: "After all, whatever veneration might be entertained for the body of men who formed our Constitution, the sense of that body could never be regarded as the oracular guide in expounding the Constitution. As the instrument came from them, it was nothing more than the draft of a plan, nothing but a dead letter, until life and validity were breathed into it, by the voice of the people, speaking through the several State Conventions. If we were to look, therefore, for the meaning of the instrument beyond the face of the instrument, we must look for it, not in the General Convention which proposed, but in the State Conventions which accepted and ratified the Constitution." *4th Cong., 1st Sess.* The same view was expressed by Albert Gallatin, in the House, Feb. 28, 1799, who believed that only the views of those who "passed and ratified" the Constitution should be received as interpretative: "The evidence of members of the Convention which framed the Constitution has sometimes been offered to prove that that body, by 'persons', meant slaves. But the evidence of those members cannot prove anything beyond their own individual intention, or, at most, the belief of what might have been the intention of some other members. Nor is, on any possible supposition, the intention of the Convention itself of any importance to decide the true meaning of the Constitution. For they were not the legislators who passed and ratified the Act, but only the framers who drew the instrument and offered it for consideration." *5th Cong., 3d Sess.*

the people in their respective State Conventions where it received all the authority which it possesses"; and again: "as presumptive evidence of the general understanding, at the time, of the language used, it must be kept in mind that the only authoritative intentions were those of the people of the States as expressed through the Conventions which ratified the Constitution." And as Jefferson wrote to the Rhode Island Legislature, on his election to the Presidency, in 1801: "The Constitution shall be administered by me according to the safe and honest meaning contemplated by the plain understanding of the people at the time of its adoption — *a meaning to be found in the explanations of those who advocated, not those who opposed it.*"[1] Hence it is essential to lay particular stress on what was said when the Constitution was discussed in the various State Conventions which met to ratify it. While these debates in these Conventions were not reported with the fullness that might be desired,[2] the striking fact remains, that so far as reported, there was no challenge, in any Convention, of the existence of the power of the Court with reference to Acts of Congress; and there were explicit acknowledgments of its existence in the debates in North Carolina, Maryland, Virginia, Pennsylvania, New York, and Massachusetts.[3]

---

[1] *Elliot's Debates*, IV, 446.

[2] James Madison said in the Jay Treaty debate in the House, March 30, 1796: "In referring to the debates of the State Conventions, as published, he wished not to be understood as putting entire confidence in the accuracy of them. Even those of Virginia, which had been taken down by the most skillful hand (whose merit he wished by no means to disparage) contained internal evidence, in abundance, of chasms and misconceptions of what was said." *4th Cong., 1st Sess.*, p. 777.

[3] *Elliot's Debates*, IV, 155–156. John Steele of North Carolina also said (*ibid.*, 71): "The judicial power of that government is so well constructed as

THE CONSTITUTION AND THE COURT 69

Thus William R. Davie of North Carolina said:

There is no rational way of enforcing the laws but by the instrumentality of the Judiciary. . . . It appears to me that the Judiciary ought to be competent to the decision of any question arising out of the Constitution itself.

Oliver Ellsworth of Connecticut said:

This Constitution defines the extent of the powers of the General Government. If the General Legislature should at any time overleap their limits, the Judicial Department is a constitutional check. If the United States go beyond their powers, if they make a law which the Constitution does not authorize, it is void; and the Judicial Power, the Judges, who, to secure their impartiality, are to be made independent, will declare it to be void.

George Nicholas of Virginia said:

Who is to determine the extent of such powers? I say the same power which, in all well-regulated communities, determines the extent of Legislative powers. If they exceed these powers, the Judiciary will declare it void, or else the people will have a right to declare it void.

Patrick Henry of Virginia said:

I take it as the highest encomium on this country that the Acts of the Legislature, if unconstitutional, are liable to be opposed by the Judiciary.

to be a check. . . . If the Congress make laws inconsistent with the Constitution independent Judges will not uphold them, nor will the people obey them." For the other opinions quoted, see *Elliot's Debates*, I, 380; II, 196, 489; III, 443, 539-541, 553; see also James Wilson's opinion, II, 445-446: "Under this Constitution, the Legislature may be restrained and kept within its prescribed bounds, by the interpretation of the Judicial Department. . . . When it (an Act) comes to be discussed before the Judges — when they consider its principles and find it to be incompatible with the superior power of the Constitution — it is their duty to pronounce it void; and Judges, independent, and not obliged to look to every session for a continuance of their salaries, will behave with intrepidity and refuse to the Act the sanction of judicial authority."

John Marshall of Virginia said:

If they (Congress) were to make a law not warranted by any of the powers enumerated, it would be considered by the Judges as an infringement of the Constitution which they are to guard. . . . They would declare it void.

James Wilson of Pennsylvania said:

If a law should be made inconsistent with those powers vested by this instrument in Congress, the Judges, as a consequence of their independence, and the particular powers of government being defined, will declare such a law to be null and void; for the power of the Constitution predominates. Anything, therefore, that shall be enacted by Congress contrary thereto, will not have the force of law.

Luther Martin of Maryland, arguing for the rejection of the Constitution, said:

Whether, therefore, any laws or regulations of the Congress, any acts of the President or other officers, are contrary to, or not warranted by, the Constitution rests only with the Judges, who are appointed by Congress to determine; by whose determination every State must be bound.

Here again, any man who has taken part in any Convention will realize that plain statements as to the existence of a power, under any new proposed Constitution or by-law, would, as a matter of common experience, be vigorously attacked and denied, if there were any considerable number of men in the Convention who believed that the power did not, or should not, exist.

Finally, the singular fact should be noted (for it is generally overlooked) that the Judiciary is the only branch of the government which has functioned precisely as the framers intended and expected. As to the feasible operation or success of the other governing bodies in the new Government, there was great scepticism and doubt expressed by the members of the Convention, and by other statesmen favorable to the adoption and experimental trial of the Constitution.[1] Thus, Franklin, Randolph, and Hugh Williamson were fearful lest the President's powers were so great that he would certainly become a king; and the country would "end in monarchy"; on the other hand, James Wilson thought the President would be so weak that he would not be "the man of the people as he ought to be, but the minion of the Senate"; and Charles Pinckney dilated on "the contemptible weakness and dependence of the Executive." George Mason was certain that "it would end either in monarchy or aristocracy"; he believed that the system of election was such that, nineteen out of twenty times, the choice of President would fall into Congress, and he thought that to refer the choice of President to the people

[1] Andrew Gregg of Pennsylvania said, in the House, Dec. 8, 1803: "It is a Constitution of experiment. The wise framers of it, with all their sagacity, could not foresee how far its various provisions would, in practice, correspond with their views or answer their expectations." *8th Cong., 1st Sess.*

John Randolph of Virginia said, in the Senate, Feb. 14, 1826: "I cannot believe that the authors of this instrument who were very sagacious men, though their sagacity did not, it could not, it is not in the nature of things, it is not in the nature of man that it should, extend to the point of seeing how this political machine, when they put it into operation, would work. . . . Men commence with the control of things — they put events in motion — but after a very little while, events hurry them away and they are borne along with a swift fatality that no human sagacity or power can foresee or control. All Governments have worked so, and none more than ours. No man ever supposed that the British Constitution, taken theoretically, was to produce the present result; no man ever supposed that the different French Constitutions, with their Councils of youngsters, were to turn out as they had done. A Government on paper is one thing — it is such a government as we find in this book. And a Government of practice is another thing." *19th Cong., 1st Sess.*

was as "unnatural as it would be to refer a trial of colors to a blind man. The extent of the country rendered it impossible that the people can have the requisite capacity to judge of the respective pretensions of the candidates."[1] Others, like Elbridge Gerry of Massachusetts and John F. Mercer of Maryland, believed that the Congress had such powers that the country would certainly become an aristocracy.[2] Gouverneur Morris referred to the system adopted as a "legislative tyranny", in which "the great and wealthy, in the course of things, will necessarily compose the legislative body. . . . It threatens this country with an aristocracy. The aristocracy will grow out of the House of Representatives." Edmund Randolph believed that the Senate would be "more likely to be corrupt than the House." John Adams wrote to Jefferson: "You are afraid of the one; I, of the few. . . . You are apprehensive of monarchy; I, of aristocracy. I would, therefore, have given more power to the President and less to the Senate." These and similar doubts as to the success of the Constitution prevailed widely among its warm friends; and even Nathaniel Gorham of Massachusetts, who presided over the Convention when it sat in Committee, expressed his disbelief "that this vast country, in-

---

[1] *Debates*, Franklin, June 4, 1787; Randolph, June 4; Williamson, July 24; Wilson, Sept. 6; Pinckney, Sept. 25; Mason, July 17, Sept. 4.
[2] *Debates*, Gerry, Aug. 14, 1787; Mercer, Aug. 14; Mason, Sept. 15; Morris, July 19, Aug. 7; Randolph, Aug. 13; Gorham, Aug. 8, 1787. *Works of John Adams*, VIII, 464, Adams to Jefferson, Dec. 6, 1787. See also Adams to Jefferson, July 29, 1791; Jefferson to Adams, Aug. 30, 1791. Charles Pinckney, in the Federal Convention, Aug. 14, said that "he hoped to see that body (the Senate) become a school of public ministers, a nursery of statesmen." Some, to-day, may even question whether this hope has been fulfilled.

cluding the Western Territories, will, one hundred and fifty years hence, remain one nation."

These misgivings have all proved to have been unfounded; the alarmist prophecies as to how the provisions for the Executive and Legislative branches would work out have all failed of fulfillment; these provisions have operated better than their framers expected, though in many instances, in a different manner from that intended.[1]

The Judiciary alone has developed precisely as planned and understood in 1787. Of course, it cannot be said that its actual decisions have entirely conformed to the views of the framers of the Constitution. For, largely owing to Chief Justice Marshall's breadth of national views in the construction and interpretation of the language of the Constitution, the Court, during its first fifty years, upheld the powers of Congress to a greater extent than the framers probably expected. Moreover, during its first seventy years, owing to the extended view which both Chief Justices Marshall and Taney took of the clause forbidding States to impair the obligation of contract, the Court curbed State legislation more rigidly and frequently than the framers anticipated. The large number of State statutes held invalid by the Court, from 1885 to 1925, under the

[1] George McDuffie of South Carolina said, in the House, Feb. 16, 1826: "In the organization of the Executive Department of the Government —that department in which it has always been found most difficult to unite the elements of liberty and power — the Convention, deriving but few and glimmering and delusive lights from history, have most signally failed of accomplishing their patriotic intentions, though this is undoubtedly the part of the system which they regarded as the least obnoxious to objection — an impressive admonition to us all how seldom in the conduct of human affairs the wisdom of man transcends the narrow horizon of his experience." *19th Cong., 1st Sess.*

due process clause of the 14th Amendment, could not have been anticipated by the framers; for they never could have conceived it possible that the peoples of the States would ever consent to such limitation of their own powers and to such an extension of Federal jurisdiction as occurred when the States ratified that 14th Amendment, eighty years after the adoption of the Constitution. Furthermore, it is to be noted that there were some parts of the Constitution — certain of the restrictions on the powers of Congress and of the President — which were not susceptible of enforcement by any Court, because they presented phases of government which could not, in the nature of things, become the subject of litigation between private individuals or between an individual and the Government. Thus the limitation on the right of Congress to appropriate money is not enforceable by the Court.[1]

Nevertheless, in spite of any specific decisions of the Court which may not have been consonant with the views of the framers, it is indubitable that, in general, it has functioned as it was intended, in 1787, that it should function. It was planned to be the power which should maintain the balance between the Nation and the States, by preventing undue encroachment of the one upon the other. This, it was intended to do. This, it has done. It was planned to be the power which should protect the citizens against violation of their rights by either Congress or the Executive. This, it was intended to do. This, it has done.

[1] See *Massachusetts* v. *Mellon, Frothingham* v. *Mellon* (1923), 262 U. S. 447.

CHAPTER THREE

THE BILL OF RIGHTS AND THE COURT

"Why had they established that fundamental law which the people themselves were as much bound to respect as their public functionaries — a rule of action for all, from which none could absolve themselves? It was because of the radical depravity and original sin of their nature, which called for wholesome restraints. In a lucid interval, they had wisely determined to tie up the hands, not only of their agents, but of themselves, that when the hour of passion should come, barriers might be opposed to their inconsiderate rashness. Every feature of our Government, both State and National, proved that the people were sensible of restraining as well the headlong impetuosity of the multitude as the inordinate ambition of the few. Where such restraint was not improved, there was no genuine liberty." — JOHN RANDOLPH of Virginia, in the House, Nov. 13, 1807. *10th Cong., 1st Sess.*

"With what show of reason can it be contended that the Federal Government is to be the exclusive judge of the extent of its own powers? A written Constitution was resorted to in this country, as a great experiment, for the purpose of ascertaining how far the rights of a minority could be secured against the encroachments of majorities — often acting under party excitement and not unfrequently under the influence of strong interests. . . . When Congress (exercising a delegated and strictly limited authority) pass beyond these limits, their Acts become null and void, and must be declared so by the Courts, in cases within their jurisdiction." — ROBERT Y. HAYNE of South Carolina, in the Senate, Jan. 26, 1830. *21st Cong., 1st Sess.*

While those who drafted the Constitution in 1787, and those who ratified it in 1788, clearly evinced their desire and intention to establish an instrument which should set definite limits of power to the Congress and the Executive, it was in 1789, when the

First Congress adopted the ten Amendments embodying the Bill of Rights, that the intention to establish the Judiciary as a curb upon usurpation of power by the other two branches of the Government became even more strikingly evident. No action ever taken by Congress was more clearly the result of a general demand for limitations on Legislative power, to be enforceable through a Judiciary. The genesis of this national Bill of Rights should be most carefully studied by the liberals and radicals in this country to-day, for they are the very persons most likely to stand in need of the protection intended to be guaranteed by this portion of the Constitution.

Radicals, especially young radicals, are a highly desirable portion of the community. It would be a stagnant world indeed if they did not comprise part of the community. The process of living and the assumption of responsibilities are likely enough to turn most men into conservatives; and it would be a deplorable and a depressing thing if young men did not start out in life more radical than their fathers. But no one should be more careful than the radical himself to make sure that proposals and panaceas, laid before him with the radical brand upon them, are, in reality, radical or progressive. For many of such proposals are, in fact, the reverse — they are reactionary — and they are regarded as radical or progressive frequently because the proposer has not known enough history to realize that what he proposes has been already tried in the past, and discarded in favor of something better. Such a reactionary proposal is that which is now made to suppress the powers of the Supreme Court. It is a

BILL OF RIGHTS AND THE COURT

reversion towards something which our ancestors fought to escape. Those who advocate this proposal should not be denounced, but they should be taught history. Their views are dangerous, only until the light is turned on. As Mr. Justice Holmes wrote a few years ago: "With effervescing opinions, as with the not yet forgotten champagnes, the quickest way to let them get flat is to let them get exposed to the air." And as the same Justice has said in a judicial opinion: "The best test of truth is the power of thought to get itself accepted in the open market." To get a thought accepted as truth, it is necessary that the thought be supported by facts and valid reasoning. Reforms cannot prevail by falsification of history.

It is highly important for all American citizens, conservatives and radicals alike, to fix firmly in their minds the fact that the document which was framed in the Federal Convention and signed on September 17, 1787 — wise, beneficial, skillful, promotive of the interest of the Union as it may have been — never was and never would have been accepted as a Constitution for these United States, by the peoples of the States; for it contained two defects and omissions, which rendered it impossible of acceptance as drafted. Those radical writers and speakers of to-day who attack the Constitution as the product solely of the professional, the wealthy, and the conservative classes, and who seek to utilize prejudices against these classes as a means of discrediting the instrument which they are alleged to have framed, make the common mistake of talking about the Constitution as if it consisted simply of the document signed on September 17, 1787.[1] It was not that document, however, which became the Constitution as finally adopted.

It is quite true, and it was quite natural, that the men who saw most clearly and felt most keenly the disastrous commercial and political conditions, existing in 1787 and due to the feeble government then prevailing, should have been those who had most at stake, the merchants, the tradesmen, the mechanics of the seaport towns, the lawyers, and the great landholders in the country — in other words, the more conservative men in the community; and hence it was quite natural that it should have been those men who took the lead in seeking the adoption of a new frame of government. But the Constitution, as so drafted by their representatives, dealt chiefly with the forms and machinery of government, and with the distribution of powers between the Nation and the States, imposing limitations on the rights and powers of both, but containing few restrictions on the power of Congress with respect to individual and human rights. So framed, however, the Constitution was at once seen to be fatally defective; and other men than those who framed it took it in hand. The two most vital defects were the absence of a guaranty of reserved powers to the States, and the absence of a guaranty to the citizens of protection against the exercise of despotic power by the new Government.

[1] Charles A. Beard, in his *Economic Interpretation of the Constitution* (1913), p. 188, said: "It was an economic document, drawn with superb skill, by men whose property interests were immediately at stake; and as such, it appealed directly and unerringly to identical interests in the country at large." This statement is not true if applied to the final Constitution containing the first ten Amendments.

BILL OF RIGHTS AND THE COURT   79

Men on all sides contended that, while the first object of a Constitution was to establish a government, its second object, equally important, must be to protect the people against the government.[1] That was something which all history and all human experience had taught.

The first thing that most of the Colonies had done, on separating from Great Britain, had been to assure to the people a Bill of Rights, safeguarding against State Legislative despotism those human rights which they regarded as fundamental.[2] Having protected themselves by specific restrictions on the power of their State Legislatures, the people of this country were in no mood to set up and accept a new National Government, without similar checks and restraints. As soon as the proposed Constitution was published,

---

[1] *The American Constitution* (1922), by Frederic J. Stimson, p. 7. Alexander Hamilton wrote in *The Federalist*, No. 51, Feb. 8, 1788: "In framing a government, which is to be administered by men over men, the great difficulty lies in this: You must first enable the government to control the governed; and in the next place, oblige it to control itself. A dependence on the people is, no doubt, the primary control on the government; but experience has taught mankind the necessity of auxiliary precaution."

[2] A Bill of Rights, drafted by George Mason, had been adopted by Virginia on June 12, 1776, even before the Declaration of Independence. Pennsylvania had followed, Sept. 28, 1776; Maryland, Nov. 11, 1776; North Carolina, Dec. 18, 1776; South Carolina in 1778; Massachusetts in 1780; and New Hampshire in 1784. So insistent, indeed, was Massachusetts, that her people turned down an earlier draft of a Constitution in 1778, because of its failure to provide such a Bill of Rights.

Richard Henry Lee, in the Congress of the Confederation, had proposed such a Bill of Rights as an Amendment, even before the Constitution was submitted to the States; and he complained in a letter to Governor Edmund Randolph, that, in the Constitution, "there is no restraint, in form of a Bill of Rights, to secure (what Doctor Blackstone calls) that residuum of human rights which is not intended to be given up to society, and which, indeed is not necessary to be given up for any social purpose. The rights of conscience, the freedom of the press, and the trial by jury, all at mercy."

Edmund Randolph, George Mason, and Elbridge Gerry, who as delegates refused to sign the Constitution, each formally stated, as one of his reasons, the lack of a Bill of Rights.

the demand for a national Bill of Rights was heard on all sides. It came especially strong from the more radical and democratic elements in the States, the farmers and the country people; but it was also supported by professional and mercantile elements in the towns. Patrick Dollard, a farmer, of Prince Frederick's Parish, said, in the South Carolina Convention, that his constituents were "nearly all to a man, opposed to this new Constitution, because, they say, they have omitted to insert a Bill of Rights therein, ascertaining and fundamentally establishing the unalienable rights of man, without a full, free, and secure enjoyment of which there can be no liberty and over which it is not necessary that a good government should have the control. . . . To make over to them [Congress] their birthright . . . they can never agree to." Without a Bill of Rights, he feared Congress as a possible despotism. Patrick Henry, a lawyer in Virginia, contended vigorously in behalf of "the great important rights of humanity . . . those valuable, inestimable rights and privileges which no people inspired with the least glow of patriotic liberty ever did, or ever can, abandon." He said that we would "exhibit the most absurd thing to mankind that ever the world saw", if we surrendered to Congress all powers "without check, limitation or control." And Thomas Jefferson wrote to Madison that "a Bill of Rights is what the people are entitled to against every government on earth, general or particular." [1]

---

[1] *Elliot's Debates*, III, 317, 442, 446–449, 461, 593–594. *Jefferson* (Ford's Ed.), Jefferson to Madison, Dec. 20, 1787; Jefferson to Noah Webster, Dec. 4, 1790.

BILL OF RIGHTS AND THE COURT 81

It was not for any mere theory, for a mere doctrinaire adherence to rhetorical, political shibboleths that these men were contending. They were thinking of facts, not theories.[1] They had lived through bitter years, when they had seen Governments, both Royal and State, trample on the human rights which they and their ancestors in the Colonies and in England had fought so hard to secure. In the seven years prior to the signing of the Federal Constitution, they had seen the Legislatures of four States — New Jersey, Rhode Island, New Hampshire, and North Carolina — deprive their citizens of the right to jury trial in civil cases. They had seen the State Legislatures of Virginia, Pennsylvania, and other States pass bills of attainder sentencing men to death or banishment without a criminal trial by jury. They had seen the Legislatures of nearly all the States deprive persons of their property without due process, by the passage of laws allowing tender of worthless paper and other property in payment of debts and of judgments. They had seen a Massachusetts Legislature impair the freedom of the press by confiscatory taxation. They had seen the Royal Government quarter troops on the inhabitants in time of peace and deny to the people the right of

[1] "These provisions were not embodied in the Constitution as mere idle speculations, and there to remain a dead letter, but as a substantial, safe, and active part of the system. The sacrifice of civil rights of personal liberty and even of life, had been so flagrant and tyrannical in the government of every country known to us in history, under the pretence of administering criminal justice, that it was believed to be fundamentally necessary to restrain and limit the several departments of our Government in this particular. . . . This constitutional right cannot be taken from the citizen, even by the supremacy of Legislative power. . . . If it may be . . . this boasted instrument becomes . . . the yawning sepulchre of our civil rights." Philemon Beecher of Connecticut, in the House, Jan. 14, 1818. *15th Cong., 1st Sess.*

assembly and of petition. They had seen the King's officials search their houses without lawful warrants.[1] They knew that what Government had done in the past, Government might attempt in the future, whether its ruling power should be Royal, State, or National — King, Governor, Legislature, or Congress. And they determined that, in America, such ruling power should be definitely curbed at the outset. There should be no uncontrolled power in the government of American citizens. Rightly had Jefferson said, "an elective despotism was not the government we fought for."

Hence it was, that the Massachusetts Convention in 1788 did not consent to ratify the Constitution until the leaders of the radical interests in that State — John Hancock and Samuel Adams — were given assurance that the State's representatives would be instructed to vote for Amendments embodying these demands for a guaranty to the rights of citizens and to the rights of the States. It was only through similar assurances that the Virginia Convention was induced to take similar action. It was in accordance with this demand that, as soon as the

---

[1] "The Constitution of the United States displays much of this spirit of jealousy against its administrators, and the Amendments to it still more. . . . This may be accounted for by the circumstances which preceded and gave rise to the American Constitution and its Amendments. The American Revolution was produced by the oppressions of a distant government, and in the formation of all the State Constitutions which preceded that of the United States, the whole of which was founded upon the fair consent of the people, the natural effect was produced, viz. that in the formation of their own governments, the people transferred a great portion of the jealousies felt against the rulers of a distant government to the rulers they were about to establish for their immediate government at home." William B. Giles of Virginia, in the House, Feb. 11, 1808, *10th Cong., 1st Sess.* "The Constitution was formed on a supposition of human frailty and to restrain abuses of mistaken powers." John Page of Virginia, in the House, Feb. 7, 1792, *2d Cong., 1st Sess.*

First Congress met, James Madison of Virginia introduced Amendments to the Constitution embodying a Bill of Rights; and it should be particularly noted that, just as the framers of the Constitution had constructed it from past experience as embodied in their State Constitutions, so now Madison took most of his Amendments from the Bills of Rights already existing in eight States, and particularly from the compilation made by George Wythe of Virginia for the Virginia Convention.[1] Not all his Amendments were found in the Bill of Rights of any one State — but at least four existed in every State — freedom of religion, freedom of the press, trial by jury, and the guaranty against being deprived of life, liberty, and property except by the law of the land, *i.e.*, by due process. Not all of the rights were of British origin. The prohibition of unreasonable search and seizure and the requirements as to search warrants, were distinctively American, and had been established for protection of the individual citizen, prior to their acceptance in England.[2] The right of

[1] Christopher Gore of Massachusetts, in the House, April 12, 1814 (*13th Cong., 2d Sess.*), referred to Virginia as "that powerful Commonwealth which has afforded to the United States almost all the precedents, as well as most of the axioms and political creeds, that regulate our faith and rule our destinies."

[2] *Law of the Federal and State Constitutions of the United States* (1908), by Frederic J. Stimson, pp. 45, 149; *Origin and Growth of the American Constitution* (1911), by Hannis Taylor, p. 234; *Constitutional Limitations* (1903), 7th Ed., by Thomas M. Cooley, p. 424; *The Constitutional History of the United States* (1901), by Frederic N. Thorpe, II, pp. 201, *et seq.*, for "Precedents for the Amendments"; *The Reasonableness of the Law* (1924), by Charles W. Bacon and Franklyn S. Morse, pp. 32, *et seq.* The New York State Constitution contained no prohibition of unreasonable search and seizure. But the minority in the Maryland Convention of 1787 said that it was "indispensable . . .; for Congress, having the power of laying excises . . . by which our dwelling houses, those castles considered so sacred by the English law, will be laid open to the insolence and oppression of office, there would be no constitutional check provided that would prove so effectual a safeguard to our citizens."

religious liberty did not exist in England to the extent prevailing in some of the States. Another right — one of the rights most cherished by radicals of to-day — that of freedom of speech, as distinct from freedom of the press, was not found in the Bill of Rights of Great Britain or of any American State, in 1788. The only right of free speech specifically guaranteed by any State was the right to speak freely on the floor of the Legislature, without being held to account in Court. The right to freedom of speech, in general, as a new and separate guaranty, was *created* by the First Amendment to the Federal Constitution, in the following language: "Congress shall make no law . . . abridging the freedom of speech"; and it is only so far as that right can be *enforced* against Congressional action that the radicals or any other persons have to-day any protection in this respect.[1] The right of a person indicted for

---

[1] Zechariah Chafee, Jr., in his *Freedom of Speech* (1920), p. 4, is incorrect in stating "thus, the guaranty of freedom of speech was almost a condition of the entry of four original States into the Union."

Frederic J. Stimson in his *Popular Law Making* (1910), p. 302, states more correctly: "It should be noted, however, that the broad principle of freedom of speech by all persons and at all places is first adopted in the American Constitution, freedom of speech in England in its historical principles extending only to freedom of speech in the House of Parliament and the right of assembly and petition at a public meeting."

The State Bills of Rights contained the following provisions:

Delaware: The press shall be free to every citizen who undertakes to examine the official conduct of men acting in a public capacity; and any citizen may print on any subject, being responsible for the abuse of that liberty.

Maryland: VIII. That freedom of speech and debates or proceedings in the Legislature ought not to be impeached in any other Court or judicature. (Note: this is only guaranteed freedom of speech for anything said on the floor of the Legislature.)

XXXVIII. That the liberty of the press ought to be inviolably preserved.

Massachusetts: XVI. The liberty of the press is essential to the security of freedom in a State; it ought not, therefore, to be restricted in this Commonwealth.

XXI. The freedom of deliberation, speech, and debate, in either House

felony to be represented by counsel did not then exist in England (nor, indeed, until the year 1836); it was an American right in 1788.

Now the important fact about these ten Amendments — a fact which is so often overlooked — is that *they* were the *essential portion* of the Constitution — the portion which was insisted upon and effected by the radical and democratic element — the portion without which the Constitution itself would never have been accepted by the American people. Consequently, when the radicals of to-day assail the present Constitution as the work of the conservative and wealthy, they show complete ignorance of the fact that these indispensable parts of the Constitution, containing restraints on Congress, are the result of radical demand in 1788; and when they now advocate making Congress the supreme judge of what it shall have the power to do, they seek to undermine and destroy the effect of the very pro-

of the Legislature, is so essential to the rights of the people that it cannot be the foundation of any accusation or prosecution, action, or complaint in any other Court or place whatsoever. (Note: this is the same as the right protected in Maryland, VIII.)

New Hampshire: XXII and XXX same as Massachusetts XVI and XXI.

North Carolina: XV. That the freedom of the press is one of the great bulwarks of liberty and therefore ought never to be restrained.

Pennsylvania: XII. That the people have a right to freedom of speech and of writing and publishing their sentiments; therefore the freedom of the press ought not to be restrained.

Section 35 of the State Constitution provides: The printing presses shall be free to every person who undertakes to examine the proceedings of the Legislature or any part of the government.

Virginia: That the freedom of the press is one of the great bulwarks of liberty, and can never be restrained but by despotic governments.

In the State Conventions which ratified the Constitution, Virginia presented a Declaration of Rights (framed by George Wythe) which it resolved should be added to the Constitution in which occurred the following: "That the people have a right to freedom of speech and of writing and publishing their sentiments. That freedom of the press is one of the greatest bulwarks of liberty and ought not to be violated."

visions of the Constitution, which the radicals of 1788 deemed necessary for their protection as Americans and as human beings.[1]

Now why is it that this Bill of Rights is so essential? The answer is found not only in the annals of politics, but in the traits of human nature itself. For both History and Anthropology tell us that unrestrained power is dangerous to men and to governments; and that men must place some check upon themselves and upon their rulers, in order to possess any liberty. Even that old republican despot, Oliver Cromwell, said, as early as 1654:[2]

> In every government, there must be somewhat Fundamental, somewhat like a Magna Charta, which would be standing unalterable. . . . Of what assurance is a Law . . . if it be in the same Legislature to unlaw it again? Is such a law likely to be lasting? It will be a rope of sand; it will give no security, for the same men may unbuild what they have built.

And this was said, in other words, by a great democratic State Judge in Virginia, in 1793: "If

---

[1] John Smilie of Pennsylvania said in the House, April 1, 1806 (*9th Cong., 1st Sess.*): "If examined, it would be found, as it originally stood, to be extremely defective. In providing for the powers of Government, it had almost entirely overlooked the rights of individuals. These defects excited great objection to the instrument. They were, however, supplied by the first Congress, and gentlemen would find that almost all the Amendments, which have been incorporated into it, go to secure the rights of individuals. . . . These Amendments constitute what might be called the marrow of the Constitution."

[2] *Letters and Speeches of Oliver Cromwell*, by Thomas Carlyle, Part VIII, Speech III, Sept. 12, 1654. See also *Reflections on the Revolution in France* (1790), by Edmund Burke, *Works*, V, 123: "Society requires not only that the passions of individuals should be subjected, but that even in the mass and body as well as in the individuals, the inclinations of men should frequently be thwarted, their will controlled and their passions brought into subjection. This can only be done by a power out of themselves, and not, in the exercise of its function, subject to that will and to those passions which it is its office to bridle and subdue. In this sense, the restraints on men, as well as their liberties, are to be reckoned among their rights."

BILL OF RIGHTS AND THE COURT

the Legislature may infringe this Constitution, it is no longer fixed; it is not, this year, what it was the last; and the liberties of the people are wholly at the mercy of the Legislature." [1]

That a Constitution must be superior to any Act of a Legislature, and that a Bill of Rights constituted the protection of the people against their Legislatures were thoroughly realized by the people themselves in this country. As early as October 21, 1776, the people of the town of Concord in Massachusetts formally resolved that "a Constitution alterable by the Supreme Legislative is no security at all to the subject, against the encroachment of the Governing Part on any or on all their rights and privileges." [2] Another striking illustration of the demand of the people for a Constitution supreme over their Legislature is found in the action of the inhabitants of Berkshire County — farmers chiefly — comprising the whole western part of Massachusetts, who, for five years, from 1775 to 1780, prevented the Courts

---

[1] Spencer Roane, J., in *Kamper v. Hawkins* (1793), 1 Va. Cases 21.

[2] *Genesis and Birth of the Federal Constitution* (1924), "The Government of Massachusetts prior to the Federal Constitution", by Frank W. Grinnell, pp. 219–220.

The whole object of a Constitution, wrote Gen. James Warren, in Massachusetts in 1788, "is the preservation of that property which every individual of the community has in his life, liberty and estate." See "A Republican Federalist", in *Massachusetts Gazette*, Jan. 9, 1788. "The Constitution is made to control the government; it has no other object," said William Harper in the Senate, *19th Cong., 1st Sess.*, April 14, 1826; see *The Supreme Court in United States History* (1922), by Charles Warren, II, 131. A writer in a Pennsylvania paper in 1782, attacking a statute of that State, as infringing on the independence of the Judges, asked: "Is our Assembly become omnipotent, as it was some years pretended that the parliament of Britain were? . . . With all due respect and reference to *our sovereigns of the year*, I will say, that if they can legislate in the face of the Constitution, in vain did the people of Pennsylvania enter into an original, explicit, and solemn compact with each other, for themselves and their posterity." *Freeman's Journal* (Phil.), Jan. 16, 1782, letter of "A Countryman."

from sitting in that County, until the people of the State should adopt a Constitution prescribing a Bill of Rights which the Courts might enforce. "Every man, by nature, has the seeds of tyranny deeply implanted within him," said the memorial of the town of Pittsfield. "Knowing the strong bias of human nature to tyranny and despotism, we have nothing else in view but to provide for posterity against the wanton exercise of power, which cannot otherwise be done than by the formation of a fundamental Constitution. Let it not be said by future posterity that in this great, this noble, this glorious contest, we made no provision against tyranny among ourselves."

The Bill of Rights constituted the restraints deliberately placed by the people, not only upon themselves (until they should see fit to remove them by the process of further amending the Constitution), but upon their own governing agents — the Congress and the President — restraints imposed for the protection of the people's liberties against unlimited and arbitrary power.[1]

A Bill of Rights has an even more necessary function. It protects the minority against the majority. Chief of the possible evils of a republican form of government, said George Mason of Virginia, in the

[1] Chief Justice Sherwood said, in 1877, in *Clark* v. *Mitchell*, 64 Mo. 564, 582: "If the Legislature of the Nation is not thus restrained and prohibited, of what avail, or of what force and effect are the most solemnly ordained constitutional guarantees? None, whatever. And if this be so, the result will be that the trinity of human rights, life, liberty and property, specially designated in the Constitution as worthy particular protection, will be held not a matter fundamentally established, but by the slender and precarious tenure of the will and caprice of the party which for the time being bears sway in the councils of the Nation. Such a result cannot be, even for a moment, contemplated without unfeigned dismay."

BILL OF RIGHTS AND THE COURT 89

Federal Convention, "is the danger of the majority oppressing the minority." Though Elbridge Gerry of Massachusetts said that he "did not deny the position of Mr. Madison that the majority will generally violate justice when they have an interest in so doing; but he did not think there was any such temptation in this country", nevertheless, all history, ancient and modern, refutes such optimism; and Madison was correct when he said that "in all cases where a majority are united by common interest or passion, the rights of the minority are in danger."[1] As a barrier to this power of the majority to oppress, the Bill of Rights stands firm; and the State Constitutions now in force in Kentucky and Wyoming specifically express this doctrine by declaring that

---

[1] *Debates*, Aug. 13, June 20, June 6, 1787. "What motives are to restrain them? . . . Religion itself may become a motive to persecution and oppression. . . . What has been the source of those unjust laws complained of among ourselves? Has it not been the real or supposed interest of the major number? Debtors have defrauded their creditors. The landed interest has borne hard on the mercantile interest. The holders of one species of property have thrown a disproportion of taxes on the holders of another species. The lesson we are to draw from the whole is, that where a majority are united by a common sentiment and have an opportunity, the rights of the minor party become insecure."

"'The declaration of the Constitution against the power of a State is paramount, not to be . . . bent to some impulse or emergency 'because of some accident or immediate or overwhelming interest which appeal to the feelings and distorts the judgment.'" Holmes, J., dissenting, in *Northern Securities Co. v. United States* (1904), 193 U. S. 400.

"A statute may only represent the sudden will of a small body of mediocre intelligence, on a new subject (or an old one) which they have never studied." *Popular Law Making* (1910), by Frederic J. Stimson.

"The guaranties of the Constitution are primarily for the protection of the minority. The majority can take care of itself. But if the majority assume the judicial power of interpretation, the rights of the minority are no longer guaranteed by the definite terms of the constitutional compact, but are subject to the will of the majority, for it is obvious that a vote is more likely to reflect the wishes of the voter than it is his judgment, since a judgment, unlike a desire, involves patient investigation, in which few will have time to engage, and dispassionate application of general rules to particular circumstances, which many will be in no frame of mind to make." *The Law and the People*, by George Sutherland, Dec. 13, 1913, *63d Cong., 2d Sess., Senate Doc. 328*.

"absolute, arbitrary power over the lives, liberty and property of freemen exists nowhere in a republic, *not even in the largest majority.*"[1] This barrier is the more necessary, because of the fact that the action of a majority may often be the result of "transient impression" (to use Madison's phrase), or of whim, prejudice, passion, temporary discontent, or lack of knowledge or investigation, and not the result of deliberately formed, cool judgment. Against legislation embodying sudden, passionate judgments of the moment, the Bill of Rights stands firm.

There is a particular reason why the liberals and radicals, above all others, should support the enforcement of a Bill of Rights; for in the early stages of the growth of any new idea or of any new economic or social movement, those who favor it are always likely to be in the minority. The political human being is inherently and primarily conservative. Social and economic reforms, as a rule, gain their way in the political field only slowly and after long argument and pressure. And, in the meantime, the majority, averse to change, often controlled by self-interest, often unduly excited over the proposed change, may, in their efforts to avert it, yield to the temptation of legislating in entire disregard of the rights of the minority. Hence, liberals and radicals have an

---

[1] "A government . . . which held the lives, the liberty and the property of its citizens subject at all times to the absolute disposition and unlimited control of even the most democratic repository of power is, after all, but a despotism. It is true that it is a despotism of the many — of the majority, if you choose to call it so. But it is none the less a despotism. . . . The theory of our governments, State and National, is opposed to the deposit of unlimited power anywhere. The executive, the legislative, and the judicial branches of these governments are all of limited and defined powers." Miller, J., in *Loan Association* v. *Topeka* (1875), 20 Wallace 655.

especial interest in seeing their fundamental rights protected and enforced, while they advocate and strive for an unpopular innovation.

Such being the purpose of the Bill of Rights in the first ten Amendments of the Constitution, again the question arises: what did their framers and those who insisted on their adoption mean should be the effect? Once more, it can be said emphatically that they were intended to be absolute legal safeguards to the citizens, strictly binding upon every agency of the new Government, including the Congress and the Executive himself. They were declarations which were to be enforced.[1] The radicals of 1788 knew full well that *only through the Courts of law could these rights be enforced.*

One does not have to infer such knowledge; for they themselves specifically stated that the chief value of the Bill of Rights lay in the existence of the Judiciary. Thus Samuel Adams of Massachusetts, a determined opponent of the Constitution up to the last moment, advocated in the Massachusetts Convention, February 1, 1788, an Amendment, proposed by Hancock, which, he said, "appears to my mind to be a summary of a Bill of Rights which gentlemen are anxious to obtain. It removes doubt which many have entertained respecting the matter, and gives assurance that, if any laws made by the Federal

---

[1] "If the prohibitions and limitations of the charters of government cannot be enforced in favor of individual rights by the judgments of the judicial tribunal, then there are and can be no barriers against the exactions and despotism of arbitrary power; then there is and can be no guarantee or security for the rights of life, liberty and property; then everything we hold dear and sacred as personal rights is at the mercy of a monarch or a mob." *History of the Celebration*, II, 370–371, speech of Judge Matthews at the Dinner of the Learned Societies of Philadelphia.

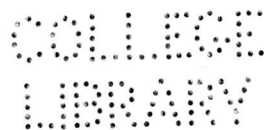

Government shall be extended beyond the power granted by the proposed Constitution, and inconsistent with the Constitution of this State, it will be an error, and adjudged by the Courts of law to be void."[1] Jefferson, writing to a friend, said: "In the arguments in favor of a declaration of rights, you omit one which has great weight with me, the legal check which it puts into the hands of the Judiciary. This is a body which, if rendered independent and kept strictly to their own department, merits great confidence for their learning and integrity." Patrick Henry said: "The Judiciary are the sole protection against a tyrannical execution of the laws. . . . They [Congress] cannot depart from the Constitution; and their laws in opposition would be void." And Richard Henry Lee wrote to Patrick Henry: "Your observation is perfectly just; that right, without power to protect it, is of little avail."

It was with the knowledge of these views, expressed by the radicals of 1788 and ringing through the country, that James Madison introduced into the First Congress, in June, 1789, the proposed Amendments; and this is how he explained their necessity to the first Congressmen who were called upon to act under the new Constitution. "If they were incor-

---

[1] *Elliot's Debates*, III, 324–335, 539–541; *Jefferson* (Ford's Ed.), I, 80. *Letters of Richard Henry Lee* (1914), II, Lee to Henry, Sept. 20, 1789; see also Gouverneur Morris in *Address to the Assembly of Pennsylvania against the Abolition of the Charter of the Bank of North America* (1785). Gouverneur Morris said in Convention, July 21, 1787: "He concurred in thinking the public liberty in greater danger from Legislative usurpations than from any other source."

It may be noted that Horace A. Davis, in *Annulment of Legislation by the Supreme Court*, Amer. Pol. Sci. Rev. (1913), VII, 568, urges that "although Adams does not expressly say *State Courts*, the strong inference is that he referred to State Courts only and was so understood by the Convention." While this is an arguable point, it is certain that Adams was insistent that the restrictions on the powers of Congress were to be enforced at least by some Court.

BILL OF RIGHTS AND THE COURT 93

porated into the Constitution," said he, "independent tribunals of justice will consider themselves in a peculiar manner the guardians of those rights; they will be an impenetrable bulwark against every assumption of power in the Legislative or Executive; they will be naturally led to resist every encroachment upon rights stipulated for in the Constitution by the declaration of rights."[1]

And to that eloquent assertion of the Judiciary as the bulwark of the rights of the citizens against the Congress and against the President, not a single member of the First Congress uttered a word of protest or denial; and with that explanation of the manner in which the rights contained in the Amendments were to be enforced, they were passed by the First Congress, submitted to the peoples of the States and ratified.[2] Radicals of to-day, who believe

---

[1] *1st Cong., 1st Sess.*, June 8, 1789.

Daniel Webster said as to Madison's authority as an interpreter of the Constitution: "Mr. Madison, all will admit, is a competent witness. He had as much to do as any man in framing the Constitution, and as much to do as any man in administering it. Nobody among the living or the dead is more fit to be consulted on a question growing out of it." *25th Cong., 1st Sess.*, in the Senate, Oct. 3, 1837.

John C. Calhoun "coincided in opinion that we were indebted to Mr. Madison at least as much as to any other man for the form of government under which we live. Indeed, he might be said to have done more for our institutions than any man now living or that had gone before him." *24th Cong., 2d Sess.*, in the Senate, Feb. 18, 1837.

[2] Robert Wright of Maryland, who had refused an appointment as a delegate to the Federal Convention in 1787, said, in the House, March 6, 1822 (*17th Cong., 1st Sess.*): "On the publication of the Constitution for the consideration and adoption of the people, I felt dissatisfied that there had been no provision for the trial by jury . . . and I am happy to say that the opposition to that instrument that gave us the name of Anti-Federalists produced the effect contemplated, the Amendments to the Constitution, which were incorporated in the Constitution, and have made us a great and happy people, and will be an indissoluble bond of union, so long as it shall be executed in the spirit of that instrument, which, it can never be forgot, was the effect of mutual concession, and must be executed with the same spirit, controlling as it does so many variant interests."

in the charge of "usurpation", should note that fact with care.

The effect of the adoption of these fundamental guarantees of rights was strikingly described by Charles Pinckney, in 1800:

> When those Amendments became a part of the Constitution, it is astonishing how much it reconciled the States to that measure; they considered themselves as secure in those points on which they were the most jealous; they supposed they had placed the hand of their own authority on the rights of religion and the press, and the as sacred right of the States in the election of the President; that they could with safety say to themselves: "On these subjects we are in future secure; we know what they mean and are at present; and such as they now are, such are they to remain, until altered by the authority of the people themselves; no inferior power can touch them."[1]

---

[1] *6th Cong., 1st Sess.*, March 28, 1800, speech of Charles Pinckney in the Senate. His remarks prior to that quoted above are of interest: "It is of essential importance in examining this bill to recur to those Amendments and the reason of their being adopted. This appears in the caption of the resolution recommending the Amendments to the adoption of the States. It is in these words: 'The Conventions of a number of the States having, at the time of their adopting the Constitution, expressed a desire, in order to prevent misconstruction or abuse of its powers, that further declaratory and restrictive clauses should be added; and as extending the ground of public confidence in the Government will best insure the beneficent end of its Constitution; therefore Congress, according to the Constitutional mode, recommended to the States to agree to, and their Legislatures to adopt such Amendments as are now officially directed to be annexed to the Constitution.'

"By this caption it appears that jealousies and suspicions existed in the States; that they were anxious to have some declaration of the principle of the system to be ascertained on the subjects of religion and the press and the rights of the people and the State Legislatures. They knew that parties would arise, and that, as in all Governments unprincipled and designing men had existed, they saw no reason to expect that their own would be without them; they therefore determined that an explicit Constitutional declaration should be annexed, expressly stipulating that the powers not specifically delegated were reserved, and that the prohibitions and reserves mentioned in the Amendments should be added, in the nature of a Bill of Rights."

CHAPTER FOUR

EARLY CONGRESSES AND THE COURT

"I believe it was generally understood when the Constitution was adopted that the Judiciary would, when necessary and proper, exercise this negative power. The different departments were expected to check and restrain each other from exceeding the proper limits. This negative power . . . has been exercised by the Courts of the United States and of most of the States, ever since the commencement of the Government, without producing any serious inconvenience." — JOHN POPE of Kentucky, in the House, Feb. 24, 1808, *10th Cong., 1st Sess.*

"It is well known . . . that the right of the Courts to decide on the constitutionality of your laws has been recognized in your laws themselves, has been exercised by the Courts, your laws have been pronounced unconstitutional and void, and that decision has not only been acquiesced in by the Legislature but the Act itself has been removed from your code of statutes." — ROGER GRISWOLD of Connecticut, in the House, Feb. 25, 1802, *7th Cong., 1st Sess.*

"Judges sworn to administer the law are bound to consider the supreme rule as being supreme . . . they have no option and must pronounce for the Constitution and against the law. . . . All this was perfectly well understood at the adoption of the Constitution; and therefore the law of 1789 passed at the very first session of Congress provides a mode by which among other things judgments of State tribunals declaring Acts of Congress void may be revised in the Supreme Court." — DANIEL WEBSTER of Massachusetts, in the House, Jan. 25, 1826, *19th Cong., 1st Sess.*

We have seen what was the intention and the expectation of both the framers and the ratifiers of the original Constitution, and the intention and expectation of the framers of the first ten Amendments and of the First Congress which adopted them, with respect to the relation of the Supreme Court to Acts of Congress.

Yet notwithstanding all this evidence of original intention, some men, at the present day — labor leaders, social reformers, so-called progressives, radicals, and others unhampered by knowledge of facts — still make the charge that the Court has usurped the power of passing on the validity of Acts of Congress.[1] They assert that the Court was *not* originally intended to possess this power; and they allege that this power was "usurped" for the first time by Chief Justice Marshall, in 1803, in giving the opinion of the Court in the famous case of *Marbury* v. *Madison*. To those making this charge, the same answer may be made which Abraham Lincoln made to Stephen A. Douglas when the latter declared that his position on slavery was that of "the fathers." To this, Lincoln replied, in his Cooper Union Speech in 1860: "He has no right to mislead others, who have less access to history and less leisure to study it, into the false belief that our fathers who framed the Government under which we live were of the same opinion, thus substituting falsehood and deception for truthful evidence and fair argument." If the evidence already furnished as to the intention of the framers of the Constitution is not sufficient to convince persons making this charge, they ought certainly to be converted, if it should be made plain to them that the early Congresses themselves did not share in this view as to "usurpation." For it was certainly those early Congresses which were primarily interested to

---

[1] See address of the late Senator La Follette before the Convention of the American Federation of Labor, June 14, 1922: "There is no sanction in the written Constitution of the United States for the power which the Courts now usurp. They have secured this power only by usurpation. . . . The usurped power of the Federal Courts must be taken away."

EARLY CONGRESSES AND THE COURT 97

combat assertion of alleged "usurped" power. It is singular that so few historical or legal writers seem to have taken the trouble to ask: "What did the members of Congress, themselves, in those early days, believe as to the Court's right to declare an Act of Congress invalid?" Few men seem, hitherto, to have made any detailed survey of the forerunner of the present day *Congressional Record*, namely the *Annals of Congress*, for the first twelve years, in order to ascertain the views of the Congresses, from the First to the Seventh. Yet a careful examination of these records (so far as printed) now discloses the fact that, in every Congress from 1789 to 1802, the power of the Court to hold Acts of Congress invalid was not only recognized but endorsed by members of both political parties, — Federalist and Anti-Federalist alike, — by members who construed the Constitution broadly as well as by those who construed it narrowly, and that there is but one specific recorded objection to the Court's power, namely by Charles Pinckney of South Carolina, in 1799, — ten years after the Constitution went into operation. The proof is overwhelming, that the early Congresses themselves then believed the Court to possess the power, to which, at this late date, to-day, some "grumbletonians" set up a challenge.[1] Contemporary views are certainly more reliable than theories and historical fiction invented over a hundred years later. American citizens and American lawyers can find no better exposition of fundamental Constitutional principles than

---

[1] It is sometimes said that Abraham Baldwin of Georgia expressed himself in 1800, as opposed to the Court's power; but his objection, if such it be, was expressed in indefinite terms. See *infra*, p. 123.

in the reports of the early Congressional debates in the House of Representatives. It was natural that, in translating the principles of the Constitution into legislation for the new Government, wide differences of opinion should arise as to the scope of those principles. Accordingly, one of the most striking, yet at the same time necessary, features of those early debates was the extent to which the discussion centered around the constitutionality of practically every important proposed bill introduced into Congress. During those discussions, many of those who had taken part in the Federal Convention of 1787 and in the State Conventions of 1787 and 1788, and who were later Members of Congress, expressed their views as to the application of the Constitution. For this reason, those early debates should receive far more attention than has been given to them by students of American history and law, since they contain a contemporaneous exposition of the fundamental provisions of the Constitution.[1] "Among other difficulties," wrote James Madison to Governor Samuel Johnston, in June, 1789, "the exposition of the Constitution is frequently a copious source, and must continue so until its meaning on all great points shall have been settled by precedents." Each po-

[1] The effect of the views of those who were fairly contemporaneous with the Constitution was interestingly stated by John G. Jackson of Virginia, in the House, Jan. 13, 1816, as follows: "I consider the decision which shall be pronounced now, as calculated to fix, perhaps for ages, the interpretation of the Constitution, in relation to one of its most important provisions . . . being given in the same age which gave birth to the Constitution (it) will possess all the weight of a precedent established almost contemporaneously with the charter." *14th Cong., 1st Sess.* See also William Vans Murray of Maryland, in the House, March 23, 1796: "We have all seen the Constitution from its cradle, we know it from its infancy, and have the most perfect knowledge of it and more light than ever a body of men in any country have ever had of ascertaining any other Constitution." *4th Cong., 1st Sess.*

EARLY CONGRESSES AND THE COURT 99

litical party, often with considerable inconsistency and lack of adherence to theory and political principles, attacked the constitutionality of bills disliked by it, and upheld the constitutionality of bills which it favored.[1] Hence it is an especially striking fact that Members of Congress, of both parties, should have been united in one sentiment at least, that under the Constitution it was the Judiciary which was finally to determine the validity of an Act of Congress. This unanimity of opinion was particularly significant in the First Congress, for, as has been well said, that body was almost an adjourned session of the Federal Convention of 1787. In this First Congress, ten of the eighteen Senators, and eight members of the House had been among the fifty-five members of that Convention, and five of the Senate and twenty-six of the House had been members of the State Conventions which ratified the Constitution.[2]

The first great constitutional debate in the first session of the First Congress was over the question whether the power of removal was vested in the President by the Constitution. And it is a singular and

---

[1] Madison to Johnston, June 21, 1789, *Writings of James Madison* (Hunt's Ed.), V, 409. Samuel Smith, a Maryland Federalist, said, Feb. 11, 1795, that he "could not comprehend what Mr. Giles would be at. Whenever a gentleman is at a loss for an argument, the Constitution is brought forward. The result would be, that when it was really useful to do so, the reference will be laughed at." *3d Cong., 3d Sess.* Nathaniel Macon, a North Carolina Anti-Federalist, said, Jan. 12, 1801: "It has been said that a part of the House are always crying out against the constitutionality of every Act they do not approve. The answer to this is very easy. There is another part of the House that never questions the constitutionality of anything. . . . One side believes it (the Constitution) has limits; the other believes it has no limits." *6th Cong., 2d Sess.*

[2] See speech of Henry St. George Tucker, in the House, Jan. 3, 1924. *68th Cong., 1st Sess.*

100 EARLY CONGRESSES AND THE COURT

striking fact that while, at that early date, all who engaged in this debate concurred in the view that the decision must ultimately rest with the Supreme Court, it was not until one hundred and thirty-six years later that the point actually came before that Court for decision.[1] In June, 1789, the debate on this question arose on a bill for a Department of Foreign Affairs which contained a specific provision that the Secretary was to be removable from office by the President.[2] This was objected to as unconstitutional. Theodore Bland, John Page, and Alexander White of Virginia, and James Jackson of Georgia opposed it on the ground that officers were removable only by the advice and consent of the Senate. Others took the view that neither the House of Representatives, the Senate, nor Congress had the power to legislate on the matter, since power of removal was one of the implied powers of the Executive under the Constitution. James Madison (who was generally a strict-constructionist), supported by the broad-constructionist, ultra-Federalists (like John Vining of Delaware, Fisher Ames of Massachusetts, and John Laurance of New York), took the ground that Congress had no power to regulate removal, but that it

---

[1] *Myers* v. *United States* (1925), argued, April 13–14, 1925, and undecided at the end of the Term of the Court.

[2] *1st Cong., 1st Sess.*, June 16, 17, 18, 19, 22, 1789, pp. 455, *et seq.;* speech of Smith, p. 459; White, p. 463; Gerry, pp. 473, 504, 573, 537; White, p. 518; Ames, p. 477; Laurance, p. 486; Sylvester, p. 562; Baldwin, p. 560. The support given to judicial review in this debate was noted by Prof. Edward S. Corwin, in *The Doctrine of Judicial Review* (1914).

See also preliminary debate on the same subject, on a bill as to the Executive Departments, May 19, 1789, pp. 368, *et seq.*

See also interesting letters of Madison to Edmund Randolph, May 31, 1789, Edmund Pendleton, June 21, July 5, 1789, Samuel Johnston, June 28, 1789, *Madison*, V, 372, 405, 409, 414.

EARLY CONGRESSES AND THE COURT 101

had the right to express its view as to the Executive by a declaratory Act, "explanatory of the meaning of the Constitution." Other Federalists, like Theodore Sedgwick of Massachusetts, opposed the removal clause as unnecessary. Some Federalists, as well as some Anti-Federalists and strict-construction Congressmen, opposed a declaratory Act as an interference with the judicial power. Thus every side of the constitutional question was presented.[1] Nothing in the debate, however, is more striking than the fact that representatives of each side of the constitutional question agreed on one point, — namely, that the Court had the power to decide the question of constitutionality.

William Smith of South Carolina, a broad Federalist, believing the President had the implied power of removal, said:

> The words should be struck out, and the question of right, if it is one, left to the decision of the Judiciary. . . . Gentlemen have said that it is proper to give a legislative construction of the Constitution. I differ with them on this point. I think it an infringement of the powers of the Judiciary . . . calls upon this House to exercise the powers of the Judges in expounding the Constitution. . . . A great deal of mischief has arisen in the several States by the Legislatures undertaking to decide constitutional questions. Sir, it is the duty of the Legislature to make laws. Your Judges are to expound them.

---

[1] See Peckham, J., in *Parsons* v. *United States* (1897), 167 U. S. 324, 329: "Then ensued what has been many times described as one of the ablest constitutional debates which has taken place in Congress, since the adoption of the Constitution. It lasted for many days, and all arguments that could be thought of by men — many of whom had been instrumental in the preparation and adoption of the Constitution — were brought forward in debate in favor of or against that construction of the instrument which reposed in the President alone the power to remove from office."

Alexander White of Virginia, a strict-constructionist, said: "I would rather the Judiciary should decide the point because it is more properly within their department." "I imagine the Legislature may construe the Constitution with respect to the powers annexed to their department, but subject to the decision of the Judges. The same with regard to the Executive; the President and Senate may construe the power in question, and as they determine respecting the power of removal, so they may act, but liable also to the decision of the Judiciary." Elbridge Gerry of Massachusetts, who was not only a strict-constructionist, but also an Anti-Federalist, who, as a member of the Federal Convention, had refused to sign the Constitution, and who was later an ardent Jeffersonian, was an especially active supporter of the Court's power, and spoke on several occasions in its behalf. He was strongly opposed to the retention of the removal clause as a declaratory Act, for, said he: "If the fact is, as we seem to suspect, that they (the President and the Senate) do not understand the Constitution, let it go before the proper tribunal; the Judges are the Constitutional umpires on such questions." Again he said: "It was said that the Judges could not have the power of deciding on the subject, because the Constitution is silent; but I ask, if the Judges are not *ex officio* Judges of the law, and whether they would not be bound to declare the law a nullity, if this clause is continued in it and is inconsistent with the Constitution." And, in opposing the power of Congress to establish the meaning of the Constitution by passing this statute, Gerry anticipated one hundred and thirty-five years ago the

EARLY CONGRESSES AND THE COURT 103

answer to Senator La Follette's proposal to give to Congress the final power to construe the Constitution. "If the power of making declaratory Acts really vests in Congress and the Judges are bound by our decisions," said Gerry, "we may later alter that part of the Constitution which is secured from being amended by the Fifth Article. . . . I would ask, gentlemen: if the Constitution has given us the power to make declaratory Acts, where is the necessity of inserting the Fifth Article for the purpose of obtaining Amendments? . . . If this is the meaning of the Constitution, it was hardly worth while to have had so much bustle and uneasiness about it." Fisher Ames, an ardent Federalist, advocating a declaratory Act, admitted that it could not bind the Judges, and said: "If we declare justly on this point, it will serve as a rule of conduct to the Executive Magistrate; if we declare improperly, the Judiciary will revise our decision." John Laurance of New York held the same view: "If the laws shall be in violation of any part of the Constitution, the Judges will not hesitate to decide against them." Peter Sylvester of New York, also favoring a declaration of Congressional view, said: "It is certain that the Judiciary will be better able to decide the question of constitutionality in this way than any other. If we are wrong, they can correct our error." Abraham Baldwin of Georgia, a strict-constructionist, said: "Gentlemen say it properly belongs to the Judiciary to decide this question. Be it so. It is their province to decide upon our laws; and if they find them to be unconstitutional, they will not hesitate to declare it so."

The next example of recognition of the Court's

power by this First Congress is found in the passage of the Judiciary Act of September 24, 1789.

In Section 25 of this Act, the Supreme Court was given jurisdiction on writ of error, of cases coming from State Courts in which were involved a decision adverse to the validity of an Act of Congress, and the Supreme Court was given express power to "reverse or affirm" the State Court decision. Power to affirm necessarily implied power to hold the Act of Congress unconstitutional, since the State Court decision, so affirmed, would have made that holding.[1] This section was enacted by Congress without any dissent, so far as appears from the reports of the debate of the Senate by William Maclay in his *Diary*, or of the House in the *Annals of Congress*.[2]

In the second session of the First Congress, debate arose over the constitutionality of the bill to fix the seat of Government, the contention being made that it was an infringement on the power of each Congress by joint resolution to fix the place to which it would adjourn. An interesting illustration of the public

[1] James A. Bayard of Delaware, in the House, Feb. 19, 1802 (*7th Cong., 1st Sess.*), pointed out that the Judiciary Act of 1789, provided that: "'A final judgment or decree in any suit in the highest Court of law or equity of a State in which a decision in the suit could be had, *where is drawn in question the validity of a treaty or statute of, or an authority exercised under, the United States*, and *the decision is against their validity*, . . . may be re-examined and reversed or *affirmed* in the Supreme Court of the United States, upon a writ of error.' Thus as early as the year 1789, among the first Acts of the government, the Legislature explicitly recognize the right of a State Court to declare a treaty, a statute, and an authority exercised under the United States, void, subject to the revision of the Supreme Court of the United States; and it has expressly given the final power to the Supreme Court to affirm a judgment which is against the validity either of a treaty, statute, or an authority of the government."

[2] It is to be remembered that the *Annals of Congress* contain no full reports of debates in the Senate until several years after 1800. The Senate sat with closed doors from April 6, 1789, until February 24, 1793, when it passed a resolution to open the doors of its legislative session at the beginning of the next session.

EARLY CONGRESSES AND THE COURT 105

understanding as to the Court's power is to be found in a letter as to this bill in the newspapers of the time, commenting on the fact that the bill was especially dangerous, because there was no way in which its validity could be brought before the Court.[1]

If laws are made which are unconstitutional because they may do no harm, Congress will soon proceed to those which may and will do harm. . . . Every law does not undergo the revision of the Judiciary; this will certainly not; the President of the United States can alone arrest its progress. . . . If the law remains unrepealed or uninvalidated by the Judiciary, the thing commanded to be done must be carried into effect. . . . The Houses will then be precluded from exercising their constitutional privileges. . . . That the clause in question is repugnant to it (the Constitution) is admitted; but it is justified on the principle that it will be inoperative; this is, however, a mistaken idea, for it will have an operation, unless formally annulled by the Judiciary, and it is impossible the construction of it can ever go before the Federal Courts. . . . The Constitution is the rock of our political salvation; it is the palladium of our rights; it is the safeguard of the rights of the States as well as individuals; it is our only bond of union. . . . When the mind pursues a favorite object with passionate enthusiasm, men are too apt, in their eager embrace of it, to overlook the means by which it is attained. These are the melancholy occasions when the barriers of the government are broken down and the boundaries of the Constitution defaced.

In the third session of the First Congress occurred the famous debate on the charter of the Bank of the

[1] *1st Cong., 2d Sess.*, Feb. 18, 24, July 6, 8, 1790, pp. 1234, 1376, 1731; see also debate on bill providing for the temporary residence of Congress at New York, Sept. 21, 1789, *1st Cong., 1st Sess.*, pp. 906, *et seq.*
Letter of "Junius Americanus" in *New York Daily Advertiser*, July 13, 1790, addressed to the President of the United States, stating that the bill relinquished the right of the two Houses of Congress to adjourn themselves by concurrent vote, without the necessity of the President's assent or signature.

United States, in which the constitutionality of that action was warmly debated, and the meaning of the "general welfare" and "necessary and proper" clauses of the Constitution was discussed with splendid ability. The Anti-Federalists and strict-constructionists, led by Madison, Jackson, Michael Stone of Maryland, and William B. Giles of Virginia, urged that the bill was unconstitutional and apparently argued that a bill ought not to be passed which would be "liable to a supervision by the Judges of the Supreme Court."[1] John Laurance, a strong Federalist of New York, on the other hand, supported the bill, saying: "It is said we must not pass a problematic bill which is liable to a supervision by the Judges of the Supreme Court; but he conceived there was no force in this, as those Judges are invested by the Constitution with a power to pass their judgment on all laws that may be passed." Elias Boudinot of Pennsylvania, another Federalist, said:

The last objection is that, adopting the bill, we expose the measure to be considered and defeated by the Judiciary of the United States, who may adjudge it to be contrary to the Constitution and therefore void. . . . This gives

[1] *1st Cong., 3d Sess.*, Feb. 1, 2, 3, 4, 7, 8, March 3, 1791, speech of Laurance, p. 1500, Smith, p. 1990.

See speech of Giles, pp. 1995–1996, in which he said: "An instance of a similar exercise of authority by the Congress which existed under the former Confederation has been mentioned in favor of its exercise by the present Congress. . . . It is to be remarked that that Act was the child of necessity and that Congress doubted its legitimacy, and the Act itself was never confirmed by a judicial decision. . . . The right of exercising that authority by the Government is at least problematical, yet is nowhere granted in express terms; the Legislature, therefore, can have no competent security against a judicial decision, but a dependent or corrupt Court. I presume that a law to punish with death those who counterfeit the paper emitted by the bank will be consequent upon the existence of this Act. Hence a judicial decision will probably be had of the most serious and awful nature; the life of an individual at stake on the one hand, an improvident act of the Government on the other."

EARLY CONGRESSES AND THE COURT 107

me no uneasiness. I am so far from controverting this right in the Judiciary that it is my boast and my confidence. It leads to greater decision on all subjects of a constitutional nature, when I reflect that if, from inattention, want of precision, or any other defect, I should do wrong, there is a power in the Government which can constitutionally prevent the operation of such a wrong measure from affecting my constituents. I am legislating for a Nation, and for thousands unborn; and it is the glory of the Constitution that there is a remedy even for the failures of the Supreme Legislature thereof.

William Smith of South Carolina said: "It is still within the power of the Judiciary to annul the law, if it shall be by them deemed not to result by fair construction from the powers vested in the Constitution." William B. Giles, an Anti-Federalist of Virginia, in opposing the bill, admitted the power of the Court to determine the question of constitutionality, and said that Congress would have no security against an adverse decision except "a dependent or corrupt Court"; he also pointed out that the question might arise in a criminal case under some law enacted to punish counterfeiting of the bank's paper, in which case the validity of the bank's charter must be decided. President Washington, having obtained the opinions as to its constitutionality from his three cabinet officers (Attorney-General Randolph and Thomas Jefferson denying it and Alexander Hamilton sustaining it), adopted Hamilton's view and signed the bill, February 24, 1791, after holding it in suspense the full time allowed by law.[1] In view of the expres-

[1] Act of Feb. 25, 1791, c. 10 (1 Stat. 191). See *Works of Alexander Hamilton* (Lodge's Ed.), III, 388, 445-493, report to the House of Representatives on a National Bank, Dec. 14, 1790; letters of Washington to Hamilton, Feb. 16,

sions used during the debate as to the power of the Supreme Court to determine the constitutionality of the charter, it is interesting to note that, within a year thereafter, Justices of that Court, sitting on circuit in Philadelphia, in April, 1792, in the *Hayburn Case*, for the first time actually held a Federal law unconstitutional. The statute involved was one which imposed on the Justices of the Supreme Court the duty of examining and passing on the claims of invalid Revolutionary soldiers, — a subject of Federal legislation by no means unfamiliar to-day. A failure to assume the duties thus imposed by Congress was likely to bring odium on the Justices and to alienate

---

1791, Hamilton to Washington, Feb. 23, 1791; *Writings of Thomas Jefferson* (Federal Ed.), VI, Jefferson to Washington, Feb. 15, 1791; Jefferson to Nicholas Lewis, Feb. 9, 1791.

See also *Writings of James Madison* (Ford's Ed.), VI, 42–46. Madison wrote to Edmund Pendleton, Feb. 13, 1791: "The arguments in favour of the measure . . . increased my dislike to it, because they were founded on remote implications which strike at the very essence of the Government as composed of limited and enumerated powers."

At President Washington's request, Madison prepared a draft for a veto in case the President decided not to sign, in which he said: "I object to the Bill because it is an essential principle of the Government that powers not delegated by the Constitution cannot be rightfully exercised; because the power proposed by the Bill to be exercised is not expressly delegated and because I cannot satisfy myself that it results from any express power by fair and safe rules of implication." To Ambrose Madison, James Madison, March 21, 1791, wrote: "The Bill remained with the President to the last moment allowed him." To Jefferson, he wrote, March 1, 1791: "We understood in Philadelphia that during the suspension of the Bank Bill in the hands of the President, its partisans here indulged themselves in reflections not very decent. I have reason to believe that the licentiousness of the tongues of speculators and Tories far exceeded anything that was conceived. The meanest motives were charged on him, and the most insolent menaces held over him, if not in the open streets, under circumstances not less marking the character of the party." For description of the manner in which the Bank Bill was debated and passed and of President Washington's attitude, see speech of John Pope of Kentucky, in the House, Feb. 15, 1811; Samuel Smith of Maryland, Feb. 18, 1811; Timothy Pickering of Massachusetts, Feb. 19, 1811; *11th Cong., 3d Sess.* Pickering said, p. 308: "It is true that Washington, cautious and circumspect beyond any man I ever knew, did suspend his decision to the last day allowed him by the Constitution."

popular sympathy.¹ Here was an occasion, therefore, when, if ever, attacks upon the Court for "usurpation" might be expected to be found. Yet, on the contrary, the records of the House of Representatives contain no criticism of the action of the Court, and the only reference is as follows: "This being the first instance in which a Court of Justice had declared a law of Congress to be unconstitutional, the novelty of the case produced a variety of opinions with respect to the measures to be taken on the occasion. At length a Committee of five were appointed to enquire into the facts . . . and to report thereon." No further action was taken, except that one Congressman suggested, amid no dissent, that a law be passed " to point out some regular mode in which the Judges shall give official notice of their refusal to act under any law of Congress on the ground of unconstitutionality." Hence, there would seem thus early, in 1792, to have been a complete recognition even by Congress itself that the Judges possessed and would continue to exercise this power.

Examination of the contemporary newspapers shows that the Anti-Federalist papers, adherents of Jefferson, expressed the hope that the Court would now proceed further and hold the Bank Act invalid. The *National Gazette* said: "It affords a hope that

---

[1] The *National Journal* (Phil.) contained an article on this legislation as follows: "Our poor, starving invalids have at length some provision made for them by Congress; and as the distresses of many of them are urgent in the extreme, it is to be hoped that not a moment's delay will be made by the public officers who are directed to settle their accounts; for although men who are accustomed to plentiful tables do not perhaps know it, it is nevertheless a melancholy truth that a few days' fasting would kill not only a feeble, war-worn veteran but even a hearty well-fed member of Congress or head of a department."

not only future encroachments will be prevented but also that any existing law of Congress which may be supposed to trench upon the constitutional rights of individuals or of States will, at convenient seasons, undergo a revision, particularly that for establishing a National Bank"; and at the close of the session, it stated that the decision of the Court, "being another resource admitted by the Constitution for its own defense and for security of the rights which it guarantees to the several States and to individual citizens . . . may be contemplated under some very pleasing aspects."[1] Madison wrote a letter to Gen. Henry Lee, April 15, 1792, in approval of this judicial curb on Congressional power, in which he referred to the fact that the decision was unsatisfactory to the upholders of the Bank Act, since they feared (and Madison hoped) that the Court would equally declare the Bank Act unconstitutional:[2]

You know that the President has exerted his power of checking the unconstitutional power of Congress. The Judges have also called the attention of the public to Legislative fallibility, by pronouncing a law providing for invalid pensioners unconstitutional and void; perhaps they may be wrong in the execution of their power, but such an evidence of its existence gives inquietude to those who do not wish Congress to be controuled or doubted, whilst its proceedings correspond with their views. I suspect also that the inquietude is increased by the relation of such a power to the Bank Law, in the public contemplation, if not in their own.

---

[1] See *National Gazette* (Phil.), April 16, 19, 23, May 11, 1792; see also *The Supreme Court in United States History* (1922), by Charles Warren, I, 70-82; 2d Cong., 1st Sess., April 13, 1792, pp. 556-557.

[2] *Letters and Other Writings of James Madison* (1865), IV.

EARLY CONGRESSES AND THE COURT 111

In the Second Congress, at its first session, in 1792, the provision of the Post-office Bill that mail stages might carry passengers without liability to State tax was attacked by many members, as beyond the power of Congress and as an encroachment on the rights of the States, "a shock to every State in the Union."[1] Thomas Fitzsimmons of Pennsylvania, replying to an argument based on the "necessary and proper" clause, said that:

> If this were once admitted, the Constitution would be an useless and dead letter; and it would be to no purpose that the States in Convention assembled had framed that instrument to guide the steps of Congress; as well might they at once have said: "There shall be a Congress who shall have full power and authority to make all laws which to their wisdom shall seem meet and proper." . . . In favor of the motion it was urged (that the necessary and proper clause) has conferred on Congress ample powers respecting the point in question. . . . The question could not involve any controversy between the United States and the individual States. It was merely a judicial question and determinable in a Court of law whether a State has a right to grant and support such a monopoly.

Nathaniel Niles of Vermont said that Congress, by passing this Act, would violate the State rights and "overleap the bounds" of its own. "This matter may occasion a legal adjudication, in order to which the Judiciary must determine whether you have a *constitutional right* to establish this regulation, and this will depend on the question whether it will be necessary and proper."[2]

---

[1] *2d Cong., 1st Sess.*, Jan. 3, 5, 1792, pp. 304, *et seq.*; speeches of Thomas Fitzsimmons of Pennsylvania, p. 304; Niles, p. 307.

[2] In the first session of the Second Congress, the constitutionality of the Cod Fisheries Bill was debated, its adherents basing the legislation on the

That the Court was relied on to curb excesses of power by Congress was evident from an article, at this time, in the *National Gazette*, an anti-Hamilton paper, with reference to the Secretary of the Treasury's report on manufactures and his attitude towards the "general welfare" doctrine:[1]

Cannot such a discretion of the National Legislature pronounce all objects whatever, to concern the general welfare? Can any usurpation of power be adjudged unconstitutional by the Judicial authority, if the Legislature can constitutionally do whatever in their discretion concerns the general welfare? . . . Does not this doc-

---

"general welfare" clause of the Constitution. This position was attacked by Hugh Williamson of North Carolina, who said that "the common defence and general welfare in the hands of a good politician may supersede every part of our Constitution and leave us in the hands of time and chance." Madison contended that the latitude argued for "would subvert the very foundation and transmute the very nature of the limited government established by the people of America. . . . Those who ratified the Constitution conceived that this is not an indefinite Government deriving its powers from the general terms prefixed in the specified powers, but a limited Government, tied down to the specified powers which explain and define the general terms." See *2d Cong., 1st Sess.*, Feb. 3, 6, 7, 8, 9, 1792, pp. 362, *et seq.*; speech of Williamson, p. 380; Madison pp. 386, 389; Giles pp. 397, *et seq.* See also debate over the general welfare doctrine on the bill to appropriate for the relief of refugees from San Domingo, *3d Cong., 1st Sess.* Jan. 16, 1794, speeches of Madison, Samuel Dexter of Massachusetts and William B. Giles *contra*, and Boudinot *pro*, pp. 170, *et seq.*

[1] *National Gazette*, Jan. 12, 1792. The article began as follows: "In the report of the Secretary of the Treasury on manufactures, it is laid down as the unquestionable meaning of the Constitution of the United States that Congress have power to provide by the application of money, for any object that concerns the general welfare, terms which he says are susceptible neither of specification nor of definition, that every object concerns the general welfare which in its operation extends in fact or by possibility throughout the Union — that it is left to the discretion of the National Legislature to pronounce upon the objects which concern the general welfare."

Madison wrote to Henry Lee, Jan. 1, 1792: "I enclose the report of the Secy. of the Treasury on manufactures. What think you of the commentary (pages 36 and 37) on the terms 'general welfare'? The Federal Government has been hitherto limited to the specified powers, by the greatest champions for latitude in expounding these powers. If not only the means, but the objects, are unlimited, the parchment had better be thrown into the fire at once." See also Madison to Edmund Pendleton, Feb. 21, 1792.

EARLY CONGRESSES AND THE COURT 113

trine in the Report knock down every boundary worth contending for between the General Government and the State Government and give an indefinite supremacy to the General Government?

In the first session of the Third Congress, there arose a long debate over the constitutionality of the tax on carriages. Its opponents claiming it was a direct tax and invalid unless apportioned as required by the Constitution.[1] The validity of a license tax on lawyers and other State Court officers was also debated. A recognition of the existence of the power of judicial review by State Courts is to be found in a speech by the strong Anti-Federalist, William B. Giles, who, opposing the bill, said that: "The tax on lawyers, physicians, and clerks was formerly a popular scheme in Virginia. The tax was adopted; but the Courts of the State afterwards declared it to be unconstitutional, and it had to be repealed."[2]

In the second session of the Third Congress the constitutionality of legislation was the topic of constant debate.[3] The Federalists attacked the Natu-

[1] *3d Cong., 1st Sess.*, May 5, 6, 7, 9, 10, 16, 29, 1794; see especially speeches of Madison and Ames, pp. 730, *et seq.* This debate is reported in much greater detail, and with many speeches omitted from the *Annals of Congress*, in *Philadelphia Gazette* and *Universal Daily Advertiser*, May 6, 7, 8, 9, 10, 1794.

[2] This speech is to be found in the above newspaper, in its report of the session of May 5, 1794, but not in the *Annals*. The Virginia statutes referred to by Giles appear to be the Act of October, 1786, c. 26, *Henning's Statutes at Large*, XII, 283; Act of Dec. 20, 1790, c. 4, *ibid.*, XIII, 114. Incidentally, it may be noted that this case of judicial review in Virginia does not hitherto seem to have been mentioned by any legal historian.

[3] *3d Cong., 2d Sess.* Jan. 2, Feb. 3, 13, 1795, speeches of Tracy, pp. 1053, 1070; Madison, p. 1054; S. Smith, p. 1166. Jeremiah Wadsworth of Connecticut said, p. 1221, that "he thanked God that the Government of the country was not left to the House of Representatives, for he believed that they would make most wretched work of it." Tracy said: "Much had been said about adhering to the Constitution strictly on former occasions; but from many things said now, it seemed as though there was no safety for the people unless the House

ralization Bill on that score, and the Anti-Federalists the Militia Bill, the Military Establishment Bill, and the Carriage Tax Bill. The validity of the latter measure aroused heated discussion, in the course of which Representatives of both political parties again recognized the existence of the Court's power of judicial review.[1] Uriah Tracy of Connecticut, a Federalist, said that "he should have no great objection to strike out the carriage tax — not that he disliked it; but many persons thought it unconstitutional. He had no doubt on that ground and believed it would be determined by the Federal Court to be constitutional. If so, it was agreed on all hands to be a good tax." Giles of Virginia, an Anti-Federalist, said: "We have all sworn to support the Constitution; and if it must be altered, we know very well that this House has no authority for that purpose. There must be authority of a different kind. As to the tax before the House, so firmly were several gentlemen persuaded of its illegality that they had determined to make an opposition to it, not as in Pennsylvania by an insurrection — but by a trial before a Court of law." As is well known, the Anti-Federalists later made up a case in Virginia to test the constitutionality of this tax; and when the Court, in *Hylton* v. *United States* (3 Dallas 171), in 1796, held that the tax was not a direct tax and hence that the law was valid, the

---

of Representatives absorbed the whole governmental power. If that House should become political cannibals and attempt to devour both of the other branches of the Legislature, he would oppose it whether it was popular or not, for he considered the Constitutional checks of the branches of this Government upon one another, as containing the most complete security for liberty that any people could enjoy."

[1] *3d Cong., 2d Sess.*, Feb. 6, 11, 1795, speeches of Tracy, p. 1194, Giles, pp. 1203, et seq.

EARLY CONGRESSES AND THE COURT 115

Virginians and other followers of Jefferson complained of the Court for its *failure* to hold this Act of Congress invalid. It is interesting to note that when, one hundred years later in the Income Tax Cases, the Court actually did hold another tax to be a direct tax and the statute imposing it to be unconstitutional, it was largely members of the Democratic party who, in 1895, opposed the very exercise of the power which the Democrats of 1796 had hoped the Court would exercise.

In the first session of the Fourth Congress, in March, 1796, during the great debate on the resolution calling on President Washington for the papers on the Jay Treaty, William Smith of South Carolina, a Federalist, referred approvingly to the decision in the Carriage Tax Case, saying: "They [the Court] took the Constitution in their hand," he said, "and tested the Act by that standard, and by that alone has their decision been governed."[1] Abraham Baldwin of Georgia, an Anti-Federalist, also cited instances of judicial review, in which the Court had

---

[1] *4th Cong., 1st Sess.*, March 7, 8, 9, 14, 23, 24, 30, 1796, speeches of Smith, p. 441; Gallatin, p. 465; Madison, p. 493; Giles, p. 506; Baldwin, p. 538; Gilbert, p. 680; Harper, p. 755. In this debate, the constitutionality of the treaty, as well as of the House resolution, and the fundamental nature of the Government as one of "limitations and checks" was discussed. The evasion of the checks was much harped upon by the Anti-Federalists, as illustrated by the following quotations from a speech by Giles: "It will be remarked by examining the history of man that the people have always been desirous to check the exercise of power in the administrators, and as uniformly have administrators endeavored to evade those checks. The same among us. The American people, sensible of this, when they, after a fortunate struggle for their liberties, were about to exercise their discretion in the establishment of a Constitution that should secure their rights and liberties, formed a Government of checks. The Americans have the reputation of a sagacious people and have showed their sagacity in framing this Constitution; but even if they had proved themselves more sagacious in devising checks, a correspondent sagacity would still have been found in the Government to evade them."

116   EARLY CONGRESSES AND THE COURT

both denied and upheld the validity of Acts of Congress, as follows:

The President had not hesitated to send back to them their laws when he thought them against the Constitution and they had given way to his reasons. The Judges had refused to execute a law intruding upon their department; it was repealed, and they passed another on the subject. . . Probably, even in making the Constitution and all that has been said upon it since, there never had been till now so many persons and so much time employed at once in searching and settling this single point. It may be said to be the first solemn decision of the question. The suability of the States was not so much talked of or believed, till it was declared by the Judges to be the meaning of the Constitution.

The Court's relation to Acts of Congress was also explained by Ezekiel Gilbert of Connecticut, saying: "The Legislature could check the Judiciary; so, the Judiciary might, in some cases, in order to guard the Constitution, check the Legislature;" and Robert G. Harper of South Carolina said: "If a case should occur in which a treaty stood opposed by a law, the Courts of Justice must decide which would supersede the other."

The second session of the Fourth Congress, in the winter of 1796–1797, again produced debates as to the "general welfare" clause and as to the constitutionality of the Relief to Savannah Fire Sufferers Bill and the Direct Tax and Indirect Tax Bills.[1]

The Fifth Congress, in 1797 and 1798, was fruitful of debates on constitutional questions. At its first

[1] *4th Cong., 2d Sess.*, Dec. 28, 1796, speeches of Aaron Kitchell of New Jersey, p. 1719; Harper, p. 1720; Baldwin, p. 1722; Giles and John Nicholas of Virginia, p. 1723. See also *ibid.*, Feb. 24, 25, 1797, speeches of Edward Livingston of New York, Ames, and Nicholas, pp. 2294, *et seq.*

EARLY CONGRESSES AND THE COURT 117

session, the validity of a proposed stamp tax on lawyers and of a proposal to deny unstamped papers admissibility as evidence was discussed, and denied by upholders of State Rights.[1] Anti-Federalists like John Dennis of Maryland, Robert Williams of North Carolina, and Giles and Nicholas of Virginia contended that a tax on lawyers might be extended to any other State officer and "thereby annihilate the State Governments", a tax on a State deed would "clash with State jurisdiction" — "nothing would give so much alarm" — "a clashing of the authorities of the two Governments" — "a violation of an attack upon State sovereignty." Nicholas expressly admitted and contended for the power of a State Court to hold the Act of Congress unconstitutional, saying:

With respect to the State Judges, he allowed that they were bound to support the Constitution and laws of the United States. They were also Judges of the law and Constitution of the United States. They will say, you had no right to pass this law, and will not execute it for you. There had been frequent instances of this sort in the State to which he belonged. . . . He was himself a Judge in an inferior grade, and his conscience would justify him in resisting the law, because he thought it did what they had no right to do.

This same view as to the power of State Judges to hold an Act of Congress unconstitutional was held by Albert Gallatin of Pennsylvania, one of the strongest Anti-Federalists, close and trusted friend and adviser of Jefferson, who said that: "The Judges of the individual States were bound to decide upon the law

[1] *5th Cong., 1st Sess.*, June 26, 27, 28, 29, 30, July 1, 1797, pp. 387, *et seq.*; pp. 417, *et seq.*

made in conformity to the Constitution of the United States. The question therefore reverted how far the law *was* made in conformity to the Constitution."

At the second session of the Fifth Congress, in 1798, excited constitutional debates took place on the Foreign Intercourse Bill, the Provisional Army Bill, the Alien Enemy Bill, and the Sedition Bill.[1] Nicholas of Virginia, during the first of these debates, referred to the existence of judicial review as follows:

> Was it true according to the practice of the Government that the Departments had no check upon each other? Did not the Judiciary consider the acts of the Executive and Legislature? Certainly they did. There were instances in which the Judges had decided upon the Constitution and laws of the country, and in one instance, he believed they had determined for them, and in another against them.

James A. Bayard of Delaware said on the same subject:

> Even the Judges, the gentleman said, are a check upon the Legislature. This arises from the nature of the Legislature, the powers of which are limited. If the Legislature transgress the bounds of their authority, their acts are void, and neither the people nor the Judges are bound by them.

In the debate in June and July, 1798, over the notorious Sedition Act this measure, which was so violently obnoxious to all Anti-Federalists, and which was supported by strong Federalists like Samuel Sewall and Harrison Gray Otis of Massachusetts, on the ground that it was warranted by the "common

---

[1] *5th Cong., 2d Sess.*, Jan. 18, 19, 22, 23, 24, 25, 26, Feb. 27, 28, March 1, 2, 5, 1798; speeches of Nicholas, p. 849; Griswold, p. 891; Bayard, p. 893; Nicholas, p. 920; Gallatin, p. 1118; Bayard, p. 1221.

EARLY CONGRESSES AND THE COURT 119

defence and general welfare", produced a further consideration of the constitutionality of legislation based on this portion of the Constitution.[1] "If such a construction be allowed," said Robert Williams of North Carolina, "what becomes of the powers of the State Governments? The preamble of the Constitution would swallow up the whole."

Albert Gallatin, an Anti-Federalist, again reiterated his belief in the power of State Courts to hold an Act of Congress invalid, saying that "the States and the State Judiciary would, indeed they must, consider the law as a mere nullity, they must declare it to be unconstitutional." Robert G. Harper, a Federalist, said:

> The gentleman from Pennsylvania says that, if this law were to pass, the Courts of Justice would declare it to be unconstitutional. If so, then, according to his own opinion, the law would become a dead letter. He did not know what the decision of the Judicial power would be.

John W. Kittera, a New York Federalist, maintained that it was for the Judges to decide whether or not the law is constitutional, saying: "The gentleman from New York (Edward Livingston) calls upon the whole people to resist this law because it is unconstitutional. This was a doctrine which Mr. K. could by no means accord with; it was a doctrine which he did not expect to have heard advanced on this floor. There is a judicial power which will sit

---

[1] *5th Cong., 2d Sess.*, June 16, 18, 21, July 5, 9, 1798; speeches of Sewall, Otis, Williams, Abraham Baldwin, and Samuel W. Dana, pp. 1954, *et seq.*; speeches of Gallatin, pp. 1982, 1996; Harper, p. 1991; Livingston, p. 2014; Kittera, p. 2016; Allen, p. 2093; Livingston, p. 2104; Gallatin, p. 2111; Macon, p. 2153.

in judgment upon our acts; but to call upon the people to resist the law was a doctrine big with mischief. If a law be unconstitutional, the Judges will refuse to execute it." And John Allen of Connecticut, also criticizing Livingston, asked if the people are to be "instructed that opposition to the laws, that insurrection is a duty whenever they think we exceed our Constitution", yet "who shall determine that point? I thought the Constitution had assigned the cognizance of that question to the Courts and so it has." Livingston replied, while practically recognizing that the Judges might decide as to constitutionality, that in the last resort the people of the United States were the Judges, and said that: "We [the Congress] are their servants. When we exceed our powers, we become their tyrants." Gallatin again expressed his view that the Alien Bill was unconstitutional, and said that "his opinion was that an appeal must be made to another tribunal, to the Judiciary in the first instance, on the subject of a supposed unconstitutional law." Bayard opposed an amendment providing that the jury should be judges of the law as well as the fact, because he said: "The effect of this amendment would be to put it in the power of a jury to declare that this is an unconstitutional law, instead of leaving this to be determined where it ought to be determined, by the Judiciary." And finally, the leading Jeffersonian Anti-Federalist in the House, Nathaniel Macon of North Carolina, said that "he was convinced that Congress does not possess the power to pass a law like the present; but if there be a majority determined to pass it, he could only hope that the Judges would exercise the power placed in them of determining the law an unconstitutional law, if upon scrutiny they find it to be so."

The significant point, which must be again emphasized, is, that in this whole excited debate, members of both political parties acceded to the view that the Judiciary had the power to hold an Act of Congress unconstitutional; and that no one expressed any contrary opinion.

The Alien and Sedition Laws were enacted on July 14, 1798, and immediately became the object of violent attack by the Anti-Federalists and the adherents of Jefferson. When indictments were found under these laws in the Circuit Courts of the United States, their opponents called loudly and continuously on these Federal Courts to declare these Acts of Congress unconstitutional. And when Justices of the Supreme Court of the United States, sitting on Circuit, rendered decisions upholding the legislation, they were vigorously assailed for their refusal to hold that Congress had exceeded its powers. It was the usurpation by Congress, not usurpation by the Courts, which was condemned. It was for failure to exercise the power of judicial review in the way desired by them that the Anti-Federalists objected to the Court, "in most poignant anathema against the Judiciary of our country."[1] And it was for the actual exercise of this power in a manner confirmatory of Federal legislation that the Federalists praised the Court.[2] Both parties, however, fully

[1] See speech of Henry Lee, Jan. 23, 1801, p. 962, *6th Cong.*, *2d Sess.*
[2] *5th Cong., 3d Sess.*, Dec. 14, 1798. John Rutledge, Jr., of South Carolina said that "the Judges who had acted under them (the Alien and Sedition Laws) had declared them to be perfectly constitutional and he was not disposed to make 'an appeal to the people' to know whether they deemed them constitutional."

recognized the legal existence of the Court's power. (Incidentally, it may be noted that, one hundred and twenty years later, the same radicals in this country who assail the *existence* of the Court's power were equally anxious with the radicals of 1798 that the Court should *exercise* its power in this particular instance and that it should hold the so-called Espionage Law of 1918 to be unconstitutional.)

In the first session of the Sixth Congress, there occurred the one solitary instance of a denial by a member of Congress of the Court's power of judicial review.[1] On March 5, 1800, Charles Pinckney, a Senator from South Carolina, arguing for his favorite bill to prevent the appointment of Justices of the Supreme Court to any other official position — a measure called forth by the appointment of Chief Justice Jay by President Washington as Special Ambassador to Great Britain in 1794, and of Chief Justice Ellsworth by President Adams as Special Ambassador to France in 1799 — used this argument in connection with the necessity of an independent and unbiased Judiciary:

It is our duty to guard against any addition to this bias, which a Judge, from the nature of his appointment, must inevitably feel in favor of the President. It is more particularly incumbent on us when we recollect that our

[1] *6th Cong., 1st Sess.*, March 5, 1800, p. 101. Pinckney, in letters of "A Republican Farmer", published in the newspapers in 1799, and in book form as *Letters from a South Carolina Planter* (1800), had said: "Upon no subject am I more convinced than that it is an unsafe and dangerous doctrine in a republic to ever suppose that a Judge ought to possess the right of questioning or deciding upon the constitutionality of treaties, laws or any Act of the Legislature. It is placing the opinion of an individual, or of two or three, above that of both branches of Congress, a doctrine which is not warranted by the Constitution, and will not, I hope, long have many advocates in this country."

EARLY CONGRESSES AND THE COURT 123

Judges claim the dangerous right to question the constitutionality of the laws, and either to execute them or not as they think proper, a right in my judgment as unfounded and as dangerous as any that was ever attempted in a free government; they, however, do exercise it, and while they are suffered to do so, it is impossible to say to what extent it might be carried. What might be the consequences if the President could at any time get rid of obnoxious laws by persuading or influencing the Judges to decide that they were unconstitutional and ought not to be executed?

No other instance, however, can be found, either in that Congress or in previous Congresses, of any similar explicit expression of opinion.[1] And on the contrary, an Anti-Federalist fully as strong in his politics as Pinckney, Thomas T. Davis of Kentucky, stated in the second session of this Sixth Congress, with reference to the Sedition Laws, that [2]:

Had the decisions of the Courts been made with all the moderation and solemnity that usually attend judicial decisions, he might answer that there had been proceedings in the United States calculated to establish the constitutionality of that law, so far as the opinion of the

---

[1] It is sometimes said that Abraham Baldwin of Georgia changed his previous views as to the power of judicial review by the Court, in a speech delivered on the Presidential Election Bill, Jan. 23, 1800 (*6th Cong., 1st Sess.*); but it is doubtful whether such was his intention. His words were as follows, p. 31: "It is true, they (the electors) as well as any other Constitutional branch of the Government, acting under that instrument, may be guilty of taking unconstitutional or corrupt steps; but they do it at their peril. Suppose either of the other branches of the Government, the Executive or the Judiciary, or even Congress, should be guilty of taking steps which are unconstitutional, to whom is it submitted, or who has control over it, except by impeachment? The Constitution seems to have equal confidence in all the branches on their proper ground, and for either to arrogate superiority, or a claim to great confidence, shows them in particular to be unworthy of it, as it is in itself directly unconstitutional."

[2] *6th Cong., 2d Sess.*, Jan. 21, 22, 23, 1801; speech of Davis, p. 917; Griswold, p. 921; Rutledge, p. 932.

Judges went. *For he must acknowledge that the Judges had the power of deciding the constitutionality of a law under which they were to act.*

In the same debate, the Federalists stated that the Judiciary had settled the question. Roger Griswold of Connecticut said:

As a constitutional question he thought no doubt could now exist, whatever might have been entertained before the question was settled on its present principles. The Judiciary had decided it to be a law effectually within the Constitution. There might be some other quorum to which gentlemen would wish to appeal, perhaps they might be better satisfied by appealing to the people, but he could not be. He believed the decision to be made in a constitutional mode, and was desirous of giving it his decided support.

John Rutledge, Jr., of South Carolina said:

Respecting the constitutionality of this law, I will only observe that our Judiciary (and they are the only appropriate judges of its constitutionality) have decided and repeatedly decided that it was constitutional. An honorable gentleman from Virginia has told us that a more high and respectable tribunal — the people — had declared it unconstitutional. Sir, I am not so good a Democrat nor so diffident of myself, as to have recourse to the people on the passage of every law, to enquire of them if it be constitutional. . . . If any proceeding of the Legislature be unconstitutional, I have the consolation of knowing the Judiciary will declare it so, and to the decisions of our venerable and profoundedly learned Judges I look up for information, whenever the constitutionality of a law is questioned, and not to the resolutions of popular and tumultuous meetings. If, upon every constitutional doubt, we are to have recourse to the people, there is an end to representative Government.

EARLY CONGRESSES AND THE COURT 125

Less than a month after these strong admissions as to the power of the Judiciary, the Federalist party enacted its famous Circuit Court Act of 1801, under the provisions of which President Adams made his much assailed appointments of the "Midnight Judges."[1] The repeal of this Act became the primary desire and determination of President Jefferson and the Anti-Federalists. Against the bill embodying this repeal, the Federalists raised the cry of unconstitutionality. The debate over the repeal became bitterly and heatedly partisan; and under the exigency of partisan politics, the Court's power of judicial review was questioned in Congress, for the first time other than in the statement by Charles Pinckney above quoted. On February 3, 1802, John Breckenridge, the Jeffersonian leader in the Senate, who had been advocating the repeal bill for over a month, rose and said, in answer to the charge as to its invalidity: "To make the Constitution a practical system, this pretended power of the Courts to annul the laws of Congress cannot possibly exist. . . . The Legislature have the exclusive right to interpret the Constitution in what regards the law-making power, and the Judges are bound to execute the laws they make."[2] This attack on the Court's power was an entire reversal of the views previously expressed by

---

[1] Act of Feb. 13, 1801, c. 4 (2 Stat. 89). For most illuminating descriptions of the attitude of the Anti-Federalists and of the country in general towards this statute, see speeches in the House in 1830 of James Buchanan, Jan. 14; James K. Polk, Jan. 20; J. W. Huntington, Feb. 16; Charles A. Wickliffe, March 16. *21st Cong., 1st Sess.*, pp. 530, 546, 566, 599.

[2] *7th Cong., 1st Sess.*, Jan. 8, 13, Feb. 3, 1803, speeches of Breckenridge, Stevens Thomson Mason of Virginia, and James Jackson of Georgia, in the Senate; speeches of John Randolph of Virginia, Thomas T. Davis of Kentucky, and Robert Williams of North Carolina, in the House.

Breckenridge; for in a debate in the Kentucky Legislature, in November, 1798, on the famous Kentucky Resolutions as to the Alien and Sedition Laws, he had denied emphatically that the Congress were "the sole judges of the propriety and constitutionality of all acts done by them", and while supporting the right of the States, in the last resort, to pass upon the constitutionality of a Federal statute, he had expressly admitted that the Judges might refuse to act under such a statute, on the ground of its unconstitutionality.[1] These views he had shared with the drafter of the Resolution, George Nicholas, another leading Anti-Federalist of Kentucky, who had written of the Alien and Sedition Laws that if enforcement were attempted, "the Courts would declare them to be void."[2] Breckenridge's view was supported in this debate in 1802, by less than half a dozen Anti-Federalists coming wholly from Virginia, Georgia, North Carolina, and Kentucky. Anti-Federalists and Federalists from the other States alike upheld the Court's power, and John Bacon, a strong Anti-Federalist from Massachusetts, stated that he "must frankly acknowledge the right of judicial officers of every grade to judge for themselves, of the constitutionality of every statute on which they are called to act in their respective spheres. *This is not only their right, but it is their indispensable duty thus to do.*"[3]

[1] See *The Kentucky Resolutions of 1798* (1887), by Ethelbert D. Warfield, pp. 93, *et seq.*

[2] Letter of George Nicholas to his friend in Virginia, Nov. 10, 1798, in *National Magazine* (June, 1799), I, 217.

[3] See report of Bacon's speech in *National Intelligencer*, March 19, July 28, 1803, publishing in full this portion of the speech which is omitted in the report in the *Annals of Congress.*

EARLY CONGRESSES AND THE COURT 127

That Breckenridge's statement as to "*pretended* power of the Courts to annul the laws of Congress" was the announcement of a novel, unexpected, and unaccepted doctrine, was pointed out by several speakers in the debate, — Archibald Henderson of North Carolina, terming it "the monstrous and unheard of doctrine which has lately been advanced", Joseph Hemphill of Pennsylvania stating that "a doctrine new and dangerous has begun to unfold itself", and Jonathan Dayton speaking of "those newly professed, though secretly harboured, doctrines which exhibit in their true colors their deformity and dangerous tendencies."[1]

On February 23, 1803, Chief Justice Marshall rendered his decision in the case of *Marbury* v. *Madison*, in which the Supreme Court for the first time held an Act of Congress unconstitutional. That its action did not constitute a "usurpation" and that its power so to act had been recognized and accepted, without question, by statesmen of both political parties in every Congress that had sat prior to the rendering of the decision, is conclusively shown by the foregoing summary.[2]

---

[1] In a debate in the Senate, Feb. 3, 1803 (three weeks prior to the decision of *Marbury* v. *Madison*), on the petition of the "midnight Judges" that the President caused a *quo warranto* proceeding to be filed to obtain a judicial decision on their claims, the power of the Court to pass on an Act of Congress was again disputed by some Southern Democrats. *7th Cong., 2d Sess.*, Feb. 3, 1803.

[2] It may be noted that at the date of this decision thirty-nine out of the fifty-five members of the Federal Convention of 1787 were still alive (sixteen having died, as follows: W. C. Houston, Brearly, Jenifer, Franklin, Livingston, Mason, Sherman, Bedford, Read, Wilson, Washington, Rutledge, Mifflin, Blair, Yates, Spaight). If the Court had "usurped" a power not given to it by the Constitution, it might have been expected that some one of these thirty-nine survivors of the Convention would have protested; but so far as appears from letters or printed publication, no one of them made any protest (except Charles Pinckney, as above noted).

CHAPTER FIVE

THE PROPOSAL TO MAKE CONGRESS THE SUPREME AND FINAL JUDGE OF ITS OWN POWERS

"Now will any one contend that it is the true spirit of this Government that the will of a majority of Congress should, in all cases, be the supreme Law? If no security was intended to be provided for the rights of the States and the liberty of the citizen, beyond the mere organization of the Federal Government, we should have had no written Constitution, but Congress would have been authorized to legislate for us, in all cases whatsoever. If the will of a majority of Congress is to be the supreme law of the land, it is clear the Constitution is a dead letter and has utterly failed of the very object for which it was designed — the protection of the rights of the minority." — ROBERT Y. HAYNE of South Carolina, in the Senate, Jan. 26, 1830, *21st Cong., 1st Sess.*

"They . . . wish that a construction be put upon the Constitution by Congress which shall be considered as the Constitution itself, and are unwilling that there should be any check to oppose it; and of course every construction put upon it by the different Legislatures will exhibit the appearance of a new Constitution, a Constitution to be tossed and blown about by every political breeze. The powers of Congress will be equal to the powers of the English Parliament, transcendent, splendid and without control." — JOSEPH HEMPHILL of Pennsylvania, Feb. 16, 1802, *7th Cong., 1st Sess.*

"It is a sound position that you should never attempt an alteration in an instrument so complicated and calculated to serve so many and opposite interests, without being able, by the test of experiment, to discern clearly the necessity of alteration, and without a moral certainty that the change shall not only remove an existing evil, but that it shall not produce any, itself." — URIAH TRACY of Connecticut, in the Senate, Dec. 2, 1803, *8th Cong., 1st Sess.*

In the foregoing chapters, it has been pointed out that the function of the Supreme Court in holding an

CONGRESS AS A FINAL ARBITER 129

Act of Congress invalid was a necessary judicial function; that a Court with such a power was embodied in the Constitution, because the framers had already been familiar, by actual experience, with the value of their State Courts in curbing by judicial decision excesses in the use of power and violations of their State Constitutions by State Legislatures; that the framers expected and intended that the Supreme Court should exercise similar power; that the general public and those who ratified the Constitution had the same expectations and intentions as to the Court; that the radicals of 1788, who secured the insertion into the Constitution of a Bill of Rights, understood that it would be a useless action unless such Bill of Rights could be enforced by a Court; and finally that the early Congresses themselves, for twelve years, recognized and endorsed the existence of this power of the Court, with hardly a dissenting vote.

At the present time, however, some labor leaders, radicals, sociologists, men and women alike, who have been made dissatisfied by some particular decision or decisions rendered by the Court in holding an Act of Congress unconstitutional, have launched an attack upon the Court, challenging the fundamental right of the Court to render *these* decisions or *any* decision, involving the validity of a Federal statute. They assail this whole function of the Supreme Court as a Court; and they advocate and demand Constitutional Amendments depriving the Court (to a greater or less degree) of all power to pass upon the constitutionality of any Act of Congress. Such an assault is, of course, of a most serious nature. It does not present a question of the correctness or incorrectness of the Judges' views as to the law involved or as to the facts of any litigation under a Federal statute. It presents the question of the whole principle on which the Court was devised as one of the three branches of government under the Constitution; what is the theory of the Court's functions as to Acts of Congress, and what would be the operation of the Government, if the Court possessed no functions in this respect? Those who make this assault, however, have a right to their opinions and must be answered. Sixty years ago, a great American Judge, Horace Gray of Massachusetts (who later sat on the Supreme Court of the United States), said: "In a free republic, it is the right of every citizen to strive in a peaceable manner by vote, speech or writing to cause the laws or even the Constitution under which he lives to be reformed or altered by the Legislature or the people."[1] The views of those who differ from us must be answered by fair statement and argument, and not by denunciation — not by the use of terms like "destroyers of the Constitution."

On the other hand, the proponents of any radical changes must equally support them by candid statement and not by mere declamation. And one thing certainly the American public may rightly demand of those who propose to alter our form of government. The public has the right to ask that those who advocate such a change shall at least state existing facts correctly and candidly, and that they shall state *all* the facts. There is nothing in the realm of governmental discussion that the public is more hungry for

[1] *Jackson* v. *Phillips* (1867), 14 Allen (Mass.), 539, 555.

CONGRESS AS A FINAL ARBITER 131

than actual facts. There is no form of intellectual diet with which it is less fed. For half-truths, suppressed information, prejudiced arguments, unfair criticism, lack of candor, too often characterize the arguments of advocates of reforms in our law and government. The public has the right to demand that the question shall not be confused and beclouded by exaggeration, suppression, or misstatement.

In previous chapters, consideration has been given to the baseless charge that the Court, in exercising its present powers, has been guilty of "usurpation." No one who paid attention to history could ever, fairly or candidly, make such an accusation. And certainly, when given the historical facts, every open-minded man or woman will agree that it is ridiculous for agitators to argue now that the Court did not and does not possess the power to set aside Congressional enactments as unconstitutional, if the members of the early Congresses themselves understood, accepted, and endorsed the Court's power.

There is one class of attack upon the Court, however, the deceptive nature of which it is less easy for the public to perceive. It consists of general statements as to fancied unjust decisions of the Court, without discrimination as to the grounds on which the decisions were rendered. A characteristic misleading statement of this nature appeared in a speech by a then leading opponent of the Court, last fall, in which, after a criticism of the Court's decisions in the Income Tax Case of 1895, the Standard Oil and Tobacco Cases of 1911, the Child Labor Cases, and the Minimum Wage Case, the speaker said: "These are only

132 CONGRESS AS A FINAL ARBITER

a very few of the cases wherein during the last few years the Court, by usurping legislative power, has nullified Acts of Congress." [1]

Here, the speaker applied the word "nullified" to two entirely different classes of cases, viz., those involving the validity of a Federal statute (like the Child Labor, Income Tax, and Minimum Wage cases) and those involving only the construction of a Federal statute (like the Standard Oil and Tobacco cases). He was using the word "nullified", therefore, in a highly deceptive manner; for it is the first class of case alone to which his proposed remedy is directed; and the second class of case, *i.e.*, that in which the Court merely construes an Act of Congress, is one in which no one has ever proposed that the Court's power to construe should be abolished. The speaker continued:

The judicial veto in practically all these cases has been

---

[1] Speech of the late Senator La Follette at New York, Sept. 18, 1924, *New York Times*, Sept. 19, 1924. As an example of a deceptive statement, see letter of Rev. Norman Thomas, socialist candidate for Governor of New York, addressed to Governor Alfred R. Smith, Sept. 27, 1924, in which he speaks of the necessity of a "curtailment of the power of the Federal Supreme Court which has heretofore declared unconstitutional anti-injunction legislation." The only decision of the Court holding any anti-injunction legislation invalid was the decision in *Truax* v. *Corrigan*, in which a *State* statute was held unconstitutional. But such a decision would not be affected at all by the proposed La Follette Amendment which is confined to decisions of the Court affecting Acts of Congress and not State statutes.

As an example of an absolute misstatement of fact, see "Supreme Court and Constitution" in *New Republic*, April 8, 1925, in which it is said: "If there be grave doubts as to the constitutionality of a statute, the Supreme Court is always anxious to remove them. Its custom is to remove these doubts effectively by holding the statute unconstitutional." This allegation as to the Court's "custom" is the exact reverse of the fact; for its "custom", as repeatedly stated by the Court from its very earliest to its latest decisions, is to the effect that it will never hold a statute unconstitutional, unless the invalidity is plain and clear beyond reasonable doubt. As Mr. Justice Sutherland has recently said in *Adkins* v. *Children's Hospital* (1923), 261 U. S. 525: "This

CONGRESS AS A FINAL ARBITER 133

levelled at progressive measures which enunciated a rule contrary to the economic or political beliefs of a majority of the men who happen to make up the Supreme Court. Tenement-house, bake-shop, workmen's compensation, eight-hour decisions and many others of a similar nature could be cited to the same effect.

This was another deceptive statement. Such an assertion would lead his audience and readers to suppose that the United States Supreme Court had declared unconstitutional tenement-house, bake-shop, workmen's compensation and eight-hour laws. But if so intended, the statement was grossly inaccurate. That Court has never declared unconstitutional any tenement-house law (either Federal or State); it has never declared unconstitutional any workmen's compensation law (Federal or State); it has never declared unconstitutional any eight-hour law (Federal or State); and the statement that "many others of a similar nature could be cited to the same effect" was untrue as applied to the United States Supreme Court. The nearest approach to truth would be the fact that in one case the Court has held invalid an Act of Congress attempting to apply a State workmen's compensation law to cases in the Federal Admiralty Courts (but it has never held invalid any Act of Congress establishing a Federal Workmen's compensation law); and in one other case, it has held invalid, twenty years ago, a State statute of New York as to

Court, by an unbroken line of decisions from Chief Justice Marshall to the present day, has steadily adhered to the rule that every possible presumption is in favor of the validity of an Act of Congress until overcome beyond rational doubt. But if by clear and indubitable demonstration, a statute be opposed to the Constitution, we have no choice but to say so."

ten-hour day labor in bakeries, — a decision which would, at the present time, probably be overruled, if the case should again arise.

The truth is that the speaker above quoted, like many other Labor and radical leaders, jumbled together cases in which the State Supreme Courts have held State laws unconstitutional, cases in which the United States Supreme Court has held State Laws unconstitutional, cases in which that Court has merely construed an Act of Congress, and cases in which that Court has held Acts of Congress unconstitutional; and by this misleading confusion of four different classes of cases, he sought to give to the public the impression that there were large numbers of cases in which the Court has held Acts of Congress invalid.

Now what are the facts?

In one hundred and thirty-five years (from 1789 to 1924) there have been exactly fifty-three decided cases in which an Act of Congress has been held unconstitutional (and one case in which a Joint Resolution of Congress has been held unconstitutional). Moreover, as some of these cases involved the same statute and merely applied the decision to a new set of facts, there have actually been held unconstitutional only forty-nine Acts of Congress and one Joint Resolution. But of these fifty-three decisions, only eleven have ever received any serious criticism; and the others have been recognized not only as correct, but as vitally important in preserving the rights of individuals and of the States as against encroachments by the Federal Government. What are these eleven, and what was their

CONGRESS AS A FINAL ARBITER 135

effect on our country?[1] Six can be easily passed over.

1. The *Dred Scott Case*, in 1857. It was cured by the result of the Civil War. It is now of only historical interest.

2. The *Legal Tender Case*, in 1870. It was reversed by the Court itself.

3. The *Monongahela Navigation Co. Case*, in 1893, as to compensation for franchises taken by eminent domain. This decision has never aroused any great antagonism.

4. The *Income Tax Case*, in 1895. This was cured by the 16th Amendment.

5. The *First Employers' Liability Case*, in 1908. This was cured by Congress itself by passing a properly worded new law.

6. The *Workmen's Compensation in Admiralty Case*, in 1919. This decision can probably be cured, at any time, by a properly drawn Federal statute.

---

[1] *Scott* v. *Sandford* (1857), 19 How. 393; *Hepburn* v. *Griswold* (1870), 8 Wall. 603; *Monongahela Nav. Co.* v. *United States* (1893), 148 U. S. 312; *Pollock* v. *Farmers' Loan & Trust Co.* (1895), 157 U. S. 429, 158 U. S. 601; *Eisner* v. *Macomber* (1919), 252 U. S. 189; *Howard* v. *Illinois Central R. R.* (1908), 207 U. S. 463; see *Mondou* v. *N. Y., N. H. & H. R. R.* (1912), 223 U. S. 1; *Adair* v. *United States* (1908), 208 U. S. 161; *Hammer* v. *Dagenhart* (1918), 247 U. S. 251; *Knickerbocker Ice Co.* v. *Stewart* (1920), 253 U. S. 149; *Bailey* v. *Drexel Furniture Co.* (1922), 259 U. S. 20; *Adkins* v. *Children's Hospital* (1923), 261 U. S. 525.

Between 1789 and June, 1924 — a period of 135 years — there was a total of only fifty-three decisions of the Supreme Court holding Acts of Congress unconstitutional. These fifty-three decisions are divided as follows:

From 1789 to 1864, inclusive	2 in	75 years
From 1864 through Oct. Term, 1885	16 in	21 years
From Oct. Term, 1886, to June, 1906, inclusive	12 in	20 years
From Oct. Term, 1906, to June, 1924, inclusive	23 in	19 years
	53 in	135 years

The increase in the last nineteen years has been largely due to the vast increase of Federal interference into matters of State concern, by Federal statutes.

Thus, there are left only five cases, as to which any one feels any deep grievance now.

7. The *Adair Case*, in 1908, holding invalid one section of an Act of Congress, making it a crime for a railroad to discharge an employee for belonging to a labor organization. Whether Labor has or has not a just grievance over this decision may be admitted to be an open question.

8. The *Child Labor Law Case*, in 1918.
9. The *Stock Dividend Case*, in 1920.
10. The *Child Labor Law Case*, in 1923.
11. The *District of Columbia Minimum Wage Law Case*, in 1923.

Even if it should be assumed that these five decisions were all erroneous, even if it should be assumed that the whole eleven decisions were erroneous, they would afford a very limited ground for demanding a revolutionary change in our form of government. Yet it is on this slight basis of facts that certain men have asserted that there exists a vast evil in the power of judicial review exercised by the Court; and it is on this basis of fact and to remedy this supposed evil, that they have called for a Constitutional Amendment completely depriving the Court of its power to pass upon the validity of Federal laws. It should be noted — what is frequently overlooked — that such a Constitutional Amendment would not fully accomplish its purpose. For if the United States Supreme Court lost its power to pass on the validity of Federal statutes, the power to do so would still remain in the State Supreme Courts, in any case involving a Federal statute coming before them. There have been many decisions by State Supreme Courts, in

CONGRESS AS A FINAL ARBITER 137

our history, holding Acts of Congress unconstitutional. Thus, the Federal Legal Tender Laws were held unconstitutional by the State Courts of Kentucky and Indiana, in 1864 and 1865; the Federal Habeas Corpus Act of 1863, relieving of responsibility officers acting under authority from the President, was held invalid by the State Courts of Indiana, Illinois, and Missouri in 1863, 1867, and 1877; the Federal Stamp Tax Act of 1864 was held invalid by the State Courts of Illinois, Indiana, Kentucky, Missouri, New York, and Wisconsin, from 1864 to 1882; the Federal Removals Act of 1866 was held invalid by the State Court of South Carolina in 1879; and the second Federal Employers' Liability Law was held invalid by the State Supreme Court of Connecticut.[1] The decisions in all these cases would have been final, if the United States Supreme Court had been deprived of its power to pass upon the validity of those Federal statutes; and the statutes themselves would not be enforced in those States. Thus, we might have the Constitution meaning one thing in one State and another thing in another State, according as the Act of Congress was upheld or not in a

---

[1] See *Griswold* v. *Hepburn* (1865), 63 Ky. 20; *Thayer* v. *Hedges* (1864), 22 Ind. 283; see also *Martin's Ex'ors* v. *Martin* (1870), 20 N. J. Equity 421 (involving the Legal Tender Act).

Other cases in which State Supreme Courts held an Act of Congress unconstitutional were *Johnson* v. *Gordon* (1884), 4 Calif. 368 (involving Section 25 of the Judiciary Act of 1789); *Re Booth* (1854), 3 Wisc. 1 (involving the Fugitive Slave Law of 1850); *Griffin* v. *Wilcox* (1863), 21 Ind. 370; *Johnson* v. *Jones* (1867), 44 Ill. 142; *Chase* v. *Mitchell* (1877), 64 Mo. 564, involving the Act of March 3, 1863, sec. 4; *Warren* v. *Paul* (1864), 22 Ind. 276; *Latham* v. *Smith* (1867), 45 Ill. 29; *Craig* v. *Dimock* (1868), 47 Ill. 308; *More* v. *Clymer* (1882), 12 Mo. App. 11; *Moore* v. *Moore* (1872), 47 N. Y. 467, *Hunter* v. *Cobb* (1866), 1 Bush (Ky.) 239; *Jones* v. *Keep* (1865), 19 Wisc. 390; involving the Stamp Tax provision of the Act of June 30, 1864, sec. 158; *State* v. *Davis* (1879), 12 So. Car. 528 (involving Rev. Stat. Sec. 463, as to removals).

State Supreme Court. American citizens may well pause to consider whether their Federal Government could exist, unless their Constitution had a uniform meaning, and their Federal laws a uniform existence and operation, in every State of the Union; also whether it would be desirable for any citizen or body or class of citizens that one State should be given an opportunity thus to discriminate in favor of or against other States, by means of a decision of its State Court construing the Federal Constitution and laws differently from the Courts of other States.[1]

This extreme demand for the complete abolition of the power of the United States Supreme Court as to Acts of Congress has been recently modified; and now the proposal, made by the late Senator La Follette and supported by other radicals and by some representatives of Labor, is that the Court's "veto power" (as they wrongly term it) shall not be taken away entirely, but that its exercise shall be subject to be overruled by Congress.

It has been proposed to provide by Constitutional Amendment that a statute enacted once may be held unconstitutional by the Court, but if enacted a second time, at least by a two-thirds majority, it shall thereafter be held constitutional and forever free from attack. Congress may overrule the Court, whenever such Congress shall say twice what it ought *not* to

---

[1] As James A. Bayard of Delaware said in the Senate, Feb. 20, 1802: "This principle would also destroy the uniformity of obligation upon all the States, which should attend every law of this Government. If a law were declared void in one State, it would exempt the citizens of that State from its operation, whilst obedience was yielded to it in the other States. I go farther, and say, if the States or the State Courts had a final power of annulling the Acts of this Government, its miserable and precarious existence would not be worth the trouble of a moment." *7th Cong., 1st Sess.*

CONGRESS AS A FINAL ARBITER 139

have said even once. A bad statute shall become good by repetition.

This plan, of course, makes Congress the supreme, and, in the last resort, the sole power in this country. For by a twice-passed statute, Congress could alter or abolish any of the powers of the President or of the Court, granted by the Constitution; alter or destroy any of the reserved powers of the States; deprive individuals of any or all of the rights guaranteed by the Bill of Rights. In other words, our entire system of government, as established by the Constitution, with its limitations of power and its checks and balances, will exist only so long and so far as Congress shall not choose to alter it.

Moreover, the plan makes of no effect any Amendment to the Constitution which the people may have adopted, or may in the future adopt; for Congress, by a twice-passed statute, may repeal or alter even that Amendment. Thus, though the Supreme Court is now bound by the provisions of a Constitutional Amendment adopted to reverse any of its decisions, Congress would be bound by no Constitutional Amendment, if it should choose to enact twice a statute violative of it. Congress, therefore, would be far more omnipotent and uncontrollable than is the present Court.

But the plan suggested goes even farther. Should it be adopted, the provisions of the Constitution requiring submission to the State Legislatures of any Amendment to the Constitution would become unnecessary. For if Congress should desire to exercise any power admittedly not authorized by the present Constitution, all that would be necessary for it to do, in order to vest itself with such a power, would be to enact a statute twice. Thus, the people would be deprived of their chance to pass upon a Constitutional Amendment. This phase of the plan should be given the most earnest consideration by all American citizens. Many who advocate this proposal talk of a demand, "that the people finally may be able to outvoice the Supreme Court and write their will into law, in spite of the Supreme Court."[1] But they forget that Congress is not "the people." The people and their Legislative body are not synonymous terms. If they were synonymous, the Constitution would have given to Congress itself the right to amend the Constitution; but this right the Constitution expressly refused to grant; it carefully provided that Congress must submit any Amendment to the people of each State through its State Legislature or State Convention.[2] In other words, the people already have the power and ability, at any time, to "outvoice the Supreme Court and write their will into law"; but the people must act in each State. It was never

[1] Thus, the late Samuel Gompers stated in a document addressed to the American Federation of Labor: "The demand is not that the Court be deprived of all power to pass on the constitutionality of legislation, but that it be deprived solely of its power of final veto. What is demanded is that the people finally may be able to outvoice the Supreme Court and write their will into law in spite of the Supreme Court." *Washington Times*, Sept. 29, 1924.

[2] Article V of the Constitution is as follows: "The Congress, whenever two thirds of both Houses shall deem it necessary, shall propose Amendments to this Constitution, or on the application of the Legislatures of two thirds of the several States, shall call a Convention for proposing Amendments, which, in either case, shall be valid to all intents and purposes, as part of this Constitution, when ratified by the Legislatures of three fourths of the several States, or by Conventions in three fourths thereof, as the one or the other mode of ratification may be proposed by the Congress; Provided that no Amendment which may be made prior to the year one thousand eight hundred and eight shall in any manner affect the first and fourth Clauses in the Ninth Section of the first Article; and that no State, without its consent, shall be deprived of its equal suffrage in the Senate."

CONGRESS AS A FINAL ARBITER 141

intended by the States which formed this Union that their State powers should be lessened, or that the power of the National Government or of the National Congress should be increased, unless the people of three fourths of the individual States should so vote.

Those who endorse the proposed new Amendment are at pains to explain that they do not desire to deprive the Court of *all* power to hold an Act of Congress invalid, but only to allow Congress to *override* the Court, should the Court exercise its power. Such a contention is deceptive; the distinction sought to be maintained is illusory. For though they state that their plan preserves to the Court power, *in the first instance*, to pass upon the validity of Acts of Congress, subject to being later overruled by Congress, nevertheless the Amendment, if adopted, could be utilized at once to deprive the Court of *all* such power. Its appearance of preserving to the Court such a right in the first instance is nothing but camouflage. American citizens should pay careful attention to the way in which the proposed Amendment might work out in practical operation, as follows. Suppose that the Constitution should be amended in accordance with this plan, so as to allow Congress the right, by passing a statute a second time, to override a decision of the Supreme Court holding the statute first passed unconstitutional, and to thus render the twice-passed statute proof against any subsequent Court decision. Then suppose that, after the Amendment is adopted, the very first statute passed by Congress should be a statute taking away *all* power in the Court to pass upon the constitutionality

142 CONGRESS AS A FINAL ARBITER

of Federal statutes; then, after the Court holds such a statute unconstitutional, suppose the Congress passes the statute a second time. If this should occur, Congress, under the Amendment, by this twice-passed statute, would have finally and completely abolished the power of the Supreme Court as to constitutionality of Federal statutes. Thereafter, *no* Act of Congress could be held either invalid or valid by the Court. Consequently, thereafter, Congress would be unlimited in power, uncheckable by any Court, and bound by no provision of the Constitution, except so far as it chose to regard it. Its own law would supersede the Amendment itself.

The advocates of the proposed Amendment profess to regard this proposed omnipotence of Congress with equanimity. They rarely pause, however, to think what it may mean. Few of them realize that they seek to place Congress in such a position that no State of this Union, and no man, woman, or child in this country, would have a single right of any kind which Congress would be obliged to respect or which Congress might not impair or abolish at any time, by a twice-passed statute. The question presented to the American people is, concretely, this: Are they willing to allow Congress, by a twice-passed statute, to do any or all the things which the Constitution (including all its nineteen Amendments) expressly forbids Congress to do? If the American people are to agree to that proposal, then the people must be willing to allow Congress, by such a statute, to do any of the following things, although each such statute would violate the present express prohibitions of the Constitution.

CONGRESS AS A FINAL ARBITER

Congress, under the proposed plan, would be permitted:

(1) to require a religious test as a qualification for office or public trust, and to pass a law respecting an establishment of religion, and to prohibit the free exercise of religion;

(2) to abridge freedom of speech or of the press;

(3) to violate the right of the people to be secure in their persons, houses, papers, and effects against unreasonable searches and seizures;

(4) to authorize the trial of any person for crime or the trial of any common-law civil suit without a jury;

(5) to try a person for any crime without presentment or indictment by a grand jury;

(6) to deprive an accused of speedy and public trial; and to refuse to allow him counsel and compulsory process for obtaining witnesses;

(7) to subject a person for the same offense to be twice put in jeopardy of life or limb;

(8) to permit the retrial of facts once established by a jury in a common-law trial;

(9) to compel a person in a criminal case to be a witness against himself;

(10) to require excessive bail and to inflict cruel and unusual punishment;

(11) to constitute any act which it chooses to be treason;

(12) to suspend the privilege of the writ of habeas corpus at any time, whether in case of rebellion or invasion or not, or whether or not the public safety may require it;

(13) to pass a bill of attainder or an *ex post facto* law;

(14) to deprive a person of life, liberty, or property without due process of law;

(15) to take private property for public use without just compensation;

(16) to impose any form of involuntary servitude;

(17) to restrict the right of the people peaceably to assemble and to petition the Government for a redress of grievance.

(18) to infringe the right of the people to keep and bear arms;

(19) to deny or abridge the right to vote on account of race, color, or sex;

(20) to legislate directly against racial discrimination in the States;

(21) to permit the manufacture, sale, transportation, importation, or exportation of intoxicating liquor for beverage purposes.

Moreover, the Constitution expressly forbids Congress to legislate as to the States with reference to the following matters; yet the new proposal would allow Congress, by a twice-passed statute:

(22) to enact a direct tax imposed irrespective of the population of the respective States;

(23) to impose a tax or duty on articles exported from a State;

(24) to give a preference by a regulation of commerce or revenue to the ports of one State over those of another;

(25) to form a new State within the jurisdiction of any other State without the consent of both.

Every one of these prohibitions to Congress contained in the Constitution, with the exception of the last four, affects the life, liberty, or property of individuals, and is in the nature of a right guaranteed to every individual in the United States by the Constitution.

Can any one believe that there would be no chance of any injurious exercise of power by Congress? Is encroachment by Congress on individual rights something which was only an imaginary danger, conjured up by the men of 1788 who insisted on the Bill of Rights?

Take one right alone — that of freedom of speech. Nothing is more important in a Republican form of government; for, as has been well said: "The first Amendment protects two kinds of interests in free speech. There is an individual interest — the need of many men to express their opinion in matters vital to them, if life is to be worth living; and a social interest in the attainment of truth, so that the country may not only adopt the wisest course of action but carry it out in the wisest way." Such a social interest can yield to nothing but the national safety. Hence in time of peace, freedom of speech should be given the widest scope. Quite rightly have Labor and the radicals insisted on this right and the right of assembly as fundamental. Yet, when they now propose to give to Congress uncontrollable power, they fail to recall that, in 1920, in time of peace, Congress was very near to passing a so-called Sedition Law which would have grossly restricted the right of free speech.

Take the right of freedom of religion. With a Congress unchecked in this respect, is it difficult to conceive of conditions arising in this country which might lead to enactment into a law of proscriptive doctrines of religious intolerance or discrimination? Take the right of freedom from unreasonable search and seizure. Should the Courts have no curb on the action of Government agents, is it difficult to conceive of actions of prohibition and other officials violating this right, or is it difficult to conceive of a law of Congress authorizing search of private houses and property without search warrant? Recall also the increasing extent to which Congress is inclined to authorize tax officials to go in investigation of private books and business operations.

Many men have been loud in their complaints against injunctions in labor disputes. Not only Labor, but all other American citizens, should note that if it were not for the fact that the Bill of Rights guarantees a jury trial in suits at common law — a right now enforceable in the Courts — every suit of every kind at common law could be begun by the objectionable injunction and could be tried by a single judge without a jury.[1] Under the proposed

[1] A striking illustration of the tendency to abolish the right to jury trial is to be seen in an official statement issued by Emory R. Buckner, United States Attorney for the Southern District of New York, as follows: "We propose to padlock the employer's place of business, and not only compel him to seek a new house of operation but compel the owner of the real estate to look sadly upon his locked premises for twelve months and be deprived of rental. A padlocking Court operates without a jury. The judge can dispose of from ten to fifty cases a day, where a jury trial would take one or two days for a single case." See *New York World*, March 6, 1925. The Prohibition Commissioner, R. A. Haynes, was also reported in the *New York World*, July 21, 1924, as saying: "There are one or two tremendous advantages of this (padlock) system over the old-fashioned criminal indictment procedure. In the first place, it is a matter of affidavits and not juries. It takes only half an hour to convince a Judge of the innocence or guilt of a violator, but it might take a jury and all the delays of a jury trial months for a similar decision." To this statement the *World* added the editorial comment: "This was precisely the 'tremendous advantage' of the English Court of Star Chamber over 'the old-fashioned criminal-indictment procedure.' And it was precisely to prevent the rise of an American Court of Star Chamber that the fathers made inviolate the right

CONGRESS AS A FINAL ARBITER 147

Amendment, nothing would prevent Congress from eliminating a jury whenever it chose. If there are any persons who think that there is no danger of Congress so doing, let them remember that already Congress has tried to enforce the Volstead Law by authorizing padlock injunctions in an equity court instead of trial by jury in a criminal proceeding; and if Congress can thus abolish a jury in the punishment of this criminal offense, it can do so with reference to any other crime of like nature. The vast increase of statutes vesting authority in administrative boards and commissions to determine the property and personal rights of individuals is another example of the tendency of Congress to encroach on right to jury trial — which, if it has not yet overstepped the constitutional line, is extremely likely to do so, in this direction.

Take the right not to be deprived of liberty without due process; and let Labor recall, at times when the public mind is excited by strikes, the suggestions in Congress for infringing liberty of action by compulsory arbitration or by prohibition of the right of strikes by railroad employees and coal miners.

Take the right to due compensation for private property seized for public use, and let every holder of railroad stocks or bonds recall the propositions in Congress to take over the railroads at less than their actual value, or to limit their income.

Take the right guaranteed by the Constitution,

---

of trial by jury in imposing upon the Federal Government Articles VI and VII of the Bill of Rights."

See especially an able article by James M. Olmstead on *Padlock Injunctions*, in *Amer. Bar Ass. Journal* (June, 1925), XI, with reference to their unconstitutionality.

that a person accused of crime must be tried in the State where the offense was committed. Is it hard to imagine a condition of affairs where, in one part of the country public sentiment might make the conviction of offenses against a certain Federal law difficult, while in other sections the reverse might be true? If under those conditions Congress should pass twice a law providing for trial of crimes in some other State than that of its commission, what then would become of the citizen's right guaranteed him by the Constitution?

During recent years, Labor and the radicals have inveighed against Congress for enacting the so-called Espionage Law, and some have attacked the Selective Draft Law; they have claimed these statutes to be violative of the Constitution; they have attacked the Supreme Court for *upholding* the power of Congress to pass these laws. Yet what is the remedy they propose? Professing vast indignation against Congress for allegedly violating their rights of free speech and liberty of action, emitting volumes of wrath on the Court for failing to protect their rights and for supporting Congress, their remedy is to put it in the uncontrollable power of Congress to keep on violating their rights, and to take away from the Court all future capacity to protect their rights even should it be so disposed. *Complaining that Congress has exercised too much power, they propose, as a remedy, to give it unlimited power.*

Finally, let each American citizen ask himself this question: If a believer in the Eighteenth Amendment, is he willing to vest in Congress the power to repeal that Amendment, by simply passing twice a statute to that effect? That is precisely what a "wet" Congress could do under the proposed Supreme Court Amendment. If he is an opponent of the Eighteenth Amendment, is he willing to vest in Congress alone the power to make mere possession of alcoholic beverage a crime or to otherwise add to the present stringency of the Eighteenth Amendment, by simply passing twice a statute to that effect? Yet that is precisely what a "dry" Congress could do under the proposed Supreme Court Amendment.

Of course, it is not to be supposed that Congress, given free rein, would entirely or constantly disregard the Constitution; it may be assumed that, in ordinary times, its effort would be to abide by the limitations prescribed by that instrument; but in periods when passionate or thoughtless public feeling has been aroused for or against some particular object, for or against some particular class or section of the community, a Congress elected on, or affected by, that issue would very probably respond to the pressure to override the opinion of the Court.

It is, moreover, the minority — those who are advocating the less popular movements — who are especially in danger. The majority can always look out for itself; but in times of emergency, or bigotry, or passion, the majority, if unrestrained by a Constitution and Court, may pay scant heed to the rights of the minority. And this may be particularly true when that minority is confined to a particular geographical section of the country, or to a particular class in the community. It is then that an enforceable Bill of Rights is essential to the citizen's liberty, and it is then that a Congress vested with uncontrolled power, and elected from the section or community of the majority, would be most likely to violate those rights. It is also not infrequent that a party in power denies to the minority that very liberty which, when itself in the minority, it ardently champions.

Moreover, it is a solemn fact that, even in times of comparative freedom from emergency or excitement, Congress, or one of its branches, has violated the provisions of the Bill of Rights at least ten times since the year 1867; and at least ten times has the Supreme Court saved the individual against Congressional usurpation of power.[1]

For Congress has already tried to authorize illegal searches and seizure of private papers and has only been prevented by the action of the Supreme Court, in 1886. Congress has tried to authorize criminal prosecution of a man after compelling him to testify before a grand jury, and has only been prevented by the action of the Supreme Court, in 1892. Congress has tried to authorize the retrial in a Federal Court of facts already tried and settled in behalf of the plaintiff in a State Court, and was only prevented by the action of the Supreme Court, in 1870, in holding the statute unconstitutional. Congress has attempted to take property for public use without due and full compensation, and has only been prevented by the action of the Supreme Court, in 1893.

[1] *Boyd* v. *United States* (1886), 116 U. S. 616; *Counselman* v. *Hitchcock* (1892), 142 U. S. 547; *Justices* v. *Murray* (1870), 9 Wall. 274; *Monongahela Nav. Co.* v. *United States* (1893), 148 U. S. 312; *Wong Wing* v. *United States* (1890), 163 U. S. 228; *United States* v. *Evans* (1909), 213 U. S. 297; *Kirby* v. *United States* (1899), 174 U. S. 47; *Ex parte Garland* (1867), 4 Wall. 333; *Kilbourn* v. *Thompson* (1881), 103 U. S. 168; *Marshall* v. *Gordon* (1917), 243 U. S. 521.

CONGRESS AS A FINAL ARBITER 151

Congress has attempted to authorize imprisonment of persons at hard labor without an indictment by a grand jury, and has only been prevented by the action of the Supreme Court, in 1890. Congress has attempted to violate the provision of the Constitution requiring the defendant in a criminal prosecution to be confronted with the witnesses against him; the citizen's rights were preserved by the Court, in 1899. Congress has attempted to allow an appeal by the Government in a criminal trial after the accused has been found not guilty by a jury, and was prevented by the Supreme Court, in 1909. Congress has attempted to make a crime out of an act which was not a crime when it was committed, and by an *ex post facto* law to punish a man for committing such an act; it was prevented by the Supreme Court, in 1867.

One branch of Congress has attempted to imprison a man without jury trial for refusing to testify in an investigation of a matter over which it had no authority whatever; and it was prevented by the Supreme Court, in 1860. It has also attempted to imprison a man without jury trial for publishing a letter containing matter alleged to be defamatory of the House, and was prevented by the Supreme Court, in 1917.

It might be supposed that Congress would have been unlikely to infringe the prohibition contained in the Constitution against bills of attainder; yet three times, in periods of excited feelings, has Congress enacted statutes violative of this provision; once, in 1807, in connection with the Yazoo land frauds in Georgia; once, in 1862, during the Civil

War; and once, in 1865, as a result of the Civil War. The first of these statutes was never tested in Court; the second was threatened with a veto by President Lincoln and was modified by Congress itself; the third was held unconstitutional by the Court.[1]

What Congress has once done, it may well try to do again. And had these infringements on personal liberty by Congress gone unchecked by the Court, they would have served as formidable precedents for even more serious infringements in times of temporary popular excitement.

It is sometimes argued that because Congress has only been held by the Supreme Court to have violated the Constitution fifty-three times in one hundred and thirty-five years, there is little danger that it would do so, in the future, even if granted

---

[1] (a) Act of March 3, 1807, c. 46 (2 Stat. 445), and debates in *9th Cong., 2d Sess.*, March 2, 3, 1807, and *10th Cong., 1st Sess.*, Jan. 4, 1808.

(b) Confiscation Acts of Aug. 6, 1861, c. 60 (12 Stat. 319), and July 17, 1862, c. 195 (12 Stat. 589); *Miller* v. *United States* (1871), 11 Wall. 268. Field, J., diss. stated: "After the bill was sent to the President, it was ascertained that he was of opinion that it was unconstitutional in some of its features, and that he intended to veto it. His objections were that the restriction of the Constitution concerning forfeitures not extending beyond the life of the offender had been disregarded. To meet this objection, which had been communicated to members of the House of Representatives, where the bill originated, a Joint Resolution, explanatory of the Act, was passed by the House, and sent to the Senate. That body, being informed of the objections of the President concurred in the Joint Resolution. It was then sent to the President and was received by him before the expiration of the ten days allowed him for the consideration of the original bill. He returned the bill and Resolution together to the House, where they originated with a message, in which he stated that, considering the Act and the Resolution explanatory of the Act, as being substantially one, he had approved and signed both. That Joint Resolution declares that the provisions of the third clause of the 5th Section of the Act shall be so construed as not to apply to any act or acts done prior to its passage, "nor shall any punishment or proceedings under said Act be so construed as to work a forfeiture of the real estate of the offender beyond his natural life." See 12 Stat. 627.

(c) Act of Jan. 24, 1865, c. 20 (13 Stat. 424); *Ex parte Garland* (1867), 4 Wall. 333.

CONGRESS AS A FINAL ARBITER 153

the powers contained in the proposed Amendment. But this argument loses sight of the fact that Congress has, in the past, been frequently deterred from passing unconstitutional legislation, by the knowledge or belief that the Court stood ready to hold such legislation invalid; and it has also been deterred by the operation of its own oath to support the Constitution. But under the La Follette Amendment, neither of these factors would operate as a deterrent; and, in fact, the oath to support the Constitution would have absolutely no meaning or effect, for the Constitution would become whatever Congress chose to make of it by a twice-passed statute. Anything which Congress decided to do by such a statute would be *rightly and lawfully* done under that amended Constitution, and anything determined upon by it would be in accordance with its oath; in other words, Congress would have not only the power but the right to disregard whatever the Constitution now commands or forbids.

To those who ask, "Have you not confidence in Congress?" the reply may well be made in the powerful words of Jefferson:

It would be a dangerous delusion if our confidence in the men of our choice should silence our fears for the safety of our rights. Confidence is everywhere the parent of despotism. Free government is founded on jealousy, not in confidence. It is jealousy and not confidence which prescribes limited constitutions to bind down those whom we are obliged to trust with power. Our Constitution has accordingly fixed the limits to which, and no further, our confidence will go. In questions of power, then, let no more be heard of confidence in man, but bind him down from mischief by the chains of the Constitution.

The liberty of the citizen depends on the enforceable restraints on the citizens' government.

Turning from the relation of the Court to the rights of individuals, let us consider, briefly, the effect of the proposed Amendment upon the relation of the Court to the rights of the States and State citizens. It has been pointed out, above, that the Constitution would never have been ratified at all, had it not been for the consent of its framers and advocates to certain Amendments — Amendments which were insisted upon by the radicals, the farmers, and the country folk of 1788. These Amendments were: first, a Bill of Rights for individuals; and second, a Bill of Rights for the States, in the form of a guaranty that all powers not expressly granted to Congress were reserved to the States.

The chief fear of the democratic radicals of 1788 was a centralized government at the National Capital. "A single consolidated government would become the most corrupt government on earth," wrote Thomas Jefferson, and again he wrote that the road on which the United States would "pass on to destruction" would be "by a consolidation first, and then corruption, its necessary consequence." Looking back over the history of nations, Jefferson sounded a warning against centralization of power when he later wrote: "What has destroyed the liberty and the rights of man in every government which has ever existed under the sun? The generalizing and concentrating all cares and powers into one body." And again: "When all government, domestic and foreign, in little as in great things, shall be drawn to Washington as the centre of all power, it will render

CONGRESS AS A FINAL ARBITER 155

powerless the checks provided of one government on another."[1] And again: "It is not by the consolidation or concentration of powers, but by their distribution, that good government is effected. Were not this country already divided into States, that division must be made that each might do for itself what concerns itself directly, and what it can so much better do than a distinct authority."

To the argument that is sometimes made by enthusiasts for extension of power by the National Government — that the latter is "more efficient" than the States, and that a centralized Government "can reach supposed ills in their entirety, when the States can only reach them partially", the question may well be asked: Is efficiency the only desideratum or test? If it is, then, as was keenly pointed out by Mr. Justice Brewer, "a centralized government with a dictator is the ideal government, for none has such efficiency and thoroughness as a government under the absolute control of a single individual."

What becomes of the States, and what becomes of our Federal form of government, if Congress, by a twice-passed statute, is to be allowed to legislate upon any subject which it may choose, regardless of the division of powers between the National and the State Governments, contained in the Constitution? Instead of a Federal Government with limited powers

[1] *Writings of Thomas Jefferson* (H. A. Washington ed.), VI, 543; VII, 216, 223. See also speech of John Clopton of Virginia, Dec. 11, 1806: "The people of the several States, therefore, see in their State Governments safe repositories of their civil rights and immunities, strong barriers against licentious interruptions of social order, convenient and easy modes of administering justice among themselves and indeed of managing all their local affairs. Hence, their fond, their invincible attachment to that species of government." *9th Cong., 2d Sess.*

and with complete reservation to the States and their citizens of all other powers and rights, Americans would have a consolidated government with unlimited powers and with no rights left to the States and their citizens, except such as Congress in its supreme autocracy might see fit to leave or to grant to them. As James A. Bayard of Delaware said in the House, long ago, in 1802: "Gentlemen tell us they are friendly to the existence of the States, that they are the friends of federative, but the enemies of a consolidated, government; and yet, Sir, to accomplish a paltry object, they are willing to settle a principle which, beyond all doubt, would eventually plant a consolidated government with unlimited power upon the ruins of the State Governments. Nothing can be more absurd than to contend that there is a practical restraint upon a political body who are answerable to none but themselves for the violation of the restraint, and who can derive from the very act of violation, undeniable justification of their conduct."

Each citizen of a State should, therefore, ask himself the question whether he favors an Amendment which will put into the power of Congress the uncontrollable power, at any time, by a twice-passed statute, to regulate the education of his children, to regulate his wages in private employment, to regulate his personal habits of any nature, to regulate his private business, and to legislate on any or all subjects of purely domestic concern, as to which the States now, under the present Constitution, have exclusive jurisdiction?

Whatever strength there may be in the argument as to the unlikelihood of Congress violating the rights of individual citizens, there is no strength whatever in any argument that Congress would not be likely to infringe upon the rights guaranteed to the States by the Constitution. For it is precisely on the ground of such violation of State Rights by Congress that most of the cases decided by the Court have been based. And experience, particularly in the present era, proves that Congress, having power to push the limits of the Federal Government beyond those set by the Constitution, would most certainly exercise that power. And when such transfer of any power from the States to the Federal Government shall be possible simply by means of a twice-passed Act of Congress, it is clear that it will only be a question of time when the States are left with little authority except of the narrowest scope.

One hundred years ago, John McPherson Berrien of Georgia made a forcible reply in the Senate to an argument that Congress should be made the judge of the meaning of the Constitution. "Is there a State in the Union," he asked, "which would have ratified that charter if such had been its provisions?" The States, he said, would utterly lack security for all their rights, if they were to be committed "to the exclusive guardianship of Congress, unrestrained in the exercise of their powers but by their own interpretation of our Federal Charter." His own experience in the Senate constrained him to this belief, "when I look to the history of the legislation of all free States, to the history of our own legislation; when I see how often the decisions of deliberative bodies are influenced by consideration of temporary expediency, how often they are swayed by the impulses of momentary feeling; when I observe, in seasons of great political excitement, with what undeviating uniformity the ranks of party are marshalled even on questions of constitutional law; when I consider that, from the very nature of the power to be exercised, every recurrence of a question, however solemnly it may have been decided, throws it open to new controversy."[1]

What would be the effect of such transfer of power to the Federal Government, upon the individual citizen, and upon the part he or she plays in the Government? That would be a very serious question — which has been well answered in a brilliant article, fitly entitled, "Destroying our 'Indestructible States'."

The successful maintenance of a self-governing democracy depends upon the intelligent interest and participation of individual citizens. Our governmental system has been peculiarly favorable to creating and preserving such a condition. The principle of local self-government, to the greatest practical extent and applying to the widest possible range of subjects, administered by the smallest governmental unit reasonably adequate for the purpose, has been the corner-stone of our institutions. It existed before the Constitution was adopted, and its preservation was an important object in the provisions which that instrument contained.

[1] James A. Bayard of Delaware, in the House, Jan. 20, 1802, *7th Cong., 1st Sess.;* John McP. Berrien, in the Senate, *19th Cong., 2d Sess.,* Jan. 31, 1827. "Destroying our 'Indestructible States'," by Bentley W. Warren, *Atlantic Monthly* (1924), CXXXIII.

Andrew W. Stevenson of Virginia, in the House, Feb. 2, 1829, said: "What mockery for the fathers of our Constitution to have told us, that, by that instrument, power was made to check power, ambition check ambition, and the State Governments (the dearest objects of their affection) to check the encroachments of the General Government . . . if the doctrines of these days are to prevail, and *this* Government is to judge, in the last resort, of the powers granted and reserved and that judgment be the supreme law! Such arguments go to the utter destruction of the landmarks between the powers of the two Governments, and bring at once all the reserved rights of the States and the people to the altar of Federal power." *20th Cong., 2d Sess.*

CONGRESS AS A FINAL ARBITER 159

The tendency to centralize represents the antipodal principle. The individual citizen is unable to follow, feels himself powerless to influence, what a government far removed from his locality, operating through unknown and inaccessible bureaus and commissions, may be doing. Consultation with his fellow citizens is useless and for the most part impossible. They represent 25,000,000 voters scattered over 3,000,000 square miles. The cost of postage alone on a single circular is a quarter of a million dollars. The increasing sense of powerlessness among these individual voters dulls their interest, lessens their participation, and produces a general atrophy in the electorate. The Central Government becomes subject to the influence only of organized minorities and blocs, each actuated by some one dominating purpose, all maintaining national headquarters at Washington and raising and using large amounts of money to carry their several purposes into effect. A vast lobby system develops at the Capital, and controls legislation and government. . . . When the States shall have been thus destroyed — as they surely will be unless present tendencies are checked — who believe that our present Union can continue? Said Madison (in *The Federalist*, No. 12): "Were it proposed by the plan of the Convention to abolish the governments of the particular States, its adversaries would have some ground for their objection; though it would not be difficult to show that if they were abolished the General Government would be compelled, by the principle of self-preservation, to reinstate them in their proper jurisdiction." Who has ever seen the keystone of an arch remain in position when its supporting members have been removed?

It is argued, as if in mitigation of the practical operation of the proposed Amendment, that the requirement that the statute shall be passed twice will make it necessary for the statute to be considered and enacted by two different Congresses, in view of the fact that after its first passage considerable time must elapse before a decision of the Court can be obtained and before a second action by Congress can ensue after the Court's decision. But a very brief consideration of what has been the actual lapse of time in certain cases in the past will show that this argument has no weight. As a matter of fact, there have been a number of cases decided by the Court holding an Act of Congress invalid within so short a time after the passage of the Act that there would have been ample opportunity for the same Congress to reënact it; and in which the La Follette Amendment might not have secured a consideration of the Act by a second and different Congress. For instance, the Adamson Law was enacted on September 3, 1916, and the decision of the Court as to its validity was rendered within six months, on March 19, 1917. The Income Tax of 1895 was enacted on August 27, 1894, and it was held invalid by the Court within nine months, on May 20, 1895. The Act imposing an Income Tax on judicial salaries was passed on February 24, 1919, and was held invalid by the Court on June 1, 1920 — within the term of the 66th Congress which enacted the law. The first Employers' Liability Act was passed on June 11, 1906, and was held invalid by the Court on January 6, 1908 — within the term of the 60th Congress. The Futures Trading Act was passed on August 24, 1921, and was held invalid by the Court on May 5, 1922 — within the term of the 67th Congress.[1]

[1] In an editorial in the *Nation*, Sept. 24, 1924, it is said: "The *Nation* is under no illusions in regard to the wisdom of Congress or the tolerance of majorities. It is sure that Congress would occasionally abuse such powers as Mr. La Follette would give it, if it had them. We think, though, that Congress

CONGRESS AS A FINAL ARBITER 161

Consideration may next be given to one argument which is adduced by the supporters of the proposed Amendment, namely, that other countries get along well enough without any such power of the Court over Acts of Congress. Some supporters go even so far as to deny that the Court's power exists in any other country. This latter statement is, of course, absolutely untrue.

Power of judicial review exists and is exercised today in the highest Courts of Australia, New Zealand, South Africa, and Canada, and also in Argentina and Brazil. In the Irish Free State, the Courts have the power to pass on the validity of legislative Acts repugnant to its Constitution and the Anglo-Irish Treaty. The doctrine of judicial review has been adopted in a more or less modified form in Roumania, Bolivia, Costa Rica, Cuba, Czecho-Slovakia, Portugal, and Venezuela.[1] As examples of cases of

---

would not often overrule the Supreme Court. It does not now pass much legislation over the President's veto. It would override the Supreme Court far less often since the decisions of the latter come months and years after the passage of an Act when passions have cooled and personalities are forgotten."

The late Samuel Gompers, in a document addressed to the American Federation of Labor, said: "This does not contemplate hasty overturning of Supreme Court decisions, nor does it contemplate the enactment of legislation over the head of the Supreme Court during a temporary wave of emotion or during any condition which might lead Congress to do what later might be regretted." *Washington Times*, Sept. 29, 1924. But see *Wilson* v. *New*, 243 U. S. 332; *Pollock* v. *Farmers Loan & Trust Co.*, 158 U. S. 601; *Evans* v. *Gore*, 253 U. S. 245; *Howard* v. *Illinois Central R. R.*, 207 U. S. 463; *Hill* v. *Wallace*, 259 U. S. 44; see also the White Slave Act passed Feb. 20, 1907, decided April 5, 1909, *Keller* v. *United States*, 213 U. S. 138; the first Child Labor Act, passed Sept. 1, 1916, decided June 3, 1918, *Hammer* v. *Dagenhart*, 247 U. S. 251.

[1] See *Spirit of the Common Law* (1921), by Roscoe Pound: "In the report of South American republics we find judicial discussions of constitutional problems fortified with citation of American authorities; in the South African reports we find a Court composed of Dutch judges, trained in the Roman-Dutch law, holding a legislative Act invalid and citing *Marbury* v. *Madison;* the Australian Bench and Bar, notwithstanding a decision of the Judicial Committee

extreme similarity to those decided by the United States Supreme Court, it may be noted that the High Court of Australia has held invalid a Commonwealth excise tax on goods not manufactured under labor conditions approved by the Commonwealth Parliament, and has based its decision on the ground that such legislation was within the sole powers of the States and not within that of the central government; on the same ground, the Court denied the validity of a Commonwealth trade-mark Act, also of a Commonwealth restraint of trade Act, also of a Common-

of the Privy Council of England, are insisting upon the authority of Australian Courts to pass upon the constitutionality of State statutes, and the Privy Council has found itself obliged to pronounce invalid a confiscatory statute enacted by a Canadian province; even Continental publicists may be found asserting it a fundamental defect of their public law that constitutional principles are not protected by an independent Court of justice."

See also *Pending Attacks on Powers of Courts to Review the Constitutionality of Legislation*, an address before the New Jersey State Bar Ass., June 7, 1924, by Robert von Moschzisker: "In Canada, both the Provincial and Dominion Courts have assumed the right to declare legislation unconstitutional, albeit they are obliged to concede that the authoritative exposition of the British North American Act rests with the Judicial Committee of the Privy Council in England. Subject to the same right of appeal to the Privy Council, the Colonial Court of New Zealand and the South African Republic apply the doctrine of judicial review, and there is even one instance of an Indian Court declaring void a legislative Act of the Governor General of India, in Council. Outside the British Empire the doctrine has been adopted, in a more or less modified form, by Roumania, Argentina, Brazil, Bolivia, Colombia, Costa Rica, Cuba, Czecho-Slovakia, Haiti, Honduras, Portugal, and Venezuela. The French Parliament is supreme, even to the extent of amending the Constitution; but Professor Garner tells us, in recent years there has developed in that country a decided tendency to extend the power of the Judiciary, and he says there are many French jurists who advocate the adoption of the American system. The latest approval of our doctrine is manifested by the new Irish Free State Constitution, which gives the Courts power to nullify legislative Acts repugnant to the Constitution or the Anglo-Irish treaty, subject, however, to the right of appeal to the English Privy Council."

For full details as to cases in foreign countries, see especially *Report of Committees of New York Bar Ass.*, Jan. 22, 23, 1919; *63d Cong., 3d Sess.*, Senate Doc. 941; *Second Report of Committee of New York State Bar Ass.*, Jan. 14, 15, 1916; *Third Report of Committee of New York State Bar Ass.*, Jan. 12, 13, 1917; *The Influence of the American Doctrine of Judicial Review on Modern Constitutional Development*, by Henry H. Wilson, *The Constitutional Review* (1925), IX.

wealth Act dealing with regulation of industries.[1]
So, too, a resolution of the Cape Parliament has been held invalid by the highest Court in South Africa.

It is to be noted, however, that in many countries, because of their own particular conditions, there is little scope for judicial review, even if it existed. Thus, very few countries other than the United States have a written Bill of Rights or have any written provision for "due process of law"; and hence there are no fixed constitutional rights of the citizens which are not subject to interference with or violation by the Legislative body. In many countries, there are no divisions of power between the National and the State Governments, no federal system, no restrictions which require to be enforced by a Court as between a National Legislature and State Legislatures, and consequently no need of the exercise of judicial review by the Courts. In several countries, martial law may practically be proclaimed by the Executive or by the Executive and Legislative, even in localities not the actual theater of war; such a condition is not possible in the United States. In many of the European countries, there is a distinct body of law applicable solely to the actions of administrative officers who are thus given certain rights distinct from those possessed by other individuals. In many countries, the facility with which written Constitutions can be amended or changed makes resort to the Courts for a

[1] See *King* v. *Barges* (1908), 6 Commonwealth L. R. 42; *Attorney General for New South Wales* v. *Brewery Employees Union* (1908), 6 Com. L. R. 470; *Huddart, Park & Co.* v. *Moorehead* (1909), 8 Com. L. R. 331; and see in general Moore's *Constitution of the Commonwealth* (2d Ed.); *Municipality of Worcester* v. *Colonial Government* (1907), 24 S. C. Cape of Good Hope 67; *Judicial Control of Legislation in the British Empire*, by Herbert A. Smith, *Yale Law Journal* (1925), XXXIV.

judicial construction of the Constitution of less necessity. Making due allowances for these differences, Professor Charles Grove Haines, in an admirable article recently published, states that "the governments of the world may, with respect to judicial review of legislation, be roughly grouped into the following classes: [1]

"1. Governments in which the Legislature interprets finally the fundamental law. Examples: England, with an unwritten Constitution; Chile, France, Italy, and Switzerland, with written Constitutions.

"2. Governments in which the authority to interpret finally provisions of the Constitution, and as a consequence to invalidate Acts in conflict therewith, is implied as a necessary requirement to maintain the equilibrium between Federal and State Governments. Examples: United States, Australia, Canada, Brazil, and Argentina.

"3. Governments in which the Constitution grants authority to the Courts to interpret the Constitution and to prevent violations of its provisions. Examples: Colombia, Czecho-Slovakia, Honduras, Irish Free State, Portugal.

"4. Governments in which the power is considered as belonging to the Courts to review the acts of coördinate departments but in which the power has been exercised so infrequently as to have little significance. Examples: Greece, Norway, and South Africa prior to 1910 . . . Austria, Germany, Italy, and Poland have followed France in denying to the Courts the power to examine into the validity of laws. To this list could be added many other countries with written Constitutions, such as Japan, Spain, and Sweden, in which it is taken for granted that the normal functions of Courts do not include the power of examining into the validity of Legislative Acts. . . .

---

[1] *Shall We Remake the Supreme Court? The Practice of Other Countries*, by Charles Grove Haines, *Nation*, May 14, 1924.

CONGRESS AS A FINAL ARBITER 165

Certain South American countries such as Brazil and Argentina not only provide for the review by the Courts of Acts of the States which may be in conflict with national powers but also have accepted the American practice of declaring void the acts of coördinate branches of the government. The Brazilian Courts, following the general purpose to adopt the American system as defined by Chief Justice Marshall, do not hesitate to declare void acts of the National Congress; eight acts have been held invalid since 1915."

Thus, it is to be seen that the United States is by no means alone in vesting its Supreme Court with power to pass upon the constitutionality of Acts of its National Legislature. Those supporters of the proposed Amendment who have the candor to admit the above facts assert, nevertheless, that there is no need for the exercise of the Court's power in the United States, because, as they allege, the citizens of Great Britain get along perfectly well without a Court possessing any such power.

In reply, it may be said that the accuracy of this statement may also be challenged. But, assuming for the moment that it be true, there is one very complete answer to the adequacy of any comparison between England and the United States. Unlike our own country, England has no federal form of government. Here, we have one and the same territory and one and the same body of citizens, over which and over whom two distinct governments operate, the National and the State, each limited in its powers by the provisions of the written Constitution. In this country, as a consequence of its peculiar federal system, one of the most important class of questions which comes before the Supreme Court is that in which the claim is advanced by one or the other of the parties to the suit that either Congress or the State Legislature has exceeded these limited powers. No such question can come before an English Court with respect to Acts of Parliament, since no such class of limitations as to National, Federal, or State powers exists in England; and naturally, therefore, there is no cause for such power of judicial review by the English Courts, there being no such limitation to be enforced by the Courts. Citation of England as a country which gets along well enough with no power of judicial review in the Courts, is, therefore, like a comparison of Switzerland with England with respect to the necessity for the existence of a navy. It is impossible to compare two countries having entirely differing conditions, for the purpose of determining the value, or otherwise, of any particular institution.

The power does exist in the United States of necessity, as has been already pointed out; because, if it possessed no Supreme Court with authority to say when Congress or a State Legislature had trespassed beyond the field assigned to them respectively by the Constitution, then both Congress and the State Legislatures would have full power to legislate at their own sweet will, utterly unrestricted by the provisions of the Constitution. And, as a natural and inevitable consequence, Congress, being the mightier body, would prevail in every instance, and national legislation might sweep away all boundaries between the Nation and the States, in any case in which Congress felt sufficiently strongly the necessity or desirability of so doing.

Passing by this point, however, let us consider the

statement of those who say that the rights of English citizens are as well guarded by an English Parliament having supreme powers and uncontrollable by a written Constitution and a Supreme Court, as are the rights of American citizens in this country. An editorial in a leading Labor Journal has recently said that: "British Judges have no such power, yet civil liberties are nowhere guarded more jealously than in Britain."[1] Similar views are expressed by many Labor writers and leaders, in support of their contention that the United States should follow, or rather revert to, the example of England and make Congress as supreme as is the English Parliament.

It seems odd that successors of those Americans who, one hundred and fifty years ago, fought hard to escape from government by the English Parliament and the King, should now be urging that the United States should adopt the institutions which were then rejected.

But if Labor, or if any American citizen, is inclined to believe that the English Parliament affords a better protection to the rights of individuals than does our American system, his attention may be directed to some concrete examples of what became of the rights of British citizens during the late war.

[1] *Locomotive Engineers' Journal*, August, 1923.
Jackson H. Ralston in his *Study and Report for American Federation of Labor upon Judicial Control over Legislation as to Constitutional Questions* (2d Ed. Oct. 1923), p. 69, said: "If its power over Acts of Congress were our only salvation, we might inquire why it is that so great a nation as England succeeds as admirably as it does without the possession or exercise of anything at all analogous in the hands of its Judiciary, and why we more than England should belittle the importance of our legislative bodies. . . . No reason is known why the people of America and their representatives under a written Constitution should be less trustworthy than are the people of England without a written Constitution."

168 CONGRESS AS A FINAL ARBITER

It is well known that in the United States the Constitution protects the American citizen in his right to jury trial, whether in time of war or of peace. Ever since the momentous decision of the *Milligan Case* in 1867 by the Supreme Court, it has been the law in this country that no American citizen may ever be tried by a military court, in any place where the civil courts are open, except a person in the army and navy (or except possibly such a person as Congress may place in the category of a war spy, in which case Congress might be held to be acting under its Constitutional power "to make rules for the government and regulation of the land and naval forces"); and no American citizen, whatever, without exception, can be punished, without trial in *some* court.

Now let us turn the page, and see what is the right of a citizen of Great Britain. On October 30, 1915, during the great war, one Arthur Zadig, a British citizen, of German origin but naturalized for over ten years, was ordered to be interned by the Home Secretary, Sir John Simon, a member of the British Cabinet. Zadig was arrested, without any indictment or court warrant, and was interned without any trial or conviction of guilt, merely on "recommendation of a competent military authority", and simply and solely because governmental regulations, issued under the defense of the Realm Act, authorized such internment of "any person of hostile origin or associations", if the Home Secretary deemed it expedient "for the public safety and defense of the Realm."

Note that Zadig was a citizen and not an enemy. He was not an "alien enemy" such as the laws of the United States allowed us to intern here (for to such

CONGRESS AS A FINAL ARBITER 169

alien enemies, even the United States Constitution affords few rights). Yet the highest Court in the land, the House of Lords, sitting as a judicial tribunal, delivered an opinion, on appeal from a decision of Lord Chief Justice Reading, and held, in effect; that neither Zadig nor any other British citizen had any right to a jury trial or to freedom from internment, if a Home Secretary should decide that he was "of hostile origin *or* association." [1]

Thus, under the English system of an uncontrollable Parliament supreme over individual rights, a British citizen without being convicted of *anything* by *any* tribunal, and on mere suspicion or belief, may be confined in prison by an order of a Government official only.

In the *Zadig Case*, the power which Parliament and the Regulations happened to grant was that of arrest and internment of a British subject without trial; but if Parliament could authorize that, it could equally authorize his execution or banishment without trial.[2]

Labor may well be asked to pause and consider what might have happened in this country in the

[1] *Rex* v. *Holliday* (1916), 1 K. B. 738; (1917), A. C. 260.

[2] And to this extreme position, the Attorney-General (then Sir Frederick E. Smith, now Lord Birkenhead) was forced, when Lord Shaw, a dissenting Justice, said, in a noble opinion:

"If there is a power to lock up a person of hostile origin and associations because the Government judges that course to be for public safety and defense, why, on the same principle and an exercise of the same power, may he not be shot, out of hand? I put the point to the learned Attorney-General, and obtained from him no further answer than that the graver result seemed to be perfectly logical. I think it — the cases are by no means hard to figure, in which a Government in a time of unrest and moved by a sense of duty, assisted, it may be, by a gust of popular fury, might issue a regulation applying, as here, to persons of hostile origin or association, 'Let such danger really be ended and done with; let such suspect be shot.'

last war or what might happen in any future wars, had our law and our judicial system been like that in *Zadig's Case*. If Congress had had the power to give to a Government official the authority to arrest and intern any citizen of the United States who, on information of a competent military officer, was believed to be of hostile origin or associations, how easily might such a power be used to influence, or coerce opinion! This was strikingly pointed out by Lord Shaw in *Zadig's Case*:

Vested with this power of proscription, and permitted to enter the sphere of opinion and belief, they who alone can judge as to public safety and defense, may reckon a political creed their special care, and if that creed be socialism, pacifism, republicanism, the persons holding such creeds may be regulated out of the war, although never deed was done or word uttered by them that could be charged as a crime. The inmost citadel of our liberties would be then attacked. For as Sir Erskine May observes, this is the greatest of all our liberties; liberty of opinion.

Would Americans, would Labor, be content to trust Congress and the Government officials with such a power, without any opportunity to test its lawfulness in court?

Note that the point is not that Zadig, as well as Milligan, may not have richly deserved the treatment they received. The point is that in the United States, the guilty as well as the innocent have rights; and the Constitution allows no Government official, by his own unchallenged will, to determine the fact of guilt or innocence.

But this right of internment without trial was not

CONGRESS AS A FINAL ARBITER 171

the only infringement on personal liberty which was lawful in Great Britain, and unlawful in the United States, even in time of war.

The Regulations, authorized under the Defense of the Realm Act, provided that any military officer, "if he has reason to suspect that any house, building, land, vehicle . . . is being or has been constructed, used or kept for any purpose in any way prejudicial to the public safety or the defense of the Realm . . . may enter, if need be by force . . . and may seize anything found therein, which he has reason to suspect is being used or intended to be used for any such purpose." Even in time of peace, when search warrants are required in Great Britain, such warrants may be obtained without any specification of the particular property for which a search is denied — thus allowing a very general search.

Let Labor contrast this with the rights of American citizens, against search and seizure, whether in time of war or peace, under Article IV of the Bill of Rights. So insistent on this right were our people that Congress passed no general statute authorizing search warrants in Federal cases until June 15, 1917, and even then such search and seizure were strictly limited and regulated. The Supreme Court has held that these rights guaranteed by the Constitution exist in war as well as in peace; and the Court has so carefully protected the citizen's right against illegal search and seizure that it has held unconstitutional an Act of Congress, passed in 1874, that very mildly violated this right. Let every citizen of a State pause and ask himself the question whether he would prefer the English system of allowing unlimited search of his house "*if need be, by force*", in time of war. Let him recall the statutes which were passed by Congress during the late war — the Wartime Prohibition Act, the Lever Food Act, the Espionage Act. Suppose that every citizen's house or automobile could have been searched by any military officer for suspected violation of any of these laws. Would Americans have been satisfied with a system which gave them no protection in Court, no right to question the legality of a statute allowing such searches and seizures?

Take one more example of interference with the life, liberty, and property of a citizen by the British Parliament which would be forbidden under the American Constitution, whether in time of war or peace. By the Regulations under the Defense of the Realm Act, the military authorities, whenever they suspected a person, whether a citizen or otherwise, "of acting or of having acted or of being about to act in a manner prejudicial to the public safety or the defense of the Realm" might prohibit such person from entering or residing in any specified place and might require him to proceed to an approved place of residence and remain there; they might also arrest without warrant any person, citizen, or otherwise, "whose behaviour was of such a nature as to give reasonable ground for suspicion" that he *had acted* or was acting in a prejudicial manner, as above.

Under this statute, on January 14, 1920, after the War with Germany was over and the peace treaty in force, but before treaties were in force with all the other enemy countries, Patrick Foy, a citizen of Great Britain, was arrested in Ireland, and, on an order of a Government official, was interned as a

CONGRESS AS A FINAL ARBITER 173

person of "hostile origin or associations" and "suspected of acting, having acted and being about to act in a manner prejudicial to the public safety and defense of the realm." Foy attempted to find out in Court whether he had any rights, and the British Court held that Patrick Foy, though *interned, without trial by any Court*, merely because he was "suspected of acting, having acted and being about to act in a manner prejudicial", had no right for relief, under British law, with a Parliament supreme over individual rights.[1]

While these instances of British legislation occurred in war time, it must be remembered, nevertheless, that Parliament has precisely the same power to act, in peace times, in any emergency which it sees fit, without any curb by a Court.

When arguments, therefore, are addressed to American citizens, citing, in advocacy of a radical change in our form of government, the advantages of the British system of an uncontrollable National Legislature, let them ponder well these instances of what a British Parliament has actually done and can do with the rights of British citizens.

Finally, in considering any Amendment to their Constitution, American citizens may well pay careful heed to the wise tests suggested, over one hundred years ago. "It has appeared to me," said Roger Griswold of Connecticut in Congress in 1803, "that every proposal to amend the Constitution ought to be tested by the nature and scope of the Constitution itself, and if it shall be found to interfere with the rights of States or with any fundamental principle of

[1] *Rex* v. *Governor of Wormwood Scrubbs Prison* (1920), 2 K. B. 305.

174 CONGRESS AS A FINAL ARBITER

the compact, it ought to be rejected, although it may provide some temporary advantages in the eyes of speculative men." And, said Uriah Tracy of the same State: "You should not attempt an alteration . . . without being able, by the test of experiment, to discern clearly *the necessity of alteration*, and without a moral certainty that the change shall not only remove an existing evil, but that it shall not produce any itself." [1]

To the proposal to curb the power of the Supreme Court, the answer can be definitely made that there is no necessity for such an Amendment to the Constitution. The Court may err on occasions. It is not infallible, and like all other human institutions it makes its mistakes. Even Presidents and Members of Congress have been known to make mistakes. But the Court's degree of errancy has been small indeed; and if power is to be taken away, simply because of possibility of an erroneous exercise of power, little authority would be left in the hands of any branch of the Government. Moreover, as President Coolidge has said: "It is not necessary to prove that the Supreme Court never made a mistake; but if the power is to be taken away from them, it *is* necessary to prove that those who are to exercise it, would be likely to make fewer mistakes." [2]

Finally, the Constitution itself contains ample provision for remedying any mistakes of the judicial branch of the Government. The experience of the

---

[1] *8th Cong., 1st Sess.*, Griswold, Dec. 2, 1803, pp. 163, *et seq.*; Tracy, Dec. 8, 1803, p. 746. *7th Cong., 1st Sess.*, Morris, Feb. 3, 1802; Henderson, Feb. 15, 1802.

[2] Speech of President Calvin Coolidge before the United States Chamber of Commerce in Washington, D. C., Oct. 23, 1924.

last twenty-five years clearly shows that if there is any change or reform in our Government which the people really want, and to which a decision of the Supreme Court is a temporary bar, such change or reform can be and is easily brought about by an Amendment to the Constitution. Hence, the present power of the Supreme Court to pass on the constitutionality of statutes can never really prevent a change actually desired by the people. The Court can only delay such change. And delay is by no means an evil. Delay produces careful consideration by the people; and if a proposed change is desirable, consideration by the people strengthens its chance of success. If the proposed change is not desirable, why give to Congress alone the right to enact it? One hundred and twenty-three years ago, Gouverneur Morris of New York said in a great debate in the United States Senate, in 1802: "The moment the Legislature of the Union declare themselves supreme, they become so. . . . The Sovereignty of America will no longer reside in the people, but in the Congress; and the Constitution is whatever they [the Congress] choose to make it." And Archibald Henderson of North Carolina said in the House, at the same time: "Concentrating judicial and legislative power in the same hands . . . is the very definition of tyranny; and whenever you find it, the people are slaves, whether they call their government a monarchy, republic or democracy."

To-day, the Constitution reads: "This Constitution and the laws of the United States which shall be made in pursuance thereof . . . shall be the supreme law of the land." Some radicals would have it read:

"Acts of Congress and such parts of this Constitution as are in accordance therewith, shall be the supreme law of the land."

Each American citizen must consider whether he is willing to trust Congress with such proposed unlimited, uncontrollable, final power, and with the supreme authority to judge the extent of its own powers, not only over the rights of individuals but over the rights of the States. And he will certainly conclude that rights of liberty, of property, and of State sovereignty are more likely to be guarded by a majority of a Court than by a majority of a Congress — a Congress which may be swayed at any particular time by political, sectional, or class appeal — a Congress which may be influenced "by the power and wealth of vested interests on one day and by the passing whim of popular passion on another day" — a Congress which may be looking to see the influence of its decisions on party success and personal chances of reëlection. He will certainly conclude that, if any body of men is to possess final and uncontrolled power of ultimate judgment as to his constitutional rights and as to the constitutional restrictions imposed on the Legislature and the Executive, such power can be more safely lodged in Judges, not dependent for election on partisan issues in passionate political campaigns, but guided only by their conscience and the Constitution, uninfluenced by hope of popular or Executive favor, undisturbed by fear as to their tenure of office so long as they are honest, and under no obligation to comply with Executive or Congressional desire or dictation.

As has been pointed out in the first chapter of this

CONGRESS AS A FINAL ARBITER 177

book, the abolition of the Court's power of judicial review would not destroy the United States as a Nation; and as Mr. Justice Holmes has said: "The United States would not come to an end." But it *would* inevitably eventually destroy our present form of Government. Instead of a federal republic with limited powers, we would become a centralized consolidated government with unlimited powers. If American citizens wish to change to that form, should they not do so directly and consciously, rather than by the indirect method, embodied in a Constitutional Amendment lessening the powers of the Supreme Court?[1]

[1] In the Introductory Chapter of my book, *The Supreme Court in United States History* (1922), pp. 16, 17, I have stated that as between the two powers vested in the Court — that of passing on the constitutionality of State statutes, and that of passing on the constitutionality of Acts of Congress, the latter power "may fairly be termed of the lesser importance." Some persons have inferred that I, therefore, did not regard the Court's possession of the latter power as of importance. This is a wrong inference. I was treating only of relative importance; and my view was that, were the Court deprived of the first power, the whole successful operation of the Nation as a united Nation would have been imperilled; for the United States could not have held together, had the different States been at liberty, each for itself, to construe the extent of their own powers. On the other hand, with the Court deprived of the second power, the United States might have held together, since Congress could have enforced its supreme will upon the States; but it would have held together under an entirely different form of Government from that which our ancestors intended or their successors desired.

CHAPTER SIX

THE PROPOSAL TO VEST IN A MINORITY OF THE COURT THE POWER TO CONTROL ITS DECISIONS

"The first principle of republicanism is that the law of the majority (*lex majoris partis*) is the fundamental law of every society of individuals of equal rights; to consider the will of the society enounced by the majority of a single vote, as sacred as if unanimous is the first of all lessons in importance, yet last which is thoroughly learned." — THOMAS JEFFERSON to F. H. Alexander Von Humboldt, June 13, 1817.

"To give a minority a negative upon the majority, which is always the case where more than a majority is requisite to a decision, is, in its tendency, to subject the sense of the greater number to that of the lesser." — ALEXANDER HAMILTON in *The Federalist*, No. 22, Dec. 15, 1787.

"When a cause has been adjudged according to the rules and forms of the country, its justice ought to be presumed. Even error in the highest Court, which has been provided as the last means of correcting the errors of others and whose decrees are therefore subject to no other revisal, is one of those inconveniences flowing from the imperfection of our faculties, to which every society must submit; because there must be somewhere a last resort, wherein contestations may end. Multiply bodies of revisal as you please, their number must still be finite, and they must finish in the hands of fallible men as judges." — THOMAS JEFFERSON to the British Minister, George Hammond, March 29, 1792.

Some persons, who disagree with the results of the decisions made by the Court in certain cases decided in the exercise of its judicial power of review of statutes, admit that its power ought not to be impaired to the extent advocated by Senator La Follette, yet, at the same time, suggest another serious modification or regulation of the Court's judicial

MINORITY DECISIONS

power, by a bill requiring that seven Justices out of nine shall occur in pronouncing an Act of Congress unconstitutional.[1] This proposal, made by Senator Borah and others, can be accurately stated in another fashion, as follows: that if *less* than seven Judges concur in pronouncing an Act invalid, the Court shall hold it to be valid; or in other words, if three Judges out of nine believe an Act to be constitutional, the case shall be decided according to the view held by the minority of the Court, and not according to the view held by the majority. That the proposed bill contemplates actual control by the minority is to be seen clearly, when one reflects that a decision of a Court is not a decision upon an abstract question or upon the general proposition of the validity or invalidity of a statute. Every decision of a Court is a positive Act, deciding and establishing which of two persons or parties, litigating before it, is right. It is a decision that X, an actual person,

---

[1] See bill introduced by Senator Borah in the Senate, Feb. 5, 1923: "That in all suits now pending, or which may hereafter be pending in the Supreme Court of the United States, except cases affecting ambassadors, other public ministers, and consuls, and those in which a State shall be a party, where is drawn in question an Act of Congress on the ground of repugnancy to the Constitution of the United States, at least seven members of the Court shall concur before pronouncing said law unconstitutional."

It may be noted that Senator Borah, in spite of his unnecessary and unwise proposal, remains an ardent admirer and upholder of the Court. See his article republished in *67th Cong., 4th Sess.*, Feb. 19, 1923, p. 3589: "One cannot be justly charged with undue national pride when he declares that the Supreme Court of the United States is the most exalted judicial tribunal in the world — not a Court beyond the possibility of error, not a Court whose opinions are deemed above the reach of fair and honest criticism, but a Court, which, whether viewed as to the reach and scope and power of its jurisdiction or as to its influence and standing, its ability, and learning, its dedication and consecration to the service of mankind, is the greatest tribunal for order and justice yet created among men. If, therefore, the machinery of the Court can be geared to a higher plane and greater accuracy, thereby insuring its judgments greater support and approval, that should be our willing task."

has certain rights as a plaintiff or defendant, and that correlatively Y, another actual person, as defendant or plaintiff, has not certain rights. John Citizen claims that he has a right against James Voter based on a Federal statute; James Voter denies this and says that he has a right based on some provision or guaranty of the United States Constitution; the Supreme Court is then called upon to decide which right shall prevail — that founded on the statute, which is made by Congress who are only the agents of the people with limited powers; or that founded on the Constitution, which is made by the whole people. The Court, in deciding, must follow the Constitution as the higher and more binding law; it must disregard the statute if it shall find that it violates the Constitution; and it must decide in favor of James Voter, who relies on the Constitution. So, also, in a case between the United States and John Citizen, if the United States relies on a statute and John Citizen on the Constitution, the Court must decide the case in favor of John Citizen; and the United States will lose, if the statute is found to conflict with the Constitution.

Senator Borah's proposal is that a minority of the Court, and not a majority, shall decide these rights, in cases where one party relies on a Federal statute and the other party relies on the Constitution. His proposal is that Congress shall step in and say to the Court: "If a case is before you in which John Citizen, a plaintiff, relies on an Act of Congress, and James Voter, a defendant, relies on the Constitution, and claims the statute to be invalid, then if only six Judges think James Voter is right, the view of the minority

MINORITY DECISIONS

of three Judges must prevail, and the Court must render its decision in favor of John Citizen.

Now the first thing to be noted about the operation of such a proposal is this: that the judgment of the Court rendered under it is not a decision of the Court itself; but it is a decision rendered by the Court at the behest of Congress; a judgment rendered, in fact, by a minority of the Court and concurred in by the majority, *not* because it represents the carefully determined judicial opinion of that majority, *but* because the command of Congress takes the place of that judicial opinion. That such a judgment would be a Congressional judgment, rather than a judicial one, may possibly be more easily perceived, if the phraseology of Senator Borah's proposal should be applied to another class of cases in the Supreme Court.

If Congress has the power to direct the Supreme Court to decide constitutional questions in any particular way, it must equally have the power to dictate to that Court how it shall decide questions of title to property and of individual rights. Now, suppose that a bill should be introduced into Congress, following Senator Borah's phraseology, but applying it *not* to constitutional law but to the law of railroad negligence, and providing as follows: "That in all cases arising between a railroad employee and a railroad corporation, where is drawn in question the Federal Employers' Liability Act, on the ground that the employee was not engaged in interstate commerce, judgment shall be rendered for the railroad corporation, unless seven out of nine Judges concur in finding that the employee was so engaged in interstate commerce." Would any one conceive that Congress had the power to dictate to a Court to make such a decision in favor of a railroad defendant? Yet there is no difference in principle between such a statute and Senator Borah's proposal. In both cases, the action of the Court would cease being Judicial, and would be simply the carrying out of a Legislative direction. Under our present Constitution, the assumption by Congress of such authority over the Judicial power would be a violation of the principle of the separation of the Legislative and the Judicial powers contained in that instrument. Only an Amendment to the Constitution can change the extent and scope of the Judicial power of the Supreme Court, and such an Amendment would undoubtedly be required to put the Borah proposal into force (as discussed later in this chapter).

Aside from this question as to the necessity of a Constitutional Amendment, what would be the practical effect of a provision so placing a minority of the Court in control, and subjecting the rights of life, liberty, and property of X and Y, to be decided in accordance with the views of three Judges instead of in accordance with the view of six Judges.

In the first place, is so radical a step necessary, in order to cure any great prevalent evil? Senator Borah said, February 5, 1923: "These five to four decisions in which important Acts of Congress are held unconstitutional have produced a vast amount of dissatisfaction throughout the country among all classes of people. A number of laws have been passed by Congress of the most vital nature which have been held unconstitutional by a five to four vote of the

MINORITY DECISIONS 183

Court. The wisdom of having a different rule obtain cannot be doubted. The question of constitutionality presents a more serious question." [1]

Now what are the actual facts about these decisions?

In the whole one hundred and thirty-five years of its existence, the Supreme Court has only decided eight cases holding an Act of Congress unconstitutional by a five to four vote. One of these eight was in 1867 — the Test Oath Act Case. [2] The other seven were the cases involving the Income Tax Law, in 1895; the Stamp Tax on Foreign Bills of Lading, in 1901; the first Employers' Liability Act, in 1908; the first Child Labor Law, in 1918; the Workmen's Compensation and Admiralty Law, in 1920; the Stock Dividend Tax in the Income Tax Law, in 1920; the Federal Corrupt Practices Act, in 1921. To these eight cases, there may fairly be added one other — the District of Columbia Minimum Wage Law Case, in 1923, in which the vote was actually five to three, but in which Mr. Justice Brandeis, who would have undoubtedly dissented, did not sit.

As has been seen in a previous chapter, the total number of Acts of Congress held invalid by the Court in one hundred and thirty-five years was only fifty-three. Of these fifty-three decisions, there were eight (as above stated) in which the vote of the Judges was five to four; there were four in which three

---

[1] See speech of Senator Borah, in *New York Times*, Feb. 18, 1923.
[2] *Ex parte Garland* (1867), 4 Wallace 333; *Pollock v. Farmers' Loan & Trust Co.* (1895), 158 U. S. 601; *Fairbank v. United States* (1901), 181 U. S. 283; *Employers' Liability Cases* (1908), 207 U. S. 463; *Hammer v. Dagenhart* (1918), 247 U. S. 251; *Knickerbocker Ice Co. v. Stewart* (1920), 253 U. S. 149; *Eisner v. Macomber* (1910), 252 U. S. 189; *Newberry v. United States* (1921), 256 U. S. 232.

Judges dissented; there were twelve in which only two Judges dissented; there were seven in which one Judge dissented; and in twenty-two cases the decisions were unanimous.

It is interesting to note, therefore, that if Senator Borah's proposal to require a concurrence of seven Judges out of nine had prevailed since the year 1789, it would have changed the decision in only four cases (other than the eight first above mentioned).[1] Certainly the fact that the Court has rendered only eight decisions by a five to four vote, and four other decisions in which three Judges dissented, cannot be deemed to constitute a very grave evil or a very startling condition of injustice — especially when it is to be noted that at least four out of these twelve decisions never received any serious criticism at all.

Nor can the fact that six out of these twelve decisions rendered by less than seven out of nine votes have been rendered within the last six years be deemed to constitute a permanent evil requiring radical and revolutionary changes in the judicial powers of the Court, unless it can be assumed with fairness that this proportion is certain or likely to continue — an assumption which there is nothing in the Court's past history to support.

Waiving, however, the fact of the nonexistence of any great prevalent evil, what would be the practical operation of Senator Borah's proposal? The form in which his proposed bill is cast is somewhat deceptive.

---

[1] The First Legal Tender Case, *Hepburn* v. *Griswold*, 8 Wall. 603, in 1870; *Keller* v. *United States*, 213 U. S. 138, in 1909, holding a portion of the White Slave Law invalid, and *United States* v. *Moreland*, 258 U. S. 433, in 1922, holding a portion of the District of Columbia Criminal Courts Act invalid; *Adkins* v. *Children's Hospital* (1923), 261 U. S. 525.

MINORITY DECISIONS

It says "at least seven members shall concur before pronouncing said law unconstitutional." But what the Court actually does is *not* to pronounce a law unconstitutional. Cases come before it, on appeal either from the inferior Federal Courts, or from the State Courts. The Supreme Court must render its judgment. It can only do one of two things; it can either *reverse* the judgment or decree of the Court from which the case comes, or it can *affirm* it.

Bearing in mind, therefore, that the statute should properly regulate the actual function of the Court, viz., its act of reversing or affirming, Senator Borah's bill, if considered by the Judiciary Committees of Congress, would properly be redrafted so as to be more consonant with previous Judiciary Acts as follows:

No decision of an inferior Court of the United States or of a State Court where is drawn in question the validity of a statute of the United States, and the decision is against its validity shall be affirmed, and no decision of such Court in favor of the validity of such statute shall be reversed, unless at least seven members of the Court shall concur in such affirmance or reversal.

Let us apply this proposal to the different ways in which a case might be presented to the Supreme Court. First, take those cases coming from an inferior Federal Court in which the latter had held an Act of Congress constitutional. In such cases, the Supreme Court would, by the Borah Bill, be forced to affirm the judgment, if three Judges agreed with it; it would be prevented from reversing the judgment, even if six Judges wished to do so; *i.e.*, the decision of the lower Court must be affirmed, unless seven out of nine Judges concurred in voting to reverse it. Doubtless, in this class of cases, *i.e.*, cases where the lower Court holds an Act of Congress to be constitutional, the Borah proposal is at least feasible, although the effect of such a minority control, as explained later in this chapter, might be deplorable. A modified form of the Borah proposal may be seen in actual operation in the State of Ohio.[1] The Constitution adopted by that State in 1912 required that "no law shall be held unconstitutional and void by the Supreme Court, without the concurrence of at least all but one of the Judges", *i.e.*, of six out of seven Judges. A case arose in 1918, involving the validity of a State election law saddling certain expenses on the counties. The inferior State Court in Ohio held the election law constitutional. On appeal to the Supreme Court of Ohio, judgment was rendered, reading as follows:

Four members of this Court are of the opinion that the section of the General Code is unconstitutional. Three members are of the opinion that this section is not repugnant to any constitutional provision. The Court of Appeals (the inferior Court) held the statute constitutional. In such cases the Constitution of Ohio requires a concurrence of six members of the Supreme Court to declare a law unconstitutional. It follows that the judgment of the Court must be affirmed.

A still more striking instance of minority rule is found in a recent decision in 1924. In this case, an employer attacked the validity of a section of the Ohio Workmen's Compensation Act requiring employers who had not taken out State insurance to

[1] *Barker* v. *City of Akron* (1918), 98 Ohio State 446; *De Witt* v. *The State* (1924), 108 Ohio State 513.

MINORITY DECISIONS

pay an award in favor of employees, within ten days after rendition of the award or be subject to a fifty per cent penalty. On decision of the case, five out of the seven Judges considered the law unconstitutional, on the ground that a fifty per cent penalty was so severe as to deter employers from resorting to the Courts and hence constituted lack of "due process." Two of the seven Judges thought the law constitutional; their view became the decision of the case; and thus a minority of two Judges assumed the affirmative power of settling the law of the State.

If either of these cases had involved laws of grave importance to individual liberty; if, for instance, it had involved a criminal statute affecting constitutional rights, or if it had involved a defendant's entire property, or the rights of a great community, how much authority would such a minority decision have? Would either the parties or the public regard it as definitely settling anything? How much confidence in the Court would the community retain after a series of such minority decisions?

But when one takes the other class of cases, viz., those in which the inferior Federal Court has held an Act of Congress unconstitutional, one is confronted with quite another situation, and a more difficult problem arises. Suppose that such a case arrives in the Supreme Court from the lower Court; suppose that six Judges of the Supreme Court concur with the inferior Federal Court in holding the statute unconstitutional, and therefore believe that the decree of the lower Court should be affirmed; but three Judges of the Supreme Court view the statute as constitutional and therefore decide that the lower Court's decree should be reversed. What is to be done in such a case? Is it possible that Congress can give the power and authority to three Judges out of nine, to *reverse* a decree of a lower Court? Can Congress say to the Supreme Court that a property right or a personal right established by decree of the lower Court as belonging to X, shall be taken away from X, and established as belonging to Y, through a reversal of the decree of the lower Court, which reversal is supported by only three Judges?[1] If that can be done by Congress, how much confidence or respect would such a reversal by a minority of the Court receive?

In order to give a full comprehension of how the proposed change in judicial power vests absolute control in the minority of the Court, and results in the startling situation of a reversal of a decree of a lower Court by a minority of the Supreme Court, attention may be called to an actual case in which this revolutionary proposal is to be seen in its actual working out. The Amendment to the Constitution of North Dakota, adopted in 1919, provides as follows:

[1] It is true that one solution of this difficulty was attempted in a statute which was defeated in Congress in 1868, during the attacks on the Court in Reconstruction days. This statute forbade any inferior Federal Court from entering a judgment holding a Federal statute unconstitutional. But it is perfectly clear that such a measure would be unconstitutional, and could only be adopted after an Amendment to the Constitution. This bill was proposed by James F. Wilson of Iowa, in the House, Jan. 13, 1869, and provided that: "If any Circuit or District Court of the United States shall adjudge any Act of Congress to be unconstitutional or invalid, the judgment, before any further proceeding shall be had upon it, shall be certified up to the Supreme Court of the United States, and shall be considered therein, and if upon consideration thereof two thirds of all the members of the Supreme Court shall not affirm such judgment, the same shall be declared and held reversed." *40th Cong., 2d Sess.*, pp. 478, *et seq.* The bill was defeated by a vote of 124 to 25; see *The Supreme Court in United States History* (1922), by Charles Warren, III, 188, 189, note 1,

MINORITY DECISIONS

"Section 89: The Supreme Court shall consist of five Judges, a majority of whom shall be necessary to form a quorum or pronounce a decision, but one or more of said Judges may adjourn the Court from day to day or to a day certain, provided, however, that in no case shall any legislative enactment or law of the State of North Dakota be declared unconstitutional unless at least four of the Judges shall so decide."[1]

Under this Constitution, a case arose in 1920, in which the District Court of Grant County had held a statute unconstitutional, and sustained a demurrer dismissing the bill. An appeal was taken to the State Supreme Court consisting of five Judges, and that Court by a minority of two Judges *reversed* the decree of the lower Court. Two Judges (Grace and Robinson, J. J.) held the statute constitutional; one Judge, being disqualified, did not sit; and two Judges held the statute unconstitutional but held that the State Constitution constrained them from giving effect to their judgment. One of these latter Judges (Birdsell, J.) said:

I am constrained to concur in the order of reversal, by reason of the provisions of the amendment to Section 89 of the Constitution. . . . There is no way to give effect to this constitutional provision unless the members of this Court respect it as a part of the fundamental law by directing a judgment to be entered in individual cases, which may not conform to their views as to what the judgment should be. Entertaining this opinion, I deem it my duty to vote for a reversal of the order, though disagreeing with my two associates.

---

[1] Initiated Vote of Nov. 5, 1918; Ratified by Legislature, Chap. 88, Session Laws, 1919; *Daly* v. *Beery*, 45 No. Dak. 287, 128 N. W. Rep. 104. See also *State* v. *Olsen*, 47 No. Dak. 617, 120 N. W. Rep. 528.

And Chief Justice Christiansen, agreeing with Judge Birdsell, said:

> While I agree that the votes of Justices Grace and Robinson are decisive of the case, I do not agree that the statute under consideration does not contravene Sections 58 and 61 of the State Constitution. On the contrary, I am firmly of the opinion that it violates both of these sections and inasmuch as Justices Grace and Robinson have filed opinions setting forth at some length the reasons why they are of opinion that the statute *does not* violate these constitutional provisions, I deem it proper to indicate the reasons why I am of the opinion that it *does*.
>
> Suppose this case had involved a statute of great importance both to the public and to the individual parties concerned, how much respect would be felt for an opinion of a Court rendered by two out of five Judges and for a decree of a Court rendered by two out of five Judges, reversing a lower Court? How firm would a plaintiff feel in a right established in such a manner by a minority of a Court? What protection would the losing defendant in such a suit feel that the Constitution gave to him?

One step further in this minority control plan must now be considered. Suppose that instead of the appeal to the Supreme Court being from an inferior Federal Court holding a Federal statute unconstitutional, the appeal is from the decree of the highest Court of a State, holding the same Federal statute unconstitutional. Such a case is of by no means infrequent occurrence. The famous case of *In re Booth* in 1858, involving the Federal Fugitive Slave Law, came up to the United States Supreme Court on writ of error to the highest Court of Wisconsin

MINORITY DECISIONS 191

which had held the Federal Law invalid. State Supreme Courts have held Acts of Congress unconstitutional on many other occasions — the Federal Stamp Tax Act of 1864, held invalid by State Courts of Illinois, Indiana, Kentucky, and Wisconsin; the Federal Court Removals Act of 1860 held invalid by the State Court of South Carolina. The famous case of *Hepburn* v. *Griswold*, in 1870, involving the Federal Legal Tender Law, came up to the United States Supreme Court on writ of error to the highest State Court of Kentucky, which had held the Law invalid. So, too, the second Federal Employers' Liability Law was held unconstitutional by the State Supreme Court of Connecticut and when it came to the United States Supreme Court, the State Court judgment was reversed. Now in such cases as these, suppose the proposed seven out of nine rule to prevail; suppose six Judges believe the statute *unconstitutional* and therefore that the State Court's decree should be affirmed, and suppose that three Judges believe the statute constitutional and that the State Court's decree should be reversed, Under the rule, the view of these three Judges must prevail, and the judgment of the highest Court of a State must be reversed by a judgment of the United States Supreme Court in which only three Judges actually concur. Is it possible that such a condition is legal or that Congress has the power to require the reversal of the judgment of a State's highest Court, by the action of a minority of the United States Supreme Court? It may well be contended that not only has Congress no such power, but that it ought not to possess any such power; and further that no self-respecting State or State Court would, for a minute, submit to the indignity of having its decrees and judgments reversed by three out of nine Justices of the Supreme Court of the United States.

That a decision by a lower Court holding a statute unconstitutional should not be reversed by a minority of a Supreme Court is plainly recognized in the Ohio Constitution of 1912 itself, which, though requiring a concurrence of all but one of the Judges, as before stated, *expressly excepts* those cases in which the State Supreme Court affirms a judgment of the lower State Court, declaring a law unconstitutional and void. Yet this very proviso of the Ohio Constitution works a singular and unfair result. For, suppose that when the case of *Smith* v. *Jones* arrives in the Ohio Supreme Court, the Judges are divided five to two against the validity of the statute on which Jones relies — then the winning of the suit by Smith or by Jones will all depend on how the lower Court decided. For if the lower Court decided against the validity of the statute, then the Supreme Court may affirm the decision and Smith will win; but if the lower Court happened to have upheld the validity of the statute, then the Supreme Court (by operation of the Constitution) may not reverse the lower Court and Jones will win, *i.e.*, either Smith will win or Jones will win according to whether the lower Court held the statute on which Jones based his right to be valid or invalid. Accordingly, in two cases presenting exactly the same facts and involving the same law, coming to the Ohio Supreme Court from two separate inferior Courts, the plaintiff might win in the one case where the lower Court happened

MINORITY DECISIONS 193

to have held the law invalid, and the defendant might win in the other case where the lower Court happened to have held the law valid. In other words, the Ohio Supreme Court ceases to be supreme, and a plaintiff or defendant wins according to the view which the lower Court took of the validity of the statute.

There remains for consideration still another phase of this proposal for minority control, which is even more important. For, while it prevents six Judges from holding a Federal law invalid, it enables three Judges to hold a law valid. A little reflection will show that this is a serious matter. As an illustration — suppose that the Volstead Law could have been held constitutional by only three Judges; suppose that the Selective Draft Law could have been held valid by only three Judges. What degree of authority would such a law possess, when the people of this country knew that six out of nine Judges believed it to be unconstitutional, and that it was the law only because, under the Borah proposal, the vote of the six would not prevail, and the vote of the three Judges in the minority would decide the case?

Present-day opponents of the Court center their dissatisfaction on those decisions of the Court which have held Acts of Congress *invalid*. It must be remembered, however, that for the first seventy-five years of the Court's existence, the attacks made upon it by its opponents were due to its decisions holding Acts of Congress *valid;* and it was because the Court upheld Congress in passing statutes, deemed by numbers of the people to violate the rights of individuals and of the States, that the Court was subjected for so many years to savage antagonism by considerable classes and sections of the country. For seventy-five years, it was the encroachments by Congress, supported by the Court, that were feared — and not at all encroachments by the Court in derogation of Congressional power. Who can say how soon again it may be the encroachments by Congress on individual and State rights guaranteed by the Constitution that may have to be curbed? And if such a time arrives, how would the American people, or any portion of them, feel, should it be possible for Congressional encroachment to be held valid by a minority of the Judges of the Supreme Court? Liberals, radicals, and conservatives alike may well give their attention to a few historical instances of opposition to Congressional assumption of power — for, despite a recent remark that "history is all bunk", the history of this country has a habit of repeating itself; and the problems of the past become, with a rapid turn of the wheel, the very serious and exciting problems of to-day.

In 1799 and 1800, there appeared the first determined political attack on Judges of the Supreme Court, arising out of their decisions on Circuit in relation to the Alien and Sedition Laws, so obnoxious to Jefferson and the Anti-Federalist party. But the attack by the latter was *not* because the Court held those Acts of Congress unconstitutional, but *because it failed to do so.*

Next came the violent attacks on the Court by Maryland, Virginia, Ohio, and the South and West in general, for its decision, in 1819, in *McCulloch* v. *Maryland*, upholding the validity of the Act of Congress chartering the Second Bank of the United

MINORITY DECISIONS 195

States. Two years later, equally violent assaults were made on the Court when, in *Cohens* v. *Virginia*, in 1821, it upheld the power of Congress to enact the famous Twenty-fifth Section of the Judiciary Act authorizing writs of error to the judgments of State Courts.

It was then that Jefferson for the first time assailed the Court's power of judicial review of Federal laws; but this antagonism to the Court then arose again, not from its exercise of its power to hold an Act of Congress invalid, but from its failure so to do.[1] It was the support which the Court gave to the wide scope of Congressional power which filled Jefferson, Madison, and their other followers with alarm. They had no fear of the Court as an instrument in restricting Congress; but they viewed the Court with grave concern as the supporter of Congressional encroachment. They deplored the Court's failure to restrict Congress.[2] It is a singular thing that all the

---

[1] No letter of Jefferson attacking the judicial power to decide the validity of statutes can be found prior to a letter to W. H. Torrance, written June 11, 1815, relating to the action of a Tennessee Court in holding invalid a Tennessee law. The series of letters written by Jefferson from 1819 to 1823, referred almost entirely to the action of the United States Supreme Court relative to State statutes held invalid, or else to its action *supporting* the validity of Federal statutes. See *The Supreme Court in United States History* (1922), by Charles Warren, I, 264–267.

[2] John Rowan of Kentucky said in the Senate, Jan. 17, 1821 (*16th Cong., 2d Sess.*, p. 425): "What is the complaint? . . . Is it that the judicial power interposed a check improperly; that, without Constitutional authority, it interposed its power to shield the citizen, to protect the liberties of the country from Legislative usurpation? No, sir. *Directly the reverse.* As far as complaint or imputation is directed towards the Judges, it rests upon the charge, *not that they did, but that they did not*, interfere to arrest the career of the Legislative usurpation." See also speech of Mahlon Dickerson of New Jersey in the Senate, Jan. 19, 1821 (*ibid.*, pp. 209, *et seq.*); see also Thomas W. Cobb of Georgia in the Senate, Feb. 23, 1825 (*18th Cong., 2d Sess.*, p. 654): "In the work of aggression, it (the Court) has ever been foremost in the march. What claim of power by the Federal Government has it not sustained?"

present-day opponents of the Court who quote Jefferson's views on the dangerous tendencies of the Federal Judiciary utterly overlook the fact that in his familiar diatribes about its being the "subtle sappers and miners, constantly working underground to undermine the foundations of our confederated fabric" — "the inroads daily making by the Federal Court" — "that body, ever acting with noiseless foot and unalarming advance", Jefferson was referring to the support which the Judiciary was giving to Congressional power as against the powers of the States, and he was alluding not at all (as has been hitherto assumed) to a denial of Congressional power by decisions of the Court.[1]

In 1824, the support to the broadest kind of Congressional power to regulate commerce, given by Chief Justice Marshall's opinion in *Gibbons* v. *Ogden*, aroused serious alarm in the Democrats. Marshall said that Congressional power extended to every species of commercial intercourse and to the rules for carrying on that intercourse. Monroe, Jefferson, and the Democrats believed that regulation of commerce in the Constitution referred only to the goods and vessels employed in trade. Jefferson wrote to Giles that "the decisions of the Federal Court, the doctrines of the President, and the misconstructions of the Constitutional compact acted on by the Legislature of the Federal branch" were all tending to usurpation of power, and he lamented the failure of the Court to limit that power.

From 1825 to 1835, the attacks upon the Court

[1] *The Supreme Court in United States History* (1922), by Charles Warren, II, 6–7.

MINORITY DECISIONS

were again directed at its support of the powers of Congress to charter the Bank, to provide for internal improvement, and to trespass on the rights of the States.¹ "What law of Congress has been enacted which tended to trench upon the rights of the States or of the citizens of the States which that Court has not affirmed to be constitutional and valid!" exclaimed John Rowan, Senator from Kentucky, in 1826. And Warren R. Davis of South Carolina, Chairman of the House Judiciary Committee, said, in 1834, referring to Federal statutes making gifts of Federal aid:

Another curse that accompanies these many projects is the constant temptation it offers alternately to the Representatives of the different States in Congress to violate and pervert the Constitution; to usurp powers never given you by the people or the States. . . . You begin by passing an unconstitutional law, which is contrived to be sent to the Supreme Court *to be consecrated by its sanction which it is certain to receive,* if its record of the past be any evidence of the future; for out of twenty-eight cases embracing question of Federal power, all but one have been decided in favor of the power claimed by that Government. . . . The Supreme Court is your great engine.

The inclination of the Supreme Court "towards the highest assertion of Federal power" was deplored by Senator James Buchanan, in 1841, in the debate on the Fiscal Bank Bill, and opposition based on the same ground was constant, throughout the debates in Congress, in 1841 and 1842, on the constitutionality of the Bankruptcy Act and the Habeas Corpus Act.

¹ *19th Cong., 1st Sess.,* April 10, 1826, p. 436; *22d Cong., 1st Sess.,* pp. 2396, *et seq.,* April 4, 1833; *25th Cong., 1st Sess.,* pp. 1605–1606, Oct. 13, 1837.

In fact, it may be said that every particle of Democratic opposition to the Court from 1789 to 1849, for sixty years, was based on the Court's support of Federal power, and *not* on its denial of it.

Then came the year 1850 and the passage of the Fugitive Slave Law. Immediately, there arose the most violent attack on the Court in all our history — this time made by the Republicans and Abolitionists — an attack which continued for ten years — not because the Court denied the constitutionality of that Act but because it refused to do so.

It thus appears that opposition to the Court's decisions for over seventy years centered on their upholding the validity of Federal laws.

Suppose, however, that Senator Borah's proposal had then been in force from 1789 to 1860, and that a concurrence of seven out of nine Judges had been required to hold a law unconstitutional, and that a minority of three Judges had been allowed to hold a law constitutional. What would have been its effect?

Even unanimous decisions of the Judges of the Supreme Court upholding the Alien and Sedition Laws as constitutional were denounced in unmeasured terms and were never accepted by the American people. How much less acceptance would such a decision have had, if those laws could have been held constitutional by a decision rendered by a minority of the Court? What would Jefferson, the Democrats, and the States of Maryland, Virginia, Ohio, and others of the South and West have thought, if they had been told that a rule of Congress was going to make it possible for a minority of the Court (three

MINORITY DECISIONS 199

out of seven Judges) to hold the Bank of the United States' charter constitutional? They were never reconciled to the actual decision so holding, even when rendered by a unanimous Court. It is not difficult to imagine how much more violent and potent would have been their opposition to the Court, to the law, and to the Bank, had the minority rule prevailed.

Marshall's decision in *Gibbons* v. *Ogden* was rendered by a unanimous Court; but his definition of "commerce", on which has been built the whole great framework of interstate commerce law to-day, was bitterly attacked, as supporting the legality of Federal aid in the building of canals, roads, railroads, and other internal improvements in the States. President Jackson's vetoes of internal improvement bills were based on the great popular antagonism to the right of the Federal Government to interfere in such matters of State concern. How much greater would have been that antagonism, had Marshall's view been shared by only a minority of the Court, *i.e.*, by only three out of seven Judges, but the views of which minority, according to the present proposed rule, would have had to prevail in deciding the case!

Suppose the Republicans and Abolitionists of the North had been confronted with this situation in 1858 — that the Fugitive Slave Law could have been upheld as constitutional by a minority of three out of nine Judges, what respect would have been likely to be paid to such a decision, when it is recalled that even a decision by a unanimous Court in the *Booth Case* was for a long time practically refused obedience by the States of Wisconsin and Ohio?

It is evident that the present proposed change would have been even more abhorrent to the opponents of the Court in the past than were the actual decisions of the Court itself. Yet, is there not every reason to suppose that this rule promulgating minority control in the Court may be equally obnoxious in the future, when one recalls that decisions of the Court upholding Congressional power may frequently be regarded as more fatal and destructive to the rights and liberties of individuals and of States than decisions denying such power?

A few possible cases that may well arise can be suggested.

Suppose that a Congress should be elected out of sympathy with the Volstead Act and that it should pass a statute making the sale of beer and light wines lawful, as nonintoxicating; suppose that six Judges held the new law unconstitutional and three thought it constitutional. Under the seven out of nine rule, the views of the three Judges must prevail over the views of the six and the new law must be held constitutional. Would the prohibitionists accept or rest easy under such a decision? When one recalls that the decision of the Court rendered by seven Judges out of nine holding the present Volstead Act constitutional has not been accepted with any great unanimity by the American people, with what feelings would they be likely to view a new statute under the Prohibition Amendment, held valid by only three out of nine Judges?[1]

[1] *National Prohibition Cases* (1920), 253 U. S. 350 (McKenna and Clark, J. J., dissenting); see also *Jacob Ruppert v. Caffey* (1920), 251 U. S. 264 (McReynolds, Day, Van Devanter, Clark, J. J., dissenting) upholding the validity of the War Time Prohibition Act of Nov. 21, 1918, and the Act of Oct. 28, 1919.

MINORITY DECISIONS 201

On the other hand, suppose a new Congress elected of an even dryer cast of mind than the past three Congresses, and suppose it should pass a law authorizing the search of private houses without a search warrant. Suppose only three out of nine Judges should consider such a statute constitutional; yet under the proposed rule, it would have to be held constitutional. How would the great mass of American householders view such a decision by such a minority of the Court?

Take another by no means improbable situation: suppose a determined movement of Bolshevists, radical communists, or Reds should endanger a portion of this country, and in a time of excitement Congress should pass such a law against sedition as was proposed two years ago, grossly infringing on the freedom of the press and freedom of speech. Suppose that six Judges thought it unconstitutional, and three constitutional. By the rule, the law would be valid and enforceable. How many convictions could be obtained from juries who knew that the law under which the indictments were framed was upheld only by a minority of the Judges?

How would the people of our Southern States regard an anti-lynching law passed by Congress, and upheld by the Court, only because, under the rule, three Judges believing the law to be constitutional would prevail in having it held so, against six Judges believing it unconstitutional?

Suppose Congress, urged on by some Nationalistic President filled with zeal for conservation of National resources, should pass an Act vesting power in the National Government to regulate the use of water in all non-navigable rivers within the States, how would the people of the Western States, now having control of such waters, view a decision upholding the validity of such an Act, made by only three out of nine Judges?

In *South Carolina* v. *United States* (199 U. S. 437), in 1905, the Court considered the validity of a Federal statute which had the effect of imposing a tax on the agents of a sovereign State selling liquor for the State, and it was upheld by a vote of six to three Judges White, Peckham, and McKenna dissenting. Judge White felt so strongly about this decision that he stated that it placed the National and State governments reciprocally "at the mercy of the other, so as to give to each the potency of destroying the other." (P. 464.) "a proposition absolutely destructive of constitutional government." (P. 472.) The decision caused great resentment in the State. Suppose that, instead of being an affirmative decision of six Judges to three in favor of the validity of a Federal law, it had been a decision in which six Judges denied the validity and three upheld it. Under the Borah proposition, the statute would still be held valid. What would have been the sentiment of a State which witnessed taxation of its agents upheld by a Court in which six Judges out of nine expressed the opinion that the United States had no power so to tax?

Now that States like North Dakota are going into the administration of commercial business like manufacturing and marketing farm products, banking, building houses, etc., the question of how far the United States can interfere by taxation with agents of

MINORITY DECISIONS 203

the State — may be a very important one to the State, and not one which the States would like to have decided by a minority of the Court.[1]

Every one of the above hypothetical cases is well within the bounds of possibility, and even of probability.

There can be but one answer. No class or section of the people of the United States would ever accept or have confidence in a judicial decision which fixed their rights and duties, by the views of a minority of the Court — of three Judges out of nine.

One argument sometimes advanced in favor of Senator Borah's proposal is as follows. It is said that the Court has, for over one hundred years, announced a rule which it will always follow in constitutional cases. This rule, as laid down time and again by the Court, is that it will not hold an Act of Congress invalid unless the invalidity is clear and shown beyond a reasonable doubt; or in other words that there is always a strong presumption in favor of the validity of the statute.[2] Advocates of the

[1] See *Green* v. *Frazier* (1920), 253 U. S. 233, in which statutes of North Dakota for these purposes were held constitutional by unanimous decision of the Court.

[2] Sutherland, J., in *Adkins* v. *Children's Hospital* (1923), 261 U. S. 525: "This Court, by an unbroken line of decisions from Chief Justice Marshall to the present day, has steadily adhered to the rule that every possible presumption is in favor of the validity of an Act of Congress until overcome beyond rational doubt."

Strong, J., in *Knox* v. *Lee* (1871), 12 Wallace 457: "A decent respect for a coördinate branch of the Government demands that the Judiciary should presume, until the contrary is clearly shown, that there has been no transgression of power by Congesss — all the members of which act under the obligation of an oath of fidelity to the Constitution."

It is to be noted, however, that Congress, in recent years, has indulged in the habit of passing bills, as to the constitutionality of which the members have had doubt themselves, with the express intention of having the Court decide the question. Thus in *Evans* v. *Gore* (1920), 253 U. S. 245, 248, the Court noted that: "Moreover it appears, when this taxing provision was adopted, Congress regarded it as of uncertain constitutionality and both contemplated and in-

Borah proposal say, the mere fact that one, two, or three of the dissenting Associates on the Court believe that an Act of Congress is unconstitutional ought to be proof to the majority of the Judges that there is a reasonable doubt about the constitutionality of the Act. Hence, it is argued that, according to the Court's own rule of behaviour, the majority should never hold a statute unconstitutional so long as there are three Judges who are unwilling to so hold. This sounds plausible; but it is, in reality, quite fallacious. To advance such a proposition is to advance something which is contrary to fact, contrary to human nature, and contrary to the manner in which every man conducts his personal or business life. Can a man never be clearly convinced of anything, if some other man supposedly equal in intelligence differs from him? If this were the case, there are few things of which any one could be convinced beyond a reasonable doubt.

The majority Judges in reaching their conclusion must, of course, take into consideration the fact that some of their Associates on the Bench differ from them; this fact must lead the majority to put their own opinion to more rigid scrutiny. But, if, after having considered this fact of dissent, and if, after having considered the presumption (which is always taken as a presumption) that Congress has acted

tended that the question should be settled by us in a case like this." It is difficult to see why the Court should continue to indulge in the presumption that Congress has acted constitutionally, if Congress itself, in passing a statute, has doubts as to its constitutionality and passes it with a view to having the doubts resolved by the Court. In such a case, it would not seem that there should be any presumption at all, one way or the other. But the Court, nevertheless, still continues to hold that it will assume that the presumption exists in favor of a Congressional statute, regardless of the attitude of those who enact it.

MINORITY DECISIONS

within its powers, each member of the majority still remains clearly convinced of the invalidity of the law, he is bound by his official oath so to decide and to uphold the Constitution as he views it.

To illustrate the fact that the holding of a different view by another man does not necessarily create a reasonable doubt, suppose that a case had been pending involving an Act of Congress, and that eight of the Court believed the Act invalid, while Judge McKenna believed it valid. The argument is made that the belief of this single man should automatically be proof to the majority that there was a reasonable doubt. Now suppose that Judge McKenna then resigned from the Bench and that before the decision was rendered by the Court and before appointment of any successor and while there was no dissenting Judge remaining on the Court, ex-Judge McKenna proceeded to publish an article again expressing his original view. Should or would ex-Judge McKenna's views expressed as a private citizen necessarily create to the members of the Court a reasonable doubt? Clearly not. Yet — what is the difference between his views expressed as a Judge and his views expressed as a citizen? It is the view of the same man; and if the majority of the Court ought to regard them as creating a reasonable doubt in the one situation, why not in the other?

Moreover, the fact that one of their number dissents need not necessarily bear the implication to the majority that the dissenter believes the statute to be valid. Under the rule that the Court will not declare a statute invalid unless such invalidity is clear, the vote of the majority necessarily means that its five Judges have been convinced beyond all reasonable doubt of the *invalidity* of the statute. But the vote of the dissenting minority Judges does not necessarily mean that these Judges have been so convinced of the *validity* of the statute. It may mean simply that the four dissenting Judges, or some of them, concur with the majority in believing the statute to be invalid, but that they do not go so far as to believe that its invalidity is free from doubt. Hence, when a Court divides five to four, it must be taken that the majority are clearly convinced of the invalidity, while the minority vote may indicate nothing more than an unwillingness to hold the statute invalid — at all events, the minority vote never necessarily indicates or implies that the minority are all convinced of the *validity* of the statute.

It has been urged by some that because a jury is required to render a unanimous verdict, so an appellate Court should be under a similar requirement. This suggestion, however, ignores the complete difference between the functions performed by a jury and those performed by such a Court. One might as well contend that because a separate jury may be drawn for each case, so a separate appellate Court should be appointed or elected for each case. Conditions applicable to the one have no relation to the other.

Moreover, the requirement of unanimity in a jury of twelve is a mere historical accident, derived from the development of the ancient common law in England; and the fact is that, at the present time, the tendency of modern constitutional and statutory law in the States of this country is towards the abolition of this requirement. Already at least ten States have provisions in their Constitutions allowing a jury to reach a verdict in civil cases by a three-quarters vote; and two States allow a verdict by a two-thirds vote. So that, even if the analogy of a verdict of a jury should be applied to the decision of the judges of the Supreme Court, there are at least twelve States which now allow a jury verdict by the concurrence of fewer jurymen than the number of Judges which the Borah proposal would require to concur.[1]

But aside from this consideration, there is one fundamental distinction between the effect of a requirement of a unanimous or of a three-quarters or two-thirds concurrence by a jury, and a similar requirement for an appellate Court. When a jury disagrees or when its verdict is not concurred in by the number required by State law, such disagreement or failure to concur does not end the case; it does not settle the rights of either party; the case comes up again before a new jury, and new trials can be had until a jury finally agrees or reaches the requisite concurrence of numbers. Quite different, on the

[1] Three quarters of nine Judges would be six and three quarters; two thirds of nine Judges would be six. The Borah proposal requires concurrence of seven. The State Constitutions providing for verdicts by three quarters of the jurymen are: Arizona (1912), California (1879), Idaho (1890), Louisiana (1913), Mississippi (1916), Nevada (1864), Oklahoma (1907), South Dakota (1889), Utah (1895), Washington (1889). The State Constitutions providing for verdicts by two thirds of the jurymen are: Missouri (1900), Montana (1889). The New Mexico Constitution (1912) leaves the entire regulation to its Legislature. See *The State Constitutions* (1918), by Charles Kettleborough.

The Supreme Court has held that, while under the Federal Constitution juries must consist of twelve men and render a unanimous verdict since the trial by jury guaranteed by that Constitution means a jury trial as known at the common law, the States are not so restricted, and that the States may provide in their own Constitutions for a jury of less than twelve and for a less than unanimous verdict. *Maxwell v. Dow* (1900), 176 U. S. 587.

other hand, would be the result of a requirement that all, or seven out of nine, of the Judges of an appellate Court should concur in a judgment holding a statute invalid. In such a case, a failure to so concur would end the suit and would settle the rights of the respective parties; it would result in a judgment against the party setting up the invalidity of the statute. Thus, it will be seen that the operation of a requirement as to concurrence of a jury is fundamentally different from the result of a requirement as to concurrence of any particular number of the Judges of an appellate Court. Accordingly, the reasons which may make such a provision advisable for a jury have no application to such a Court.

The Borah proposal to change the operation of the judicial power of the Supreme Court has been discussed from the standpoint of its being obnoxious, unfair, unjust, unworkable, and as destructive of popular confidence in the Court's judgments. Consideration should now, however, be given to the question whether the statute embodying the proposal would be constitutional and whether Congress has any power to interfere in this manner with the decision of the Court. That it would be unconstitutional hardly admits of doubt.

Unlike the inferior Federal Courts, which may be erected by Congress and given such powers, broad or limited, as Congress may choose, the Supreme Court is the creation of the Constitution itself. Its powers as a Court, *i.e.*, the powers inherent in a Court as a judicial tribunal, are not derived in any way from Congress. When the Constitution said in Article III, Section 1: "The judicial power of the United

States shall be vested in one Supreme Court," it used the words "Supreme Court" in the sense in which such words were used at the common law, and meant a tribunal possessing such powers as were inherently possessed by a "Court" at common law.[1] Thus, as was said in *Ex parte Robinson* (19 Wallace 508), in 1874, "the power to punish for contempt is inherent in all Courts. . . . The moment the Courts of the United States were called into existence and invested with jurisdiction over any subject they became possessed of this subject;" and while, in that case, it was decided that since the inferior Federal Courts were created by Congress, they might be controlled as to their powers by an Act of Congress, it was also said: "The Act, in terms, applies to all Courts; whether it can be held to limit the authority of the Supreme Court, which derives its existence and powers from the Constitution, may perhaps, be a matter of doubt."[2]

---

[1] "The Federal law adopts for its various requirements in respect of Federal tribunals or magistrates . . . the Common Law conception of Courts of Justice and of Judicial character or status." *Principles of the Federal Law* (1917) by Heman W. Chaplin, sec. 577.

[2] See also *Bessette* v. *W. B. Conkey Co.* (1904), 194 U. S. 324.

Power of a Court to punish for contempt as well as other powers is incidental to the grant of judicial power. See Johnson, J., in *United States* v. *Hudson & Goodwin* (1812), 7 Cranch 32, 34: "Certain implied powers must necessarily result to our Courts of Justice from the nature of their institution. . . . To fine for contempt, imprison for contumacy, inforce the observance of order, etc., are powers which cannot be dispensed with in a Court, because they are necessary to the exercise of all others; and so far our Courts no doubt possess powers not immediately derived from statute." And see Johnson, J., in *Anderson* v. *Dunn* (1821), 6 Wheaton 204, 227: "Courts of justice are universally acknowledged to be vested, by their very creation, with power to impose silence, respect and decorum, in their presence, and submission to their lawful mandates. . . . It is true that the Courts of justice of the United States are vested, by express statute provision, with power to fine and imprison for contempts: but it does not follow, from this circumstance, that they would not have exercised that power without the aid of the statute . . . on the contrary, it is a legislative assertion of this right, *as incidental to a grant of judicial power.*"

But if power to punish for contempt is a power inherent in a Court, and if, as the Court intimates, Congress cannot regulate the power of the Supreme Court in cases of contempt, certainly the power of a Court to *decide* a case in accordance with its own views, and not in accordance with the views or direction of any other body, is a still more inherent power. At common law, the word "Court" has a well-defined meaning, as a tribunal possessing certain powers. So, too, the word "jury", as used in the Constitution, had a defined meaning at common law, as a body consisting of twelve men which must vote unanimously to convict. It is well known that Congress has no power to change this common law jury or its powers. In the same way and at common law, in all tribunals, judicial, administrative, and corporate, the vote of the majority (or the vote of a majority of whatever was declared to be a quorum of the tribunal) was held to control. Hence, this power to decide by a majority of its members (or of its quorum) is such an inherent portion of the judicial power possessed by a Court created by the Constitution as to be uncontrollable by Congress.

The Borah proposal is an attempt by Congress to exercise judicial power and to dictate to the Supreme Court how it shall decide a constitutional question. A majority of the Court finds that X has a right under the Constitution, and that Y has a conflicting claim under a Federal statute. Congress would direct the Court to decide for Y in conformity with the Act of Congress under which he claims, and in conformity with the views of the minority of the Court, and against the Constitution as the majority of the Court

MINORITY DECISIONS 211

understand it. Certainly this is an attempt to substitute Congressional decision for judicial decision — an attempt which constitutes a palpable usurpation by Congress of the judicial power vested by the Constitution exclusively in the Supreme Court.[1] Numerous State Courts have considered and held invalid State legislative attempts at "unconstitutional assumption of judicial functions." In 1858, the New Jersey Court of Appeals held invalid a statute which declared that no judgment of the Supreme Court should be reversed unless a majority of the members of the Court of Appeals who were competent to sit should concur in such reversal.[2] In 1879, the Tennessee Supreme Court held unconstitutional a statute which directed the Supreme Court as to manner of procedure when it reversed a lower Court on certain subjects; and it said:

That the Legislature has the power to prescribe such rules as may be necessary to enable this Court to exercise its appellate jurisdiction is not questioned; but after that jurisdiction has once rightfully attached under such rules as may be prescribed by law, the Court, as a coördinate branch of the State government under the Constitution, has power to make and enforce its decrees without any direction from the Legislature.[3]

[1] See *James* v. *Appel* (1904), 192 U. S. 129, in which Holmes J. seems to intimate that a legislative direction of a judgment by a Court would be invalid.
Congress may not decide on a question of the meaning of a contract; to do so will "invade the province of the Judiciary." *Commonwealth* v. *Beaumarchais*, 3 Call. (Va.) 169; see also *Ratchiffe* v. *Anderson*, 31 Gratt (Va.) 105, 107.
See also *Judicial Independence*, by Judge Henry B. Brown, *American Bar Ass. Proc.* (1912).

[2] *Clapp* v. *Ely* (1858), 27 New Jersey Law 622.

[3] *Northern* v. *Barnes* (1879), 70 Tenn. 603: "No authority need be cited to show that the Legislature has no constitutional power to prescribe or regulate the decrees of this Court, however desirous it may be to expedite the administration of justice. . . ."

In 1895, the Pennsylvania Supreme Court held that a statute imposing on the Courts a specific construction of a previous law was invalid: "It is a legislative mandate to the Courts to perform their judicial functions in a particular way."[1] So, in 1904, the Indiana Supreme Court said that while the Legislature "may prescribe rules of procedure and pleading by which both Courts and the parties in a cause are bound, nevertheless, it cannot, under the Constitution, encroach on the judicial domain by prescribing the manner and mode in which the Court shall discharge their judicial duties."[2] In New York, the Court held, in 1904, that a statute requiring it to designate a day for hearing preferred causes was invalid, saying: "One of the powers which has always been recognized as inherent in Courts . . . has been the right to control its order of business and so to conduct the same that the rights of all suitors before them may be safeguarded. This power has been recognized as judicial in its nature and as being a necessary appendage to a Court authorized to enforce rights and redress wrongs. . . . The Courts are not puppets of the Legislature."[3] And, in Wisconsin, in 1868, the Court held that a statute which required jury trials in equity cases was invalid, as depriving the Court (which was vested by the Constitution with equity jurisdiction) of one of the

---

[1] *Commonwealth* v. *Warwick* (1895), 172 Pa. 140: "The practical effect of the Act of 1867, in the present case would be to compel this Court to 'construe' the expression 'next city election' used in the Act of 1854 to mean not the 'next' but the 'next but one.' It was clearly beyond the legislative power to thus usurp the judicial functions or to distort language."

[2] *Parkison* v. *Thompson* (1904), 164 Ind. 609; see also *Sander* v. *State* (1882), 85 Ind. 318.

[3] *Riglander* v. *Star Co.* (1904), 90 N. Y. Supp. 772.

MINORITY DECISIONS 213

powers inherently possessed by an Equity Court, and said that to determine questions of fact as well as of law was "one of the established elements of judicial powers in equity, so that the Legislature cannot withdraw it and confer it upon juries."[1] That the Legislature may not order a final judgment of a Court to be vacated was held in Connecticut in 1898.[2]

The fact is that, under the Constitution, Congress has the power to decide how many Justices shall compose the Court, and how many Justices shall compose the working Court, *i.e.*, the quorum; Congress has also the power to say when and where the Court shall meet; but there its power stops, and when these Justices come together in the place prescribed for them, then, by virtue of the general power inhering in all such bodies, they have the uncontrollable power to make, by their majority, the judicial decision which such a Court is entitled to make at common law.[3]

Those who defend the new proposal base the right of Congress thus to restrict judicial power upon that portion of Article III, Section 2 of the Constitution, which provides that (after the grant of original jurisdiction to the Supreme Court) "in all the other cases before mentioned, the Supreme Court shall have appellate jurisdiction, both as to law and fact, with such exceptions, and under such regulations, as the

---
[1] *Callanan* v. *Judd* (1868), 23 Wisc. 343.
[2] *State* v. *R. R. Co.* (1898), 71 Conn. 43; see also *Martin* v. *Land Co.*, 94 Va. 28; *Chicago, etc. R. R.* v. *The People*, 219 Ill. 408.
[3] See full and able discussion of this question in the debate by Samuel S. Marshall of Indiana, George W. Woodward of Pennsylvania, and Richard D. Hubbard of Connecticut, over a proposition to require a two-thirds concurrence, in the House, Jan. 13, 1868. 40th Cong., 2d. Sess.

Congress shall make." They say that their proposal is one of the "exceptions" and "regulations" which Congress is allowed to make. But they entirely fail to note that the Constitution provides for these "exceptions" and "regulations" by Congress, *only* in respect to the "appellate jurisdiction", of the Supreme Court, and not in respect to the "judicial power" of the Supreme Court over the cases of which Congress shall have given it appellate jurisdiction, and *after* such appellate jurisdiction shall have vested.[1]

"Appellate jurisdiction" and "judicial power" are two entirely distinct things; and authority granted to Congress to regulate the one does not imply or vest any authority to regulate the other. Judicial power comprises the functions exercised by the Court *after* it has obtained jurisdiction. The appellate jurisdiction is something which lies entirely within the discretion of Congress; but how the Court shall proceed to exercise its appellate jurisdiction after Congress has once granted it, is something over

---

[1] Senator W. E. Borah in an able and interesting article, in defense of his bill, in the *New York Sunday Times*, Feb. 18, 1923, contends that because Congress assumes the power to fix the number constituting a quorum of the Supreme Court, and because it assumes the power to vest certain powers in single Justices, it, therefore, has the power to control the number of Justices who must concur in a decision on a specific question.

The power, however, to establish what shall constitute a quorum of the Court is, of course, simply a part of the undisputed power of Congress to say how many Justices shall compose the Court; a "quorum" is nothing else than the number of Justices who shall compose the working Court. Congress can certainly say that the Court shall not be a Court ready to act, unless a certain number of Justices are present. After that number are present, however, Congress has no power to control or direct its decisions.

As to Borah's other argument that Congress has frequently legislated as to the powers of single Justices, it has been decided that legislation which affects the powers of individual Judges, as distinguished from the Court itself, is not an interference with the judicial functions of the Court, see *State* v. *Taylor*, 68 N. J. Law 276.

which Congress has little, if any, authority. The powers of the Court to act *as a Court*, after Congress has granted jurisdiction of the parties and subject matters, are inherent judicial powers, — the powers which inhere in a Court at common law to decide and pronounce a judgment and carry it into effect, between opposing parties who bring a case before it for decision.[1]

Only an Amendment to the Constitution can change the extent and scope of the judicial power of the Supreme Court which inhered in that body at the time of the adoption of the Constitution.

When all is said and done, however, the fact is that this complaint about five to four decisions holding Federal statutes invalid is largely insincere, or rather a mere camouflage of the real complaint. The real grievance felt by the Court's critics is not the number of Justices who joined in setting aside the Federal statute; it is rather the fact that the statute was set aside at all.

For instance, take the reformers who favor Congressional action on Child Labor. Were they any more satisfied with the second Child Labor Law decision setting aside the Child Labor Tax Law which was rendered by a vote of eight to one Judges, than they were with the first decision setting aside the Child Labor Interstate Commerce Law, which was rendered by a vote of five to four? On the con-

---

[1] *Miller on the Constitution*, 314; *Bouvier* (1914), II, 1140.
To apply to a completed transaction laws which were in force at the time is a judicial act. *Ross* v. *Oregon* (1913), 227 U. S. 150, 163. "A judicial inquiry investigates, declares and enforces liabilities as they stand on present or past facts and under laws supposed already to exist." *Prentis* v. *Atlantic Coast Line Co.* (1908), 211 U. S. 210, 226.

trary, they attacked the Court equally for *both* decisions.

Labor bitterly assailed the Court for its decision in the *Adair Case* in 1908, holding invalid the Federal statute making it a criminal offense to discharge employees for membership in a labor union. The vote of the Court, however, was seven to two, exactly the number prescribed by the Borah Bill. Was it any greater satisfaction to Labor that the vote was seven to two instead of five to four? Would they not have equally attacked any decision against them, even if unanimous?

The *Stock Dividend Case* was decided in 1920 by a vote of five to four. But would those who denounced the Court's decision have found it any more acceptable if the vote had been seven to two or even unanimous?

The farmers attacked the decision of the Court in the *Connolly Case* in 1902, holding the Illinois State Anti-Trust Law invalid for discrimination in excluding from its operation combination of farmers and live-stock owners. The vote of the Court was seven to one. Was it any greater satisfaction to the opponents of this decision that this vote was seven to one instead of five to three?

The *District of Columbia Minimum Wage Case* in 1923 was decided by a vote of five to three, but even if it had been unanimous, the social reformers interested in that legislation would not have been any better pleased.

The *Dred Scott Case*, by which the Constitution was held to extend slavery into the Territories, was decided by the exact proportion of Judges now proposed by Senator Borah — seven to two. Was the decision any more satisfactory to the antislavery men than if the Court had divided five to four?

The questions answer themselves. It was not the size of the vote of which the loser in each case complained. It was the adverse decision itself.[1] In other words, whether the Court is lauded or assailed — all depends on whose toes are trodden upon — and not upon the number of Judges who do the treading. One of the strongest arguments against the Borah proposal, therefore, is that, in its application, it would not satisfy even its proponents.

Summing up the proposal, it may be said that it is a proposal to allow Congress to dictate to the Court how the rights of parties litigating before it shall be decided — a proposal to place it in the power of a minority of the Judges to determine the rights of those parties — to empower a minority of Judges to reverse a judgment of a lower Court or of a State Court — to empower a minority of Judges to hold an Act of Congress constitutional. Such minority decisions would never command the confidence, respect, or support of a people, who, in practically every other affair of life, are accustomed and willing to submit to the considered judgment of the majority; and even if the proposal should be practicable of operation, it would never satisfy those who support it, for their real dissatisfaction with the Court lies, *not* in the proportion of dissenting Judges, *but* in

---

[1] *Hammer* v. *Dagenhart* (1918), 247 U. S. 251; *Bailey* v. *Drexel Furniture Co.* (1922), 259 U. S. 20; *Adair* v. *United States* (1908), 208 U. S. 161; *Eisner* v. *Macomber* (1920), 252 U. S. 189; *Connolly* v. *Union Sewer Pipe Co.* (1902), 184 U. S. 540; *Adkins* v. *Children's Hospital* (1923), 261 U. S. 525.

the actual decision which the Court makes, regardless of the number of Judges joining in the decision.

NOTE

It should be carefully observed that Senator Borah's proposal is not novel in American history. Three times have similar proposals been made in Congress — in 1823, 1826, and 1868, — that the concurrence of more than a majority of the Supreme Court should be required to hold an Act of Congress unconstitutional; and, moreover, nine times — in 1823, 1824, 1825, 1826, 1827, 1829, and 1868 — have similar proposals been made in Congress for a requirement of concurrence of more than a majority of the Supreme Court to hold a State statute unconstitutional. No one of these proposals has ever passed Congress. They are as follows:

(1) *8th Cong., 1st Sess.*, Dec. 10, 1823, by R. M. Johnson of Kentucky, in the Senate — concurrence of at least 7 [out of 10] Judges in any opinion "which may involve the validity of the laws of the United States or of the States respectively."

(2) March 11, 1824, by Martin Van Buren of New York in the Senate — "no law of any of the States shall be rendered invalid without the concurrence of at least 5 [out of 7] Judges of the Supreme Court, their opinions to be separately expressed."

(3) May 17, 18, 1824, by Thomas Metcalfe of Kentucky in the House — "in any case now or hereafter depending in the Supreme Court, in which shall be drawn into question the validity of any part of the Constitution of a State or of any part of an Act passed by the Legislature of a State, unless two thirds of the whole number of Justices composing

MINORITY DECISIONS 219

the said Court shall concur in pronouncing such part of the said Constitution or Act to be invalid, it shall not be held or deemed invalid."

(4) *18th Cong., 2d Sess.,* Jan. 26, 1825, by Robert P. Letcher of Kentucky in the House — concurrence of 5 [out of 7] Judges in any case "in which shall be drawn in question the validity of any part of the Constitution of a State or of any Act passed by the Legislature of a State." Judges to be "required by law to give their opinions with their respective reasons, therefor, separately and distinctly."

(5) *19th Cong., 1st Sess.,* Daniel Webster said in the House, Jan., 25, 1826, that at the last session, several propositions were brought forward by Charles A. Wickliffe of Kentucky, "among which was one requiring a certain definite majority when the Supreme Court passed a sentence which went to invalidate any law enacted by one of the States of the Union."

(6) *19th Cong., 1st Sess.,* April 7, 1826, by John Rowan of Kentucky, in the Senate: "that the Supreme Court shall in no instance decide that the Constitution of any State or any provision thereof or the law of any State, or any Act of Congress, or any part or portion thereof, or of either of any of them is invalid or void by reason of any supposed collision between them or any part or portion of them, or any or either of them, and the Constitution of the United States or any article, section or clause thereof, unless at least 7 [out of 10] of the Justices of said Court shall concur in that decision."

(7) *19th Cong., 2d Sess.,* Jan. 22, 1827, by Charles A. Wickliffe of Kentucky, in the House — concurrence of 5 [out of the 7] Judges, "in all cases in which is drawn in question the validity of any law of a State."

(8) *20th Cong., 2d Sess.,* by P. P. Barbour in the House requiring concurrence of 5 [out of 7] Judges in cases

involving the validity of a State law. See also *Public Documents of 20th Cong., 2d Sess.*, House Report No. 34, Jan. 2, 1829.

(9) *40th Cong., 2d Sess.*, pp. 478 *et seq.*, by Thomas Williams of Penn. in the House, Jan. 13, 1868, that "in all cases of writs of error from and appeals to the Supreme Court of the United States, where is drawn in question the validity of a statute of, or an authority exercised by, the United States, or the construction of any clause of the Constitution of the United States, or the validity of a statute or an authority exercised under any State on the ground of repugnance to the Constitution or laws of the United States, the hearing shall be had only before a full bench of the Judges of said Court, and no judgment shall be rendered or decision made against the validity of any statute or any authority exercised by the United States except with the concurrence of all the Judges of said Court."

James F. Wilson of Iowa moved an amendment that if any Circuit Court or District Court of the United States should declare an Act of Congress invalid, its judgment should be reversed unless two thirds of all the members of the Supreme Court should concur in affirming the judgment.

In addition to these proposals, John Forsyth of Georgia, in the Senate, Jan. 5, 25, 1826 (*19th Cong., 1st Sess.*), proposed that "no final judgment shall be pronounced affecting the rights, liberty or life of any citizen of the United States by less than a majority of the entire number of Justices including the Chief Justice." T. P. Moore and Charles A. Wickliffe of Kentucky, in the House, Jan. 25, 1826 (*19th Cong., 1st Sess.*), proposed bills requiring similar concurrence of a majority of the Court (*i.e.*, 6 Judges out of 10)

MINORITY DECISIONS

in any case "in which shall be drawn in question the validity of any Act of Congress or treaty of the United States, of any part of the Constitution of a State, or of an Act passed by the Legislature of a State."

Full details as to these various proposals will be found in the author's *The Supreme Court in United States History* (1922), II, Chapters 17 and 30.

CHAPTER SEVEN

LABOR AND THE SUPREME COURT

"I do solemnly swear that I will administer justice without respect to persons, and do equal right to the poor and to the rich, and that I will faithfully and impartially discharge and perform all the duties incumbent upon me as Justice of the Supreme Court of the United States, according to the best of my abilities and understanding, agreeably to the Constitution and laws of the United States: So help me God."

(Form of oath taken by each Justice of the Court, in accordance with the provisions of the Federal Judicial Code, section 257.)

"An enlightened and independent Judiciary is the safeguard of the poor against the tyranny of the rich; it is the safeguard of the citizen against the tyranny of his Government. . . . Our Judiciary is the sheet-anchor of safety against popular fury, or the more destructive though less violent attacks of usurpation." — JOHN G. JACKSON of Virginia, in the House, Jan. 31, 1805. *8th Cong., 2d Sess.*

The representatives of organized Labor have been particularly active in opposition to the Supreme Court's power to pass upon the validity of Acts of Congress.[1] The Court has been frequently denounced by them as prejudiced against Labor in its decisions. And either through misapprehension of the purport of those decisions, or through lack of knowledge as to the facts, the impression has been given to Labor that the proposal for a Constitutional Amendment made by the late Senator La Follette would relieve Labor from decisions obnoxious to it — whereas the truth is that special Labor interests were con-

---

[1] See Reports of Proceedings of the 42d and 43d Annual Conventions of the American Federation of Labor (1922) (1923); articles by John Ford, Samuel Gompers, Meyer London, in *American Federationist* (April, May, 1923) XXX.

LABOR AND THE SUPREME COURT

cerned in very few of the cases in which Acts of Congress have been held invalid.

There exists so much misunderstanding as to what the Supreme Court has actually decided in Labor cases that it is highly desirable that a complete statement should be made. What are the actual facts as to the Court's record in cases specifically involving Labor?

The Court has decided about one hundred of such cases. Of these, not more than twenty were decided in a manner which Labor might term adverse to its supposed interests. But of these twenty, it should be particularly noted that only six involved the constitutionality of an Act of Congress. Of the others, six involved questions of statutory construction under the Sherman and Clayton and other Federal Laws; two involved no question of statute, State or Federal, but simply decided questions of general law; six involved the constitutionality of a State statute.

First, let Labor note that, so far as regards the six decisions construing the Sherman and Clayton or other Acts and the two merely deciding questions of general law, Congress may at any time, by appropriate legislation, alter the law as laid down by the Court. Labor should, therefore, direct its efforts towards Congress, rather than on the Court; for whenever Labor can persuade Congress that these eight decisions were wrong, Labor has it in its own control to change them. No Amendment to the Constitution taking away the power of the Court is necessary; and no such Amendment would have the slightest effect upon the power of the Court to render these decisions.

224 LABOR AND THE SUPREME COURT

The twenty decisions alleged to be adverse to Labor, considered in detail, are, briefly, as follows.

1. CASES CONSTRUING THE CLAYTON, SHERMAN, OR OTHER ACTS.

(a) The first case was that of *Ex parte Lennon*, in 1897, in the Ann Arbor Railway strike. But the only point decided was that the lower Federal Court which had held the defendant in contempt had jurisdiction of the case, under the Federal Judiciary Acts, since the bill for injunction was brought solely to enforce provisions of the Interstate Commerce Act. If Labor objects to this decision, it has a perfect remedy by persuading Congress to refuse the use of injunctions in the enforcement of that Act.

(b) The next case was the *Danbury Hatters Case*, in 1908. In this case, the Court held that the use of the primary and of the secondary boycotts, and of lists of "unfair" dealers in an attempt to break up the plaintiff's interstate trade was a violation of the Sherman Act and could be enjoined.[1]

Objection by Labor to this decision cannot be cured by attacks on the Supreme Court; but Labor can attain its object by persuading Congress to change the law as to injunctions. Congress has already, by the Clayton Act, legalized the use of the primary boycott in disputes between employers and employees. Congress has full power to forbid similar use of injunction in cases of secondary boycott, if Labor can show good reasons for such additional legislation.

[1] *Ex parte Lennon* (1897), 166 U. S. 548; *Loewe* v. *Lawlor* (1908), 208 U. S. 274; *Lawlor* v. *Loewe* (1915), 235 U. S. 522.

LABOR AND THE SUPREME COURT 225

It is sometimes alleged by Labor that the Supreme Court has held that an Act of Congress forbidding injunctions in labor disputes would be unconstitutional; but the allegation is not true. Not only has the Court in several cases recognized the validity of the Clayton Act, which forbade injunctions in certain labor matters, but it has specifically stated in its decision in *Truax* v. *Corrigan*, in 1921, that the reasons which impelled it to hold invalid a particular anti-injunction law of Arizona did not apply to Congress and the Clayton Act.[1]

(c) The next case was the *Gompers Case*, in 1911, in which the Court held that a boycott instituted by means of letters, circulars, and printed matter, if intended to restrain interstate trade, could be injoined as a violation of the Sherman Act.[2] Here again it lies within the power of Congress to forbid an injunction in such a case and to legalize the acts complained of. It is to Congress Labor should turn.

(d) The next case was that of the *Duplex Printing Company*, in 1921, in which the Court, construing Section 20 of the Clayton Act, held that this section was not intended by Congress to legalize a secondary boycott, and that, on the facts in the case, such a boycott was an unlawful restraint of interstate trade. The correctness of this decision may be doubtful, but whether the Court properly interpreted the Act of Congress or not, Labor has a perfect remedy to cure the decision.[3] It can secure from Congress the enactment of a statute which shall legalize a secondary

---

[1] *American Steel Foundries Co.* v. *Tri City Central Trades Council* (1921), 257 U. S. 184; *Truax* v. *Corrigan* (1921), 257 U. S. 312.
[2] *Gompers* v. *Buck's Stove & Range Co.* (1911), 221 U. S. 418.
[3] *Duplex Printing Co.* v. *Deering* (1921), 254 U. S. 443.

boycott, if such be the desire or intent of Congress. No attack on the Court and no Constitutional Amendment is necessary.

(e) The next case was that of the *American Steel Foundries Case*, in 1921, in which the Court held that the kind of picketing employed in that strike did not come within the meaning of the term "peaceful persuasion", as used in the Clayton Act. The decision was an interpretation of the statute as applied to the facts in the case. Here, again, if Labor thinks that the kind of picketing used in that strike ought to be legalized, it is entirely in the power of Congress to so provide, as soon as Labor can convince Congress of the justice of its claim.

(f) The next case was that of the *Coronado Coal Company*, in 1922, in which the Court unanimously held that an unincorporated labor union might be sued in its own name for its actions. In this case, the Court construed the term "association", as used in the Sherman Act, as well as on general principles of law. If the Court was wrong, Congress can remedy the situation.[1]

---

[1] *United Mine Workers* v. *Coronado Coal Co.* (1922), 259 U. S. 344. That all Labor does not regard this decision as adverse may be seen from the comment of *The United Mine Workers Journal*, quoted in *Literary Digest*, June 17, 1922, as follows: "Although the Supreme Court says in the Coronado decision that labor unions can be sued for damages for destruction of property in a strike, it also makes certain limitations and restrictions upon that rule. It says an international union cannot be held in damages for what is done in a local strike, unless it authorizes, sanctions or ratifies the strike. Second, coal mining and the manufacture of goods is not interstate commerce, even though the coal or the goods may be shipped from one State to the other. Interruption of coal mining, the Court says, is not an interruption of interstate commerce. Both of these features are of great importance. Besides, if a labor union is such an entity as can be sued, it must also be such an entity as can sue. Then, since this principle is established, labor unions ought to make use of the injunction process and damage suits against union-busting employers for the protection of the rights of their members as the employers do for their own benefit."

LABOR AND THE SUPREME COURT

Such are the six decisions construing Federal statutes adversely. In each case, Labor can gain nothing by a Constitutional Amendment; it *can* gain by Congressional legislation.

But if Labor were inclined to treat the public fairly, it would be candid enough to point out that while, in these six cases, the Court had rendered decisions which it regarded as unfavorable, the Court had also rendered decisions in Labor's favor.

Thus, in the *Gompers Case*, although holding, as a matter of law, the boycott to be unlawful, the Court decided the case, on its merits, twice favorably to Mr. Gompers, holding first that he was entitled to jury trial on the question of criminal contempt, and second that the statute of limitations had run against an indictment for such contempt.[1]

While attacking the picketing decision in the *American Steel Foundries Case*, Labor neglects to state that the Court warmly upheld the right of the labor union to interfere by persuasion and appeal to induce a strike against low wages, as constituting no violation of the Sherman or Clayton Acts.

Labor attacks the *Coronado Coal Company Case*, because it sustained the legal liability of labor unions; but it gives no credit to the Court for its actual decision in that case, — a decision extremely favorable to Labor. Amidst all the assault on the Court, who is ever told that in this case a unanimous Court reversed a judgment which a jury had rendered against the labor union for $600,000, plus $120,600 interest, and $25,000 counsel fees — a total of

---

[1] *Gompers* v. *Buck's Stove & Range Co.* (1911), 221 U. S. 418; *Gompers* v. *United States* (1914), 233 U. S. 604.

$745,000? Furthermore, the Court's actual decision was of high importance to Labor, holding as it did that a conspiracy to obstruct mining at particular mines, though it may prevent coal from going into interstate commerce, is not a conspiracy to restrain that commerce, under the Sherman Act, "unless the obstruction to mining is intended to restrain commerce in it or has necessarily such a direct, material and substantial effect to restrain it that the intent reasonably must be inferred." Moreover, in 1925, the Court rendered another decision in this case, sustaining the same doctrine of *law*, but holding that, on the particular facts presented against the local union, there was evidence that should have been submitted to the jury as to the definite intent of the union to restrain interstate commerce; it is to be noted that the Court, at the same time, held that there was no evidence against the International Union. In 1924, a similar case in favor of Labor was decided, in which a leather workers' strike in St. Louis was held not to constitute a conspiracy in violation of the Sherman Act.[1] At the same term, the Court held that a combination and agreement between the National Window Glass Workers' Union and their employers regulating a wage scale and time

---

[1] *United Leather Workers International Union, Local Lodge or Union 2066*, v. *Herkert & Meisel Trunk Co.* (1924), 265 U. S. 457. In this case the Court held that a strike intended by the strikers to prevent, through illegal picketing and intimidation, continued manufacture was not a conspiracy to restrain interstate commerce, and did not violate the Sherman Anti-Trust Act, even though the products of the manufacturers, when made, were, to the knowledge of the strikers, to be shipped in interstate commerce to fill orders in other States, in the absence of evidence that the strikers interfered or attempted to interfere with the free transport and delivery of the products when manufactured to their destination in other States, or with their sale in those States. See also *Coronado Coal Co.* v. *United Mine Workers of America* (1925), 268 U. S. 000.

LABOR AND THE SUPREME COURT 229

and places of employment was not a conspiracy to restrain interstate commerce and did not violate the Sherman Anti-Trust Act.[1]

While attacking the Court's decisions in the *Hatters* and *Gompers Cases*, that the use of lists of "unfair" dealers constituted an unlawful act, Labor fails to mention the fact that the use of a similar list of "unfair" dealers by Capital was also held unlawful by the Court in the *Retail Lumber Dealers Case*.[2] In both cases, such a black list was held to violate the Sherman Act.

Still more recently, a decision has been rendered in the *Michaelson Case*,[3] which will be of very great service to Labor. In this case, the Court held that the provisions of the Clayton Act, providing for jury trial in criminal contempt cases in Labor disputes, were mandatory and not merely permissive and absolutely required the Federal Judges to grant such jury trial; and the Court also held, contrary to the decision of the lower Federal Courts, that these provisions of the Clayton Act were constitutional.

That the decisions of the Court are not always "on the side of the wealthy and powerful" is shown by the fact that, for every one case holding a

[1] *National Association of Window Glass Manufacturers and National Window Glass Workers* v. *United States* (1923), 263 U. S. 403.
[2] *Eastern States Retail Lumber Dealers Assn.* v. *United States* (1914), 234 U. S. 600.
[3] *Michaelson et al.* v. *United States ex rel. Chicago, St. Paul Minneapolis and Omaha Railway Co.* (1924), 266 U. S. 42. See also *Pettibone* v. *United States* (1893), 148 U. S. 197, in which the Court quashed an indictment against members of the Miners' Union; and see decisions favorable to Labor, relating to the Transportation Act of 1920, *Penn. R. R.* v. *U. S. Railroad Labor Board* (1923), 261 U. S. 72; *Robertson* v. *U. S. Railroad Labor Board* (1925), 268 U. S. 000.

230 LABOR AND THE SUPREME COURT

labor union, there have been at least eight cases holding business combinations, to be violative of the Sherman Act — including such great combinations of wealth as the Trans-Missouri Freight Association, the Wholesale Tile Trust, the Northern Securities Company, the Packers Trust, the Tobacco and the Standard Oil Trusts, the Union Pacific and Southern Pacific Railroad combinations, the Reading Railroad Coal Trust, the Retail Lumber Trust, the Hardwood Manufacturers Trust, the Linseed Oil Trust, and many others.

2. CASES DECIDED ON GENERAL PRINCIPLES OF LAW.

The first of the cases decided on general principles of law, irrespective of any Federal statute, which Labor regards as adverse, is the *Debs Case*.[1] As to this decision, there has been much misunderstanding by the public. In the first place, it should be made clear just what the Court did *not* decide. It did *not* decide whether the terms of the injunction issued by the lower court were or were not in accordance with established rules of law; it expressly refused to decide that point; second, it did *not* decide whether Debs and his fellow members in the Union had or had not violated the injunction; third, it did *not* decide whether the lower court rightly sentenced Debs for contempt. All that the Court *did* decide was that the Federal Government was entitled, on general principles of law, to bring a bill for an injunction to prevent obstruction of its mails and of interstate commerce, and that the lower court,

[1] *In re Debs* (1895), 158 U. S. 564.

therefore, had jurisdiction of such a suit, and having jurisdiction had power to decide on the question of contempt. As to the correctness of the lower Court's decision the Supreme Court declined to rule. It is probable that the injunction issued was, as a matter of law, too broad and would have been so held had it ever come before the Supreme Court on the merits, but it never did.

There is in this case, therefore, no ground for assault by Labor upon the Court. If Labor is of the opinion that the Federal Government should *not* have the right to protect its mails and commerce by an equity suit, and that it should be confined to use of the army or criminal indictment, Labor has a perfect remedy in Congress. If it can persuade Congress that the Federal Government should be left helpless in an equity Court, the whole matter can be remedied by legislation. If Congress had the power to pass the Clayton Act forbidding the use of injunctions in certain labor controversies between private employers and employees, it has similar power to restrain injunctions in controversies in which the Government is interested.

The next case decided on general law principles was the *Hitchman Coal & Coke Company Case*, in 1917.[1] In this case, the Court held that a combina-

---

[1] *Hitchman Coal & Coke Co.* v. *Mitchell* (1917), 245 U. S. 229. The opinion in this case contained many dicta which have confused both the Bar and the public; but the actual decision was explained in *American Steel Foundries* v. *Tri-City Central Trades Council* (1921), 257 U. S. 184, as follows: "There the action was by a coal mining company of West Virginia against the officers of an International Labor Union and others, to enjoin them from carrying out a plan to bring the employes of the complainant company and all the West Virginia mining companies into the International Union, so that the Union could control, through the Union employes, the production and sale of coal in West Virginia, in competition with the mines of Ohio and other States. The plan thus pro-

tion by the United Mine Workers to procure concerted breaches of contract by the plaintiff's employees constituted a violation of the plaintiff's legal rights. Here again, if Labor can persuade Congress that in labor disputes an outside union should be allowed rightfully to perform the actions which constituted the injury in this case, Congress has the power to restrain the issue of injunction in Federal Courts directed against such actions, just as it has restrained by the Clayton Act the issue of injunctions against certain other forms of actions. It is useless, therefore, for Labor to assail the Court, when it has a remedy in Congress.

Nor should Labor, in all candor, omit to state that even in this class of cases, decided on general law principles, the Court has decided cases favorably.

Thus, in the *Paine Lumber Company Case*, in 1917, the Court held that no injunction could issue to restrain members of the Carpenters and of the Woodworkers Union from conspiring to refuse to work on the plaintiff's material made by nonunion labor.[1] So, in a case decided as late as 1922, the Court stated

jected was carried out in the case of the complainant company by the use of deception and misrepresentation with its non-union employes, by seeking to induce such employes to become members of the union, contrary to the express term of their contract of employment that they would not remain in complainant's employ if union men, and after enough such employes had been secretly secured, suddenly to declare a strike against complainant and to leave it in a helpless situation, in which it would have to consent to be unionized. This Court held that the purpose was not lawful, and that the means were not lawful, and that the defendants were thus engaged in an unlawful conspiracy which should be enjoined. The unlawful and deceitful means used were quite enough to sustain the decision of the Court, without more. The statement of the purpose of the plan is sufficient to show the remoteness of the benefit ultimately to be derived by the members of the International Union from its success, and the formidable country-wide and dangerous character of the control of interstate commerce sought. The circumstances of the case make it no authority for the contention here."

[1] *Paine Lumber Co.* v. *Neal* (1917), 244 U. S. 459.

LABOR AND THE SUPREME COURT 233

that black listing by employers might be held unlawful, regardless of the Sherman Act.[1] The decision of the two *Gompers Cases*, favorably to the defendant, before mentioned, must be noted as showing that the Court is quite as willing to afford its protection to Labor as to deny it.

3. CASES DECIDED ON THE CONSTITUTIONALITY OF STATE STATUTES.

Before considering the six cases in which the Court has held adversely to Labor in deciding upon the constitutionality of State statutes, let us review briefly those cases in which State labor laws have been *upheld*. To these, Labor seldom refers. There are at least sixty of such cases, and the variety and radical nature of many of the laws sustained is remarkable.

In the first place, the Court has upheld every single State employees' liability law brought before it, and every other statute abrogating or modifying the fellow-servant doctrine.[2]

In the second place, the Court has upheld every State workmen's compensation law brought before it.[3]

[1] *Prudential Ins. Co. v. Cheek* (1922), 259 U. S. 530.
[2] Iowa — *Mo. Pac. Ry. v. Mackey* (1888), 127 U. S. 205; Minnesota — *Minn. etc. R. R. v. Herrick* (1888), 127 U. S. 210; Kansas — *Chicago etc. R. R. v. Pontius* (1895), 157 U. S. 209; Indiana — *Tullis v. Lake Erie etc. R. R.* (1899), 175 U. S. 348; L. & N. R. R. v. *Melton* (1910), 218 U. S. 36; Mississippi — *Mobile etc. R. R. v. Turnipseed* (1910), 219 U. S. 35; *Easterling Lumber Co. v. Pierce* (1914), 235 U. S. 380; Iowa — *C. B. Q. R. R. v. McGuire* (1911), 219 U. S. 549; Arkansas. — *Aluminum Co. v. Ramsey* (1911), 222 U. S. 251; Minnesota — *Minn. Iron Co. v. Kline* (1905), 199 U. S. 593; Nebraska — *Mo. Pac. R. R. v. Castle* (1912), 224 U. S. 541; Arizona — *Arizona Employers' Liability Cases* (1919), 250 U. S. 400; Oklahoma — *Chicago, R. G. & P. R. R. v. Cole* (1919), 251 U. S. 54.
[3] Ohio — *Jeffrey Mfg. Co. v. Blagg* (1915), 235 U. S. 571; *Valley Steamship Co. v. Wattawa* (1917), 244 U. S. 202; Washington — *Northern Pac. R. R. v. Meese* (1916), 239, U. S. 614; *Mountain Timber Co. v. Washington* (1917),

234 LABOR AND THE SUPREME COURT

Third, the Court has upheld the validity of every State law as to the employment of women brought before it.[1]

It has upheld the Illinois child labor law; the Oregon ten-hour day law in factories; the Utah miners' eight-hour day law; the Kansas eight-hour day public work law;[2] the New York citizens' labor preference public works law.

It has upheld laws of New York requiring semi-monthly cash wage payments; of Virginia against payment to employes in merchandise; of Tennessee requiring redemption in money of store orders given to employes for wages; of Arkansas requiring payment of all unpaid wages to railroad employes when discharged; of Missouri and Oklahoma requiring corporations to give service letters to employes leaving or discharged.[3]

243 U. S. 219; Iowa — *Hawkins* v. *Bleakly* (1917), 243 U. S. 210; New York — *N. Y. Central R. R.* v. *White* (1917), 243 U. S. 188; (So much of the New York law as applied to interstate commerce was held to violate Federal power in *Erie R. R.* v. *Winfield* (1917), 244 U. S. 170, and so much of the New York law as attempted to apply it to suits in the Federal admiralty Courts was held unconstitutional in *Southern Pacific Co.* v. *Jensen* (1917), 244 U. S. 205.) Texas — *Middleton* v. *Texas Power & Light Co.* (1919), 249 U. S. 152; New York — *N. Y. Central R. R.* v. *Bianc* (1919), 250 U. S. 596; *Ward & Gow* v. *Krinsky* (1922), 259 U. S. 503; Ohio — *Thornton* v. *Duffy* (1920), 254 U. S. 361; Indiana — *Lower Vein Coal Co.* v. *Industrial Board* (1921), 255 U. S. 144; California — *Madera Sugar Pine Co.* v. *Industrial Acc. Com.* (1922), 262 U. S. 499.

[1] Oregon (eight-hour law) — *Muller* v. *Oregon* (1908), 208 U. S. 412; Massachusetts — *Riley* v. *Massachusetts* (1914), 232 U. S. 671; California (eight-hour law) — *Miller* v. *Wilson* (1915), 236 U. S. 373; *Bosley* v. *McLaughlin* (1915), 236 U. S. 385; Arizona (women in hotels) — *Dominion Hotel Co.* v. *Arizona* (1919), 249 U. S. 265; New York (women in restaurants) — *Radice Inc.* v. *New York* (1924), 264 U. S. 292. Oregon (women and minors' wage and working hours law) — *Stettler* v. *O'Hara* (1913), 243 U. S. 629.

[2] *Sturges & Burn Mfg. Co.* v. *Beauchamp* (1913), 231 U. S. 320; *Bunting* v. *Oregon* (1917), 243 U. S. 426; *Holden* v. *Hardy* (1898), 169 U. S. 366; *Atkin* v. *Kansas* (1903), 191 U. S. 207; *Heim* v. *McCall* (1915), 239 U. S. 175.

[3] *Erie R. R.* v. *Williams* (1914), 233 U. S. 685; *Keokee Coke Co.* v. *Taylor* (1914), 234 U. S. 224; *Knoxville Iron Co.* v. *Harbison* (1901), 183 U. S. 13;

LABOR AND THE SUPREME COURT 235

It has upheld State laws for the protection of railroad employees, laws of Arkansas requiring full train crews, and full switching crews; Iowa law forbidding railroads from contracts limiting liability for injuries, etc.; Indiana railroad safety appliance law.[1]

It has upheld State laws for the protection and benefit of coal miners — the Illinois coal mining law; Kansas powder in coal mines law; Arkansas law forbidding contracts for wages on basis of screened coal mined; Indiana law prescribing width of entries in bituminous coal mines; Pennsylvania law requiring boundary pillars in coal mines; Ohio anti-screen coal mine law; Indiana coal mine washhouse law.[2]

Other State laws in the interests of Labor upheld by the Court have been the Kansas law requiring safeguards on dangerous machinery; the Illinois law for protection of elevators and hoists; the Ohio mechanics lien law; the Japanese alien laws of California and Washington; and the New York rent control and housing emergency laws.[3]

In view of this record of steady support of legislation in behalf of and protection of Labor, and ren-

---

Dayton Coal & Iron Co. v. *Barton* (1901), 183 U. S. 23; *St. Louis etc. R. R.* v. *Paul* (1899), 173 U. S. 404; *Prudential Ins. Co.* v. *Cheek* (1922), 259 U. S. 530; *Chicago etc. R. R.* v. *Perry* (1922), 259 U. S. 548.

[1] *Chicago etc. R. R.* v. *Arkansas* (1911), 219 U. S. 453; *St. Louis etc. R. R.* v. *Arkansas* (1916), 240 U. S. 518; *C. B. & Q. R. R.* v. *McGuire* (1911), 219 U. S. 549; *Southern R. R.* v. *R. R. Com.* (1915), 236 U. S. 439.

[2] *Consolidated Coal Co.* v. *Illinois* (1902), 185 U. S. 203; *Wilmington Star Mining Co.* v. *Fulton* (1907), 205 U. S. 60; *Williams* v. *Walsh* (1912), 222 U. S. 415; *McLean* v. *Arkansas* (1909), 211 U. S. 539; *Barrett* v. *Indiana* (1913), 229 U. S. 26; *Plymouth Coal Co.* v. *Pennsylvania* (1914), 232 U. S. 531; *Rail & River Coal Co.* v. *Yaple* (1915), 236 U. S. 338; *Booth* v. *Indiana* (1915), 237 U. S. 391.

[3] *Bowersock* v. *Smith* (1917), 243 U. S. 29; *Chicago etc. Co.* v. *Fraley* (1913), 228 U. S. 680; *Great Southern etc. Co.* v. *Jones* (1904), 193 U. S. 532; *Terrace* v. *Thompson*, *Porterfield* v. *Webb* (1923), 263 U. S. 197, 225; *Marcus Brown Co.* v. *Feldman* (1921), 256 U. S. 170; *Levy Leasing Co.* v. *Siegel* (1922), 258 U. S. 242.

dered generally in cases in which the corporations and employers contended that the statutes were invalid, it may fairly be said that it is not only uncandid, and unfair to the public, but also ridiculous for any one to state that [1]:

Always these decisions of the Court are on the side of the wealthy and powerful and against the poor and weak, whom it is the policy of the lawmaking branch of the Government to assist by enlightened and humanitarian legislation.

As against these sixty cases upholding State labor laws, there are only six in which the Court has held the State statute invalid.[2]

(a) The *Lochner Case*, as to the New York ten-hour day bakers' law, decided in 1905, on insufficient argument and before the new form of brief devised by Louis D. Brandeis came into vogue. This case would probably be decided differently now.

(b) The *Smith Case*, as to the Texas law requiring all train conductors to have served two years as freight brakemen or conductors, decided in 1914. No fair or just man, Labor leader or otherwise, now attacks this decision.

(c) The *Coppage Case*, as to the Kansas law forbidding employers to require or influence persons not to join or remain in labor unions as a condition of securing or continuing in employment, decided in 1915. This decision by a divided Court may properly be criticized and is likely to be overruled some day.

---

[1] See speech of the late Senator La Follette at New York, Sept. 18, 1924.
[2] *Lochner* v. *New York* (1905), 198 U. S. 45; *Smith* v. *Texas* (1914), 233 U. S. 630; *Coppage* v. *Kansas* (1915), 236 U. S. 1; *Truax* v. *Raich* (1915), 239 U. S. 33; *Adams* v. *Tanner* (1917), 244 U. S. 590; *Truax* v. *Corrigan* (1921), 257 U. S. 312.

LABOR AND THE SUPREME COURT 237

(d) The *Raich Case*, as to the Arizona law requiring 80 per cent. of employees to be qualified electors or native-born citizens of the United States, decided in 1915. Few fair men will wish to defend this law or oppose this decision.

(e) The *Tanner Case*, as to the Washington law forbidding private employment agencies from receiving fees from persons seeking employment, decided in 1917. As to the correctness of this decision, there may well be opposing views.

(f) The *Corrigan Case*, as to the Arizona law prohibiting in labor disputes injunctions against picketing if unaccompanied with violence, decided in 1921. This decision affords a just grievance to Labor; but it is based so largely on the construction of the State statute given by the Arizona State Court, that the decision may easily be modified should a case arise under an anti-injunction statute in another State.

In addition to the above six cases, holding State statutes invalid, there are two decisions in which State hours of labor laws have been held invalid, *only so far* as they were applied to interstate commerce employees in the particular cases.[1]

Such being the total number of decisions adverse to Labor, holding State labor laws invalid, even if it be assumed that every one of those six decisions was wrong, would this justify a movement on the part of Labor to abolish or impair the power of the Court to pass on the validity of State laws? Apart from the disastrous effect of such a measure upon the maintenance of the National Government, would Labor benefit by such a proposal?

[1] *No. Pac. R. R.* v. *Washington* (1912), 222 U. S. 370; *Erie R. R.* v. *New York* (1914), 233 U. S. 671.

Let Labor recall that the compulsory arbitration law of Kansas, so obnoxious to it, was upheld by the State Supreme Court, but was held unconstitutional by the United States Supreme Court in 1923.[1]

Let Labor recall that the law of Nebraska forbidding the teaching of the German language in the schools, upheld by the State Supreme Court, was held unconstitutional by the United States Supreme Court, in 1923.[2]

Let Labor recall that the validity of the Oregon law forbidding to a parent the right to send his child to a parochial or private school, was denied by the United States Supreme Court, in 1925.[3]

Let Labor recall that the State Courts of New York held its workmen's compensation law unconstitutional, while the United States Supreme Court has upheld every State workmen's compensation law which has come before it.

4. Cases Decided on the Constitutionality of Acts of Congress.

Of the twenty cases decided adversely to Labor, it has been shown that fourteen have nothing to do with validity of Acts of Congress. Of the cases in which the Court has held unconstitutional Federal laws relating to Labor, there are only six.[4]

---

[1] *Charles Wolff Packing Co.* v. *Court of Industrial Relations* (1923), 262 U. S. 522; *ibid.* (1925), 267 U. S. 552.

[2] *Meyer* v. *Nebraska* (1923), 262 U. S. 390.

[3] *Pierce* v. *Society of the Sisters of the Holy Names of Jesus and Maria,* (1925), 268 U. S.

[4] *Howard* v. *Illinois Central R. R.* (1908), 207 U. S. 463 ; see *Mondou* v. *N. Y. N. H. & H. R. R.* (1912), 223 U. S. 1; *Adair* v. *United States* (1908), 208 U. S. 161; *Hammer* v. *Dagenhart* (1918), 247 U. S. 251; *Knickerbocker Ice Co.* v. *Stewart* (1920), 253 U. S. 149; *Bailey* v. *Drexel Furniture Co.* (1922), 259 U. S. 20; *Adkins* v. *Children's Hospital* (1923), 261 U. S. 525; see also *Washington* v. *Dawson Co.* (1924), 264 U. S. 219.

LABOR AND THE SUPREME COURT

(a) The first *Employers' Liability Case*, in 1908. This was later cured by an amendment of the Act, confining its operation to interstate transactions, so that this decision had no permanent effect.

(b) The *Adair Case*, in 1908, holding invalid one section of an Act of Congress making it a crime for a railroad to discharge an employee for belonging to a labor organization.

It may well be admitted that Labor had a right to feel aggrieved at this decision, especially as it was based on the lack of power of Congress, under its authority over interstate commerce, to enact the section held invalid. This section was part of a railroad arbitration statute, and it would seem that the provision as to discharge might validly be made a part of a general scheme of regulation of labor disputes on interstate railroads. On the other hand, had the discharge section been a separate law, unconnected with arbitration, many men might reasonably think that the Court was correct in saying that so long as an employee had the legal right to quit service because his employer employed nonunion labor, the employer should have the same legal right to discharge from service any one who joined a union; that equality of right was of the essence of American principles; that in the absence of a contract no person ought to be compelled by Congress to retain the personal services of another. As to this decision, at all events, it is fair to admit that there may reasonably be differing views.

(c) The first *Child Labor Case*, in 1918.
(d) The second *Child Labor Case*, in 1923.
The decision in these cases may be cured by a

Constitutional Amendment whenever the requisite number of States favor it.

(e) The *Workmen's Compensation in Admiralty Case* in 1919. This decision can probably be cured at any time by a properly drawn Federal statute.

(f) The *District of Columbia Minimum Wage Case,* in 1923.

To these six cases directly affecting Labor, there may be added four more decisions affecting the general public, and holding Acts of Congress invalid.[1]

The first *Legal Tender Case,* in 1870;

The *Monongahela Navigation Co. Case,* in 1893, as to compensation for franchises;

The *Income Tax Case,* in 1895;

The *Stock Dividend Case,* in 1919.

With this total of ten cases, there will have been included practically all the cases since the Civil War in which the action of the Court in holding an Act of Congress unconstitutional is now seriously criticized — ten cases in sixty years.

On the other hand, the public should note — and Labor utterly fails to call this to public attention — how many Acts of Congress of interest to Labor have been held constitutional by the Court. A few of these, since 1910, have been:[2] the second Federal Employers' Liability Act; the very important

---

[1] *Hepburn* v. *Griswold* (1870), 8 Wall. 603; *Monongahela Nav. Co.* v. *United States* (1893), 148 U. S. 312; *Pollock* v. *Farmers' Loan & Trust Co.* (1895), 158 U. S. 429, 158 U. S. 601; *Eisner* v. *Macomber* (1919), 252 U. S. 189.

[2] *Mondou* v. *N. Y. N. H. & H. R. R.* (1912), 223 U. S. 1; *Strathearn S. S. Co.* v. *Dillon* (1920), 252 U. S. 348; *Sandberg* v. *McDonald* (1918), 248 U. S. 185; *Smith* v. *Kansas City Title Co.* (1921), 255 U. S. 180; *Southern R. R.* v. *United States* (1911), 222 U. S. 20, see also *Johnson* v. *So. Pac. Co.,* 196 U. S. 1; *Wilson* v. *New* (1917), 243 U. S. 332; *Block* v. *Hirsh* (1921), 256 U. S. 135; *Stafford* v. *Wallace* (1922), 258 U. S. 495; *Board of Trade of Chicago* v. *Olsen* (1923), 262 U. S. 1; *Michaelson et al.* v. *United States ex rel. Chicago, St. Paul,*

La Follette Seamen's Act of 1915; the Farm Loan Act; the Railroad Safety Appliance Acts; the Adamson Eight-hour Law; the District of Columbia Rent Control Act; the Packers and Stockyards Act of 1921; the Grain Futures Act of 1922; the Clayton Act of 1914 as to regulation of injunctions, and jury trials in contempt cases. During the term of Court ending in June, 1924, the following Acts of Congress were held constitutional; the Act which extended to seamen the right to jury trial and all the remedies available to railroad employees under the Federal Employers' Liability Act; the Act which provided that the Federal Government might take all excess of earnings of interstate railroads over reasonable return on the investment and might hold such excess earnings for development of railroad transportation generally.[1]

In the face of this recent record of the Court in upholding the validity of Acts of Congress, how untrue and unfair was the statement made by a late Labor leader, in 1924, that:[2]

In years of effort, we finally prevailed upon Congress to enact laws to safeguard the welfare and interests of the people. In *every instance* in the last fifteen years, despite our efforts, the Courts of the country have annulled them and declared them null and void.

Because of these six decisions holding Acts of Congress invalid, affecting Labor, and because of

Minneapolis & Omaha Railway Co. (1924), 266 U. S. 42. See also the Railroad Employees' Hours of Labor Act, *B. & O. R. R.* v. *Interstate Commerce Commission* (1911), 221 U. S. 612.

[1] *Panama Railroad Co.* v. *Johnson* (1924), 264 U. S. 375; *Dayton Goose Creek R. R.* v. *United States* (1924), 263 U. S. 456; *Myers* v. *United States* (1924), 264 U. S. 95.

[2] *New York Times*, Sept. 20, 1924.

four more at most, Labor has been demanding a revolutionary change in our form of government, viz., a Constitutional Amendment depriving the Court of its power to pass finally upon the validity of Federal laws.

When the complaints of the Court by Labor, the radicals and others, are more closely analyzed, it will be found that they consist chiefly in dissent from what they claim is the Court's interpretation of the phrase, "due process of law." The Fifth Amendment provides that "no person . . . shall be deprived of life, liberty or property, without due process of law." This Amendment, as has long been held by the Courts, was intended to apply and does apply only to legislation by Congress or to acts by officers of the Federal Government and does not apply to the States (the latter being placed under the same restriction by the Fourteenth Amendment). It is alleged against the Court that in construing this general phrase, "due process of law", as applied to Federal legislation of a social and economic nature, *i.e.*, statutes of the kind which, if enacted by State Legislatures, would be known as "police power" legislation, the Justices of the Court "invoke their own social and economic views as against the social and economic views of the majority of Congress."[1]

[1] *The Red Terror of Judicial Reform*, in the *New Republic*, Oct. 1, 1924: "These broad guarantees in favor of the individual are expressed in words so undefined, either by their intrinsic meaning, or by history, or by tradition, that they leave the individual Justice free, if indeed they do not actually compel him, to fill in the vacuum with his own controlling notions of economic, social and industrial facts with reference to which they are invoked. These judicial judgments are thus bound to be determined by the experience, the environment, the fears, the imagination of the different Justices. For it cannot be too often made clear that the meaning of phrases like 'due process of law' and of simple terms like 'liberty' and 'property' is not revealed within the Constitution;

Incidentally, it may be stated that it is not a fact that the Justices do, consciously, act in this manner. In case after case, they have denied any right or power so to do. Mr. Justice Brandeis has but recently said that: "No principle of our constitutional law is more firmly established than that this Court may not, in passing upon the validity of a statute, enquire into the motives of Congress. Nor may the Court enquire into the wisdom of the legislation. Nor may it pass upon the necessity for the exercise of a power possessed, since the possible abuse of a power is not argument against its existence."[1] But here again, however, people are misled by half-truths, suppressions of fact, and misstatements. Thus, a recent writer in an article on the La Follette proposed Amendment said: "These are the clauses —

their meaning is derived from without." See also letter of Prof. Edwin Borchard in the *Nation*, Oct. 29, 1924; *Judicial Review versus Doctrinaire Democracy*, by Robert H. Hale, *Amer. Bar Ass. Journal* (sec. 1924), X.

[1] *Hamilton* v. *Kentucky Distilleries Co.* (1919), 251 U. S. 146. See White, J., in *McCray* v. *United States* (1904), 195 U. S. 27: "No instance is afforded from the foundation of the Government where an Act which was within a power conferred was declared to be repugnant to the Constitution, because it appeared to the judicial mind that the particular exertion of the Constitutional power was either unwise or unjust. To announce such a principle would amount to declaring that in our constitutional system the Judiciary was not only charged with the duty of upholding the Constitution, but also with the responsibility of correcting every possible abuse arising from the exercise of their conceded authority. So to hold would be to overthrow the entire distinction between the legislative, judicial and executive departments of the Government, upon which our system is founded, and would be a mere act of judicial usurpation. The decisions of this Court from the beginning lend no support whatever to the assumption that the Judiciary may restrain the exercise of lawful power, on the assumption that a wrongful purpose or motive has caused the power to be exerted. If it be said that a statute like the one before us is mischievous in its tendencies, the answer is that the responsibility therefor rests upon legislators, not upon the Court."

See also Moody, J., in *Twining* v. *New Jersey* (1908), 211 U. S. 106: "Under the guise of interpreting the Constitution, we must take care that we do not import into the discussion our personal views of what would be wise, just and fitting rules of government to be adopted by a free people, and confound them with constitutional limitations."

'due process' and 'equal protection of the laws' — which have brought forth the most abundant crop of judicial nullifications."[1] This statement is false and misleading if sought to be applied to National legislation held invalid by the Supreme Court. For it is a fact that only five cases can be cited in which the Court construed "due process" to invalidate an Act of Congress. Let us note that the *Child Labor Cases* did not involve any question of "due process" under the Fifth Amendment, for the decisions were based on a construction or interpretation by the Court of the meaning of the words "regulate commerce among the several States" and "to lay and collect taxes", in Article One, Section 8, of the Constitution. Hence, there exists no great evil as to "due process" decisions sufficient to warrant a fundamental change in the Constitution with respect to the judicial power relating to Acts of Congress.

Most of the complaints with reference to the Court's action under the "due process" clause will be found to be directed against its decisions holding State statutes violative of this clause of the Fourteenth Amendment. But the Court's power to hold State laws invalid is not based on the same reasons or derived from the same source as its power relative to Federal laws; and the proposals made by Senator Borah and by the late Senator La Follette do not assume to control the Court's decisions as to State statutes.[2] Furthermore, the facts are again mis-

[1] *New Republic*, Oct. 1, 1924.

[2] Writers frequently overlook this difference between the function of the Court in holding an Act of Congress invalid, and its function in holding a State statute invalid. As an example of such confusion, see *Social Policy and the Supreme Court*, in *The New Republic*, July 15, 1924: "The Fourteenth Amendment, in plain truth, deals with 'law' very differently from ordinary

represented even as to such decisions; for it will be found that the number of State laws of the class known as "social justice" legislation held invalid by the Court is comparatively few.[1]

Labor and its representatives may well ponder the very suggestive words of Senator McCumber, in the debate over the Clayton Act, in 1914:[2]

There are no people in this country who are more deeply concerned in maintaining the constitutional power of the Courts than are our laboring people. Paralyze the arm of the Court and a tyrannical power will take its place in the future as it has always taken its place in the past. . . . Let every laboring man pause before he strikes the protector of his own liberties.

And each individual working man should ask himself the question: Have I such implicit trust in the correctness and justice of every thing done by Congress as to be willing that Congress should legislate as to my rights, at its own sweet will, unfettered by any bounds of a written Constitution, or by any restraining hand of a Federal Judiciary sworn to uphold the Constitution? Is the party in power in any particular Congress so just in its views and actions, so protective of the minority, so truly representative of the wishes, rights, and liberties of the people, that I am ready to trust it with unlimited power?

law in its incidence, in its raw material and in the stuff that determines decisions. The multitudinous cases . . . are, in essence, judgements upon social policies. . . . It it sheer pedantry to prove that power to declare legislation invalid antedated our Constitution. It is wholly confusing to assert that other nations today entrust their Courts with questions of constitutionality. What matters is that no other nation entrusts its Courts with *such questions* of constitutionality as our Supreme Court has to deal with under the Fourteenth Amendment."

[1] See *The Progressiveness of the United States Supreme Court*, by Charles Warren, *Columbia Law Rev.* (April, 1913), XIII; *A Bulwark to the State Police Power*, by Charles Warren, *ibid.* (Dec. 1913), XIII.

[2] *Cong. Rec. 63d Cong., 1st Sess.*, p. 13965, Aug. 13, 1914.

CHAPTER EIGHT

THE INDEPENDENCE OF THE COURT

"The morals of your people, the peace of the country, the stability of the government rest upon the maintenance of the independence of the Judiciary. It is not of half the importance in England that the Judges should be independent of the Crown, as it is with us that they should be independent of the Legislature. . . . Is it not our great interest to place our Judges upon such high ground that no fear can intimidate, no hope can seduce them?" — JAMES A. BAYARD of Delaware, in the House, Feb. 20, 1802. *7th Cong., 1st Sess.*

"It seems to have been supposed, at the time this subject was before the Nation, to be necessary to interpose some barrier to protect the rights of the minority against the persecuting spirit of an overbearing majority and to secure an accused individual against oppression and injustice from the strong arm of power. The independence of the Federal Judiciary was deemed a valuable safeguard against the encroachments of the Federal Government on the rights of the people and the sovereignty of the States." — JOHN POPE of Kentucky, in the House, Feb. 24, 1809. *10th Cong., 2d Sess.*

"The Constitution does not proceed upon the supposition of the infallibility of Congress, or upon the supposition of Executive infallibility. Every member of Government, who is sworn to support the Constitution, is to perform his public trust according to what he believes to be the true construction of the rule of duty to which he is bound by oath. . . . The Judges of Courts of the United States are considered as not bound to afford any agency or aid toward carrying into effect a Legislative provision which is unconstitutional." — SAMUEL W. DANA of Connecticut, in the House, Feb. 2, 1809. *10th Cong., 2d Sess.*

"The independence of the Judiciary is at the very basis of our institutions." — WILLIAM HARPER of South Carolina, in the Senate, April 14, 1826. *19th Cong., 1st Sess.*

One of the favorite forms of attack upon the Supreme Court's exercise of the power to pass upon the validity of Acts of Congress is to allege that it makes the Court superior to Congress, that it destroys the

INDEPENDENCE OF THE COURT

independence of one of the three coördinate branches of the Government. Thus, Jackson H. Ralston, long the counsel for the American Federation of Labor, in an exhaustive report on the subject in 1923, wrote:

> And stating the proposition in other terms, if we concede that there are three coördinate branches of the government, is not such a concession fatal to the idea that one branch can destroy the work of the others on some theory of its own, relative to the subject of constitutionality? . . . The argument is made that when Congress passes an unconstitutional Act, such Act is in excess of its powers under the instrument creating it, and should not be enforced. But this is reasoning in a circle, because no power is given to any body other than Congress to determine the question of constitutionality; and the Courts, as has been explained, cannot do it without Congress ceasing to be coördinate and becoming a simple subordinate branch of the government.

This charge, however, is unfounded; it proceeds from a complete misunderstanding of fundamental principles of the American Constitution. When we speak of the three coördinate branches of the Government, if we mean by "coördinate" that the Congress, the Executive, and the Judiciary are each a complete governmental body exercising its own peculiar functions, we use the word accurately. If, on the other hand, we mean by "coördinate" that each of the three branches of the Government is *completely independent of the other*, and not subject to be affected in any way by the other — the meaning which apparently those who share Mr. Ralston's views give to the word — then it is entirely untrue that the Constitution was ever intended to make, or did make, the three branches "coördinate" to that extent.

When in the State Constitutions of Virginia and of other States, it was provided that "the Legislative, Executive and Judicial powers of government ought to be forever separate and distinct from each other", the phrase was used only in a very general way. As a matter of fact, as Madison said in *The Federalist*: "If we look into the Constitutions of the several States, we find that, notwithstanding the emphatical, and in some instances, the unqualified terms in which the maxim has been laid down therein, there is not a single instance in which the several departments of power have been kept absolutely separate and distinct." And as William R. Davie said in the North Carolina Convention of 1788: "It is true the great Montesquieu and several other writers have laid it down as a maxim not to be departed from that the Legislative, Executive and Judicial powers should be separate and distinct. But the idea that these gentlemen had in view has been misconceived and misrepresented. An absolute and complete separation is not meant by them. It is impossible to form a government upon these principles. Those States who had made an absolute separation of these three powers their leading principle had been obliged to depart from it. It is a principle, in fact, which is not to be found in any of the State Governments. . . . The meaning of this maxim I take to be this — that the whole Legislative, Executive and Judicial powers should not be exclusively blended in any one particular instance." [1]

[1] *Elliot's Debates*, IV, 121, 122.

INDEPENDENCE OF THE COURT

And when the framers of the Constitution established a new Federal Government with three independent branches — a President, a Congress, and a Supreme Court — they did not intend, nor did they provide, for a Government in which these three branches should be absolutely independent of each other. The framers constituted a Government in which not only should each branch have limited powers for itself, but each branch should also have a curb or check on the operation of the other. This is what is meant when we speak of the American Government as being one of "checks and balances."

This fact that the three branches were not absolutely and entirely independent of each other was pointed out clearly in debates in the early Congresses. "The more checks there are to any Government, the more free will its citizens be," said James Jackson of Georgia, in the First Congress, in 1790. Uriah Tracy of Connecticut said, in the Third Congress, in 1795, that he "considered the constitutional checks of the branches of this Government upon one another, as containing the most complete security for liberty that any people could enjoy."[1] These checks placed by the framers of the Constitution upon the absolute independence of the respective branches of the new Government were as follows.

The President was not entirely independent; for his power of appointment of officers and his making of treaties were subjected to confirmation "with the advice and consent" of the Senate; his veto of legis-

[1] See especially *1st Cong., 1st Sess.*, speeches of Jackson, June 19, 1789, p. 553; Stone, p. 564; Madison, June 22, 1789, p. 581; Jackson, July 23, 1790, p. 1790; Tracy, Jan. 2, Feb. 3, 1790, pp. 1053, 1070.

lation was subject to being overruled by a two-thirds vote of both branches of Congress; and his proper performance of his duties was to be insured by impeachment by the House of Representatives in case of his failure so to perform.

The Supreme Court was not entirely independent; for its members were subject to confirmation by the Senate; its membership could be added to, or (in case of death or resignation of a Judge) reduced in number, by Congress; its salaries were dependent on appropriations by Congress; and its members, in case of misperformance of duties, were subject to impeachment by the House; its sentences in criminal cases were subject to the President's power to pardon, and even its exercise of inherent judicial power to commit to prison for criminal contempt was subject to the similar power in the President to pardon the contemning offender.

The Congress was not entirely independent; for its bills were subject to veto by the President; its laws, enacted in pursuance of the Constitution, could be repealed by treaties made by the President and the Senate acting together; and its enacted laws, if not made in accordance with the Constitution or "pursuant thereto", could be disregarded by the Supreme Court.

Thus, each branch was "coördinate" to a limited extent only; and each was subject, in a certain degree, to action by the other interfering with its uncontrolled powers and with its entire independence. As was said by Chief Justice Taft, in a recent opinion: "Complete independence and separation between the three branches, however, are not attained,

INDEPENDENCE OF THE COURT 251

or intended. . . . Independence of each of the other is qualified and is so subject to exception as not to constitute a broadly positive imposition or a necessarily controlling rule of construction."[1]

To say, therefore, that the power of the Court to pass on the validity of Acts of Congress destroys Congress as a "coördinate" branch is to evince a complete misunderstanding of the intentions of the framers of the Constitution; for they never planned for a Congress that should be "coördinate" in the sense of being "unrestricted in power."

Moreover, if the curb by the Supreme Court on Congress destroys the latter as coördinate power, the question may well be asked: Why does not a curb by the Supreme Court on the President destroy him also as a coördinate power? If Congress is to be allowed to violate the Constitution without being checked by the Court, why should not the President also be allowed to violate the Constitution without any similar check?

Yet it is well known that if a case arises in Court in which an action of the President violative of the Constitution is set up by a party to the suit, either as a defense or as a ground of action, the Court will not hesitate, and in the past has not hesitated, to declare such Presidential action to be void and of no effect and hence incapable of affording to any person a

---

[1] *Ex parte Grossman* (1925), 267 U. S. 87. Chief Justice Taft concluded his opinion: "It goes without saying that nowhere is there a more earnest will to maintain the independence of Federal Courts and the preservation of every legitimate safeguard of their effectiveness afforded by the Constitution than in this Court. But the qualified independence which they fortunately enjoy is not likely to be permanently strengthened by ignoring precedent and practice and minimizing the importance of the coördinating checks and balances of the Constitution."

252 INDEPENDENCE OF THE COURT

valid defense to the suit or a valid basis for recovery in the suit.[1] At this point, it is only necessary to cite, as an example, the famous decision of the Supreme Court in the *Milligan Case*, in 1867, holding President Lincoln's action in authorizing trial by Military Commission in places where the civil Courts were open to be in violation of the Constitution and therefore void.

Is there any reason why Congress should be more "coördinate" as to its actions than the President? Is there any reason why the Legislative branch of the Government should be more privileged to violate the Constitution than the Executive branch, without being curbed by the Supreme Court?

The answer is: that the Constitution was intended to afford a means to curb both. And in performing its action under the Constitution, the Supreme Court has, in fact, actually curbed both.

It is frequently forgotten, however, in the discussion of the question, that this judicial curb is never applied directly to either Congress or the President.

[1] *The Judicial Review of Executive Acts*, by Albert Levitt, *Michigan Law Rev.* (1925), XXIII. David Barton of Missouri said, in the Senate, March 17, 1830: "The founders of the republic and the people of the United States when they adopted the Federal Constitution were especially jealous of the powers of the President and the encroaching spirit of Executive will. To that point all their principal fears were concentrated; and the history of that day shows that it was with some difficulty the people of the United States could be induced to adopt the Union, lest the President with the powers then accorded to him should become the destroyer of their liberties. Their fears of Executive encroachment were not idle chimera of the fancy. . . . The histories of all nations which have lost their liberties lay before them and they saw on their pages that arbitrary Executive discretion and will . . . had been the destroyers of national liberty throughout the greater part of the world . . . and the fathers did intend, and the most of them have left this world in the paternal confidence that they had effected the object, to establish a government of law and of checks and restraints upon Executive will, in which no case should exist in which the fate of the humblest citizen whether in private or public life could depend upon the arbitrary will of a single man."

INDEPENDENCE OF THE COURT 253

The Court does not "veto" or "annul" an Act of Congress. It is because this fact is so often overlooked that much of the talk has arisen about interference with Congress by the Court, and about the Court as "superior" to Congress. As a matter of fact, the question of violation of the Constitution does not arise directly between the Court and Congress, or between the Court and the President. It only arises in some suit brought in a Court, in which a plaintiff to the suit alleges that he has a right against the defendant based on an Act of Congress or on an action of the President, and in which the defendant alleges that the plaintiff has no such right because the Act of Congress or the Presidential action was an infringement of the Constitution; or else it arises in some suit in Court in which a defendant bases his defense on an Act of Congress or on a Presidential action, and the plaintiff alleges that such Act or action is no valid defense because it was violative of the Constitution. The Supreme Court's duty is, then, simply to decide whether these contentions, by the plaintiff or by the defendant respectively, are valid, and whether, in fact and in law, the Act of Congress, or the Presidential action, was or was not in accordance with the provisions of the Constitution.

The Supreme Court, as has been pointed out in earlier chapters, decides individual cases. It does not determine questions, though a case in Court may, of course, present facts as to which in Congress there may be differences of political view. But as John W. Noell of Missouri very rightly said, in the House, in 1860: "These modern solons have discovered a great distinction between questions which they call political and those which are not political. *Every question, while it is pending here (i.e., in Congress) is a political question, and every question when it is transferred to the Judiciary is a judicial question. No law passed by Congress affecting the rights of persons or the rights of property but must be decided upon and enforced by the Judiciary. . . . No man contends that a judgment or opinion of the Federal Judiciary can tie the hands of Congress; but every man . . . ought to know that when we enact a law, its validity and constitutionality must be determined by the Judiciary."*

Opponents of the Court sometimes quote Jefferson, Jackson, and Lincoln as opposed to the judicial power to pass upon the constitutionality of statutes. In citing these Presidents as authority, they fall into the common mistake of failing to note the distinction between the decision of a *case* and of a *question*. Jefferson, Jackson, and Lincoln, each, explicitly acknowledged the Court's power to render decisions binding upon the parties to the case and holding Acts of Congress invalid; but their contention was that these decisions did not bind the President when he came to exercise his Executive power of veto with reference to a subsequent similar statute, and did not bind the Congress in exercising its Legislative power to enact subsequent similar statutes, subject to the liability that such statutes would also be held invalid by the Court in subsequent litigated cases.[1]

---

[1] See *The Supreme Court in United States History* (1922), by Charles Warren, I, 264–266, II, 222–224, III, 52–54; and see especially letter of Jefferson to W. C. Jarvis, Sept. 28, 1820, *Works* (Ford's Ed.), X, 160; see also *Are the*

INDEPENDENCE OF THE COURT 255

In a preliminary draft of his first Message, Jefferson wrote:

> Our country has thought proper to distribute the powers of its Government among three equal and independent authorities, constituting each a check on one or both of the others, in all attempts to impair its Constitution. To make each an effectual check, it must have a right, in cases which arise within the line of its proper functions, where, equally with the others, it acts in the last resort, and without appeal, to decide on the validity of an Act according to its own judgment and uncontrolled by the opinions of any other department. . . .

In other words, Jefferson claimed the right to pass upon the validity of an Act of Congress, in the per-

---

Departments of Government Independent of Each Other? by Sydney G. Fisher, *Amer. Law Rev.* (1887), XXI.

See citations of Jefferson and Jackson, in an attack on the Supreme Court by Roscoe Conkling, in the House, April 16, 17, 1860, and reply of John W. Noell, April 25, 1860. *36th Cong., 1st Sess., and App.*

Samuel W. Dana of Connecticut said, in the House, Feb. 2, 1809: "The Constitution does not proceed upon the supposition of the infallibility of Congress or upon the supposition of Executive infallibility. . . . Every member of government who is known to support the Constitution has to perform his public trust according to what he believes to be the true construction of the rule of duty to which he is bound by oath. According to this principle . . . the Judges of Courts of the United States are considered as not bound to afford any agency or aid toward carrying into effect a Legislative provision which is unconstitutional." *10th Cong., 2d Sess.*

John McPherson Berrien of Georgia said, in the Senate, Jan. 24, 1827: "The decisions of that tribunal are entitled to respect. They are authoritative, so far as, in the exercise of their constitutional powers, they have decided that a given subject is beyond the control of Legislative power, because since the interpretation of the laws is confided to them, and so long as it is confided to them and since their precedents are binding, future legislation on the same subject would be futile." *19th Cong., 2d Sess.*

Hugh Lawson White of Tennessee said, in the Senate, July 11, 1832, that while the Court's decision "is final and conclusive between the parties, as an authority it does not bind the Congress or the President. I hope neither of them will ever view them as authority binding on them." *22d Cong., 1st Sess.*

formance of his constitutional functions as President, in exactly the same fashion as he recognized the right of the Court so to do in performing its judicial functions.

And Jackson's attitude was explained by Chief Justice Taney as follows:

He has been charged with asserting that he, as an Executive officer, had a right to judge for himself whether an Act of Congress was constitutional or not, and was not bound to carry it into execution if he believed it to be unconstitutional, even if the Supreme Court decided otherwise. . . . Yet no intelligent man who reads the message can misunderstand the meaning of the President. He was speaking of his rights and his duty, when acting as a part of the Legislative power, and not of his right or duty as an Executive officer. For when a bill is presented to him and he is to decide whether, by his approval, it shall become a law or not, his power or duty is as purely Legislative as that of a Member of Congress, when he is called on to vote for or against a bill. . . . It is true that he may very probably yield up his preconceived opinions in deference to that of the Court, because it is the tribunal especially constituted to decide the questions in all cases wherein it may arise, and from its organization and character is peculiarly fitted for such inquiries. But if a Member of Congress, or the President, when acting in his Legislative capacity, has, upon mature consideration, made up his mind that the proposed law is a violation of the Constitution he has sworn to support, and that the Supreme Court had in that respect fallen into error, it is not only his right but his duty to refuse to aid in the passage of the proposed law. . . . But General Jackson never expressed a doubt as to the duty and obligation upon him in his Executive character to carry into execution any Act of Congress regularly passed, whatever his own opinion might be of the constitutional question.

Lincoln's attitude was shown in his Inaugural Address in 1861:[1]

> I do not forget the position, assumed by some, that constitutional questions are to be decided by the Supreme Court, nor do I deny that such decisions must be binding in any case, upon the parties to a suit, as to the object of that suit, while they are also entitled to very high respect and consideration in all parallel cases by all other departments of the Government. And while it is obviously possible that such decision may be erroneous in any given case, still the evil effect following it, being limited to that particular case, with the chance that it may be overruled and never become a precedent for other cases, can better be borne than could the evils of a different practice.

It is one of the glories of the American Federal Judiciary that both the Supreme Court and its Justices have shown as complete independence of the Executive as of the Congress. And they have never hesitated to curb any usurpation of power by the Executive or to hold invalid an Executive action, if it was an action unwarranted by the Constitution or by a constitutional statute. Furthermore, the Supreme Court has not hesitated to curb the officers of the law and the Judges of the inferior Courts, whenever the latter have acted in violation of the Constitution; and in a number of instances where the rights guaranteed to individuals by the Bill of Rights in the Constitution — such as the right against unrea-

---

[1] See Lincoln's speech at Galena, Ill., Aug. 1, 1856, when he said: "I grant you that an unconstitutional act is not law; but I do not ask and will not take your construction of the Constitution. The Supreme Court of the United States is the tribunal to decide such a question, and we will submit to its decisions; and if you do also, there will be an end of the matter. Will you? If not, who are the disunionists, — you, or we?" *Works of Abraham Lincoln* (Federal Ed., 1905), II; see *ibid.*, III, Lincoln's speeches at Springfield, Ill., June 17, 1858, and at Chicago, July 10, 1858.

sonable search and seizure, the right not to be forced to testify against oneself, and similar rights — have been infringed, the Supreme Court has held the actions of United States attorneys, police officers, magistrates, and Judges to be invalid, and to constitute a ground for setting aside a conviction or an imprisonment of the citizen complaining of the action.[1] Do those who wish Congress to be free to act in conflict with the Constitution, unchecked by the Court, also wish the Executive or the inferior Judiciary to be similarly free? And if not, what reason can be advanced why the Legislative branch of the Government should be allowed to violate the Constitution, but the Executive and the Judiciary forbidden so to do? The question has been strikingly put by a President of the American Bar Association: "Shall we say that when an American stands before the Court demanding rights given him by the supreme law of the land, the Court shall be deaf to his appeal? Shall wrongs visited upon him by the illegal excesses of Congresses or Legislatures be less open to redress than those which he may suffer from Courts, or sheriffs, or military tyrants or civilian enemies? If this be so, if in any such case the ears of the Court are to be closed against him, it is not the power of the Court that has been reduced but the dearly bought right of the citizen that is taken away."[2]

[1] See especially *Ziang Sung Wan* v. *United States* (1924), 266 U. S. 1; *Boyd* v. *United States* (1886), 116 U. S. 616; *Silverthorne Lumber Co.* v. *United States* (1920), 251 U. S. 380, and cases cited; *Gouled* v. *United States* (1921), 255 U. S. 298; *Note* on "Restricting Liberty without Due Process of Law", in *Michigan State Bar Journal* (1925), IV, 357.

[2] Address before the American Bar Association, Aug. 29, 1923, at Minneapolis, Minn., by John W. Davis.

INDEPENDENCE OF THE COURT 259

Early in history, at a dinner given in Washington in 1801, the following toast was offered: "The Judiciary of the United States — independent of party; independent of power; and independent of popularity." To this might have well been added — "independent of Presidents; and independent of politics."

That the Court has, from the outset, proved itself to be fully as ready to curb the President as Congress, if either had exercised power not granted, is shown by many episodes in its history; and their independence was evinced by the Justices of the Court within three years after the inauguration of the first Court, when, in August, 1793, they made it plain that they would not render any decision or give any judicial opinion even to the President, unless in an actual case litigated by parties before them as a Court. And although it appears that it was the popular expectation that they would render advisory opinions (in the same manner as the Justices of the Massachusetts Supreme Judicial Court did under the State Constitution), they refused, very firmly though respectfully, to render to President Washington an advisory opinion which he had sought from them on the complicated questions then arising out of the neutral attitude of the United States in the War between Great Britain and France. In his letter to Washington, announcing this refusal by the Court, Chief Justice Jay said that "the lines of separation drawn by the Constitution between the three departments of the government", " these being in certain respects checks upon each other . . . afford strong arguments against the propriety of our extrajudicially deciding the questions alluded to."[1]

Eight years later, in 1801, a case arose involving one of the pet measures of the Federalist Administration, the retaliatory war statute directed against French depredations on American commerce; but when the Federalist leader, James A. Bayard, attempted in argument to read the instructions issued by the Federalist President, Adams, construing the statute, all the Judges (themselves Federalists) opposed the attempt; and Judge Paterson stated that he had "no objection to hearing them, but they will have no influence on my opinion. We are willing to hear them as the opinion of Mr. Bayard but not as the opinion of the Executive." On a similar attempt being made, in a case in 1804, President Adams' warm Federalist adherent, Judge Chase, stated that he was always against reading the instructions of the Executive, because "if they go no further than the law they are unnecessary; if they exceed it, they are not warranted."[2] This was exceedingly plain language to be addressed by the Judiciary to the Executive.

Four years later, in 1808, an even stronger instance of judicial independence occurred in a case involving an issue of the most heated nature. The famous Embargo Act provided that ships laden with provisions should be denied clearance if, *in the opinion of the Collector of Customs*, intended for foreign ports. President Jefferson had issued peremptory instructions to collectors to deny clearance to *all* vessels

[1] *The Supreme Court in United States History* (1922), by Charles Warren, I, 109–111.
[2] *Talbot* v. *Seaman* (1801), 1 Cranch 1; *Murray* v. *Charming Betsy* (1804), 2 Cranch 64.

INDEPENDENCE OF THE COURT 261

laden with provisions, thus eliminating the discretion which the statute gave to the collector. A case involving this situation arose in the Circuit Court in Charleston, South Carolina, before William Johnson, a Justice of the Supreme Court. Johnson was a young man, of thirty-six; he had been appointed to the Bench, only four years before, by President Jefferson as the first Democratic Judge on the Supreme Court. Every influence and condition would seem to tend to incline him to decide in favor of the President, and to uphold the President's pet embargo. Without hesitation, however, he proceeded to hold the President's action to be unauthorized by the law and that the "collector is not justified by the instructions of the Executive in increasing restraints upon commerce"; and he pointed out to the President that "the officers of our Government from the highest to the lowest are equally subjected to legal restraint." So incensed was Jefferson that he caused his Attorney-General to issue an opinion denying the accuracy of Johnson's decision and instructing collectors to pay no attention to it. But the Judge himself did not waver from his position of courageous independence, and he replied publicly to the Attorney-General's opinion, and reasserted his previous ruling.

Four years later, in 1812, another Justice of the Supreme Court, Joseph Story, a Democrat, strikingly showed his independence of the Democratic President — James Madison — who had appointed him upon the Court, only ten months prior to the decision in question. Story was a young man of thirty-three. The War of 1812 had begun, and the

262 INDEPENDENCE OF THE COURT

Administration was vitally interested in prosecuting and convicting the cases of Americans who had been guilty of unlawful trade with the enemy, England. Such a case came up before Judge Story, in which the defendant pleaded that a proclamation of President Madison reviving an embargo law, under which the indictment had been found, was illegal. Judge Story was thus called upon to decide upon the legality of the action of a President who had just appointed him to office, and upon its legality as bearing upon a class of case in which the President and his Administration were vitally desirous of obtaining convictions.[1] Story, in spite of his youth and his personal and political predilections, without hesitation held the action of the President to have been illegal, and the prisoner went free. "For the Executive Department of the Government, this Court entertain the most entire respect," said the Judge, but "it is our duty to expound the laws as we find them in the records of State; and we cannot, when called upon by the citizens of the country, refuse our opinion, however it differs from that of very high authorities. I do not perceive any reasonable ground to imply an authority in the President to revive this Act, and I must, therefore, with whatever reluctance, pronounce it to have been, as to this purpose, invalid."

In 1818, the Court again reaffirmed the cardinal principle of the Anglo-Saxon system of law that no man — not even the President of the United States — is above the law. A case arose involving the question whether certain Government officials, who had been sued for damages for making seizure of a vessel under

[1] *The Schooner Orono* (1812), 1 Gallison 137.

INDEPENDENCE OF THE COURT 263

alleged violation of the neutrality laws, could justify their action by alleging that it was done by express order of President Madison. Attorney-General Rush argued in their behalf that it has been "the wise policy of the law, by enactments and decisions coextensive with the range of public office, to throw its shield over officers while acting under fair and honest convictions." But as the counsel for the plaintiff pointed out, unless the act could be justified under some express authority, it was illegal, and "were it otherwise, the President would be a despot." The Court, through Judge Story, held that as no statute authorized the President to direct seizure by the civil officers, his order constituted no protection to them, if rights of an individual had been trespassed upon. Thus, for a third time and with regard to the instructions of three different Presidents (Adams, Jefferson, and Madison), the Court in its short career had shown its independence of the Executive, and its determination to prove to all that ours is a "government of laws and not of men."[1] Frequent other instances have occurred of independence by the Judges of Presidents who appointed them to the Bench. Thus, Henry Baldwin, appointed by President Jackson, gave the leading opinions in the Spanish land fraud cases during the 1830's, in which the Court took a position directly opposed to Jackson's vigorous views on the subject. In 1838, the Court consisting almost wholly of Judges appointed by the Democratic Presidents, Jackson and Van Buren, rendered a decision against Jackson's personal friend and Postmaster-General in a case around which much bitterness of

[1] *Gelston* v. *Hoyt* (1818), 3 Wheaton 246.

feeling had centered.¹ In 1866, the Court, on which five out of nine Justices then sitting had been appointed by President Lincoln, held that the action of that President in establishing military tribunals, in places where the civil Courts were open and not in the actual theater of war, was illegal, and that a man sentenced to be hung by such a tribunal was unconstitutionally sentenced and must be released. And Lincoln's personal friend, Judge David Davis, in delivering the opinion of the Court, uttered the great sentiment: "The Constitution of the United States is a law for rulers and people, equally in war and in peace, and covers with the shield of its protection all classes of men, at all times and under all circumstances." Its provisions, he said, could not be suspended, "during any of the great exigencies of the government" — not even by the President of the United States; for if they could be so suspended, "such a doctrine leads directly to anarchy or despotism."² And in connection with this case, a decision of the Illinois Supreme Court, also holding as unlawful military arrests made by order of President Lincoln, and further holding as unconstitutional the attempt of Congress to validate them by the Act of March 3, 1863, should ever be remembered as a splendid exposition of the duty of Courts:

We are not unconscious of the fact that the decision which we are obliged to make in the present case on the facts appearing in the record . . . attributes to our late lamented President the unlawful exercise of power and therefore implies a certain degree of censure. None can

[1] *Kendall* v. *Stokes* (1838), 12 Peters 542.
[2] *Ex parte Milligan* (1866), 4 Wallace 2; *Johnson* v. *Jones* (1867), 44 Ill. 142, 161.

INDEPENDENCE OF THE COURT

have a higher appreciation than the members of this Court of the unselfish patriotism and purity of motive of that great Magistrate. If he exercised a power not given by the Constitution, he undoubtedly did so under a full conviction of its necessity in the extraordinary emergencies wherein he was called to act. But neither our honor for his memory, nor our confidence in his honesty, can be permitted to sway our judgment here. . . . If this plaintiff has been wrongfully restrained of his liberty, he has right to call upon us so to declare, without fear, favor or affection. It is unfortunate that cases having a political or partisan character should come before the Courts, but when they do so, we must declare the law as we believe it to exist. If we can know any other motive than the simple wish to expound it, or if, when our convictions are clear, we should hesitate to declare them without reference to what party it may please or what offend, we should betray the solemn trusts which the people have committed to this Court and bring dishonor on the administration of justice.

Sixteen years later, the Court again proved its independence of the Executive when it restored to the heirs of General Lee the land taken by the United States Government for Arlington Cemetery, and which was then in the possession of military officers under the orders of the President of the United States. To the plea urged by the Attorney-General that the Court ought not to entertain jurisdiction of the suit against these Federal officers, Justice Miller, speaking for the Court, said: "No man in this country is so high that he is above the law. No officer of the law may set that law at defiance, with impunity. All the officers of the Government, from the highest to the lowest, are creatures of the law and are bound to obey it . . . Shall it be said . . . that the Courts cannot give a remedy when the citizen has been deprived of his property by force . . . without any process of law, and without any compensation, because the President has ordered it and his officers are in possession?"[1]

That the Justices of the Supreme Court have proved themselves independent of the political parties from whose ranks they were appointed has been seen from early days.

Thus, the Court over which John Marshall presided and which rendered the great series of decisions upholding the extended scope of National powers and the broad construction of the Constitution — in the cases of *McCulloch* v. *Maryland, Cohens* v. *Virginia, Gibbons* v. *Ogden, Brown* v. *Maryland,* and *Weston* v. *Charleston* — from the years 1819 to 1830, consisted of one Federalist appointed by John Adams, a Federalist President, and six Democrats appointed by Thomas Jefferson, James Madison, and James Monroe, Presidents who held narrower views of the construction of the Constitution.

The constitutionality of the Fugitive Slave Law of 1850, a law detested by Whigs, free soilers, and Republicans of the North, was upheld by Northern and Southern pro-slavery and anti-slavery Judges, alike, in the famous case of *In re Booth* in 1859.

After the Civil War, Republican Justices appointed by Republican Presidents joined with Democratic Justices appointed by Democratic Presidents, in rendering both the majority and the minority opinions in most of the great constitutional cases.

Chief Justice Chase, in the first *Legal Tender Case,*

[1] *United States* v. *Lee* (1882), 106 U. S. 196.

rendered an opinion holding unconstitutional laws which he himself as Secretary of the Treasury had favored and administered under President Lincoln, who appointed him upon the Court.

In the *Slaughterhouse Cases*, in 1873, presenting a question involving the political doctrines of the two political parties, and in which a decision the other way would have practically destroyed most of the rights of the States, a Democratic Judge and a Judge with Democratic leanings joined with three Republicans and against a Republican Chief Justice, two Republican Judges and one Democratic Judge. During Chief Justice Waite's term of office, eight Acts of Congress — all Republican legislation — were held invalid by a Court almost exclusively Republican.

In the *Insular Cases*, in 1900, when the Democratic party strongly supported the position that the Constitution followed the flag, a Democratic Judge joined with Republican Associates on the Bench to establish the contrary principle.

When the appointment of a Democratic Chief Justice, Edward D. White, was made by a Republican President, Taft, in 1910, it was pointed out in a prominent law review that during the preceding eighteen years of the Chief Justiceship of Melville W. Fuller (the Democrat whom White succeeded) there had only been one case involving a constitutional question on which all the Republican Judges had lined up on one side and all the Democratic Judges on the other.[1]

[1] *Chief Justice Fuller*, by Robert P. Reeder, *Amer. Law Reg.* (1911), LIX; see also address of Senator George F. Hoar before the Virginia Bar Association, *Virg. Law Reg.* (1899), IV.

Another proof that the Court has shown itself independent of politics is to be found in the striking fact that its history reveals instance after instance of the same Court being attacked for exactly opposite reasons by each of the two political parties. Thus, in 1819, the Democrats reviled Chief Justice Marshall's decision in favor of the hated Bank of the United States in *McCulloch* v. *Maryland*, as having "saddled a monster of iniquity upon us" and as having intentionally been rendered to prop up and save "this objectionable monopoly" — the Bank. Yet, within five years, these same Democrats were praising Marshall's opinion in *Gibbons* v. *Ogden* because it put an end to an even more objectionable monster — the great steamboat monopoly in New York. This was the first trust case in this country, and in 1824 (just as in 1904 in the *Northern Securities Case*) the Supreme Court demolished the trust.

From 1830 to 1833, the Court was condemned by President Jackson, because, as he claimed, in the *Florida Land Claim Cases*, it had surrendered to New York and foreign bankers and land speculators — the "big business" of those days. Yet, four years later, after its *Charles River Bridge Case* decision in 1837, the Court was equally attacked and condemned by the Whigs, as the destroyer of property and as the enemy of all investors in corporate stock. "The vested-rights class cry out bloody murder," said a Boston Democratic paper; and Chancellor James Kent wrote that the decision "injures the moral sense of the community and destroys the stability of contracts. . . . I have lost my confidence and hopes in the constitutional guardianship and

INDEPENDENCE OF THE COURT 269

protection of the Supreme Court." A leading Whig Review said that the decision "merits the severest animadversion that wounded justice and indignant patriotism can bestow."

Eleven years later, in 1848, when the Court upheld the right to take chartered rights by eminent domain, in *West River Bridge Co.* v. *Dix*, it was praised by the *Boston Post*, as having dealt "a great blow at monopoly" and "triumphantly sustained the republican doctrine that a corporation has no more right than individuals." But nine years later, in 1854, the same Court was assailed with the contrary cry that it was corporation-ridden, when, by its decision in the *Bank Tax Emption Cases*, it held an Ohio statute invalid. "An outrageous decision by the truly Federal Court," said a leading Ohio newspaper. "The sober mind may begin to wonder how this unrighteousness can possibly be imposed upon a community or a democratic form of Government."

In 1873, after the famous *Slaughterhouse Cases*, the Court was attacked as too conservative and as pro-monopoly. Yet within four years, after the Granger Law decisions — *Munn* v. *Illinois*, and other cases — it was equally attacked as too radical and anti-corporation, and, in the *Sinking Fund Cases* in 1879, as anti-railroad.

Labor attacked the Court in 1908, because of its decision in the *Danbury Hatters Case*, and claimed that this case and the *New York Bakers' Ten-Hour Law Case* (*Lochner* v. *New York*) proved that the Court favored the capitalist and the employer. And yet these cases were decided by a Court composed of practically the identical Judges who decided the *Northern Securities Company Case*, in 1904, in which a great capitalist holding company was dissolved, and in which the Court, through Judge Harlan, said:

> Disaster to business and widespread financial ruin, it has been intimated, will follow the execution of its provisions. Such predictions were made in all the cases heretofore arising under that Act. But they have not been verified.... But even if the Court shared the gloomy forebodings in which the defendants indulge it could not refuse to respect the action of the legislative branch of the government, if what it has done is within the limits of its constitutional power.... This Court has no function to supervise such legislation from the standpoint of wisdom or policy.

This, by the way, was a five to four decision *in support of the Federal statute*. The trust's opponents found no fault with such a close decision, when it went their way.

Within the past few years, radical papers like the *Nation* have been found assailing the Court for its alleged suppression of freedom of speech in the *Espionage Law Cases*, and yet praising it for protecting freedom of speech in the *Nebraska Foreign Language Teaching Case*.

In 1923, Labor attacked the Court for its *Minimum Wage Law* decision which held invalid a statute allowing a District of Columbia Board to fix wages; but Labor praised the same Court for holding invalid, in the same year, the Labor Court Act of Kansas, which also allowed a Board to fix wages and to establish compulsory arbitration.

It thus appears that those who have attacked the

INDEPENDENCE OF THE COURT 271

Court for a decision to-day have often been the very persons to praise it for another decision to-morrow. What better proof of the independence of our Judiciary could be asked?

When, therefore, radical changes in our Constitution affecting the functions of the Court are suggested, simply because some few decisions of the Court have displeased certain classes or sections of the community, when the American people are asked to amend their Constitution simply for the purpose of avoiding the effect of these few decisions, when it is proposed to allow Congress full scope to deprive the minority of their rights, when it is proposed to allow a minority of the Court to hold a statute void, when these remedies are proposed to cure a temporary evil which can at any time be cured by such Amendments as the Constitution already makes ample provision for, each American citizen should consider well whether the remedy would not be greater than the supposed ill. The Court with its present functions may not at all times satisfy every one; it may not effect what appears to every one to be justice. But the question for each citizen to ponder is: Will the Court be better able to do justice, if its powers are weakened? Is it wise, in order to gain a temporary advantage, to bring about a permanent loss of the Court's full ability to protect and to enforce the citizens' constitutional rights? Those were wise words which Alexander Hamilton uttered in *The Federalist*, in 1788: "No man can be sure that he may not be to-morrow the victim of a spirit of injustice, by which he may be a gainer to-day."

In 1808, John Randolph of Virginia, in a bitter

political debate on the Embargo Bill, excitedly exclaimed: "What are Constitutions themselves in the mighty concussions of parties?"[1] Eighty years later, a less noted politician, in less elegant language, asked: "What is the Constitution between friends?" It is the good fortune of the American people that there is one branch of the Government possessed with the power to answer: "The Constitution is to be upheld, regardless of parties or of friends, whenever Congress or the President shall overstep the bounds set by that instrument."

NOTE. For proof that the Courts of the States, prior to the adoption of the Federal Constitution (page 49, *supra*), were frequently holding State statutes invalid, as in contravention of the treaty between the United States and Great Britain, see letter of Jefferson as Secretary of State to George Hammond, the British Minister, May 29, 1792, *American State Papers, Foreign Relations*, I, 201, 208, 209. "Mr. Channing, the Attorney of the United States in that State (Rhode Island) (No. 19) speaking of an Act passed before the treaty says: ' This Act was considered by our Courts as annulled by the treaty of peace and subsequent to the ratification thereof, no proceedings have been had thereon.' The Governor of Connecticut in his letter (No. 18) says: 'The sixth article of the treaty was immediately observed, on receiving the same with the proclamation of Congress; the Courts of justice adopted it as a principle of law.' . . . In Pennsylvania, Mr. Lewis, Attorney for the United States, says in his letter (No. 60): 'The Judges have uniformly and without hesitation declared in favor of the treaty, on the ground of its being the supreme law of the land.' . . . In Maryland in the case of *Mildred* v. *Dorsey*, cited in your letter a law of the State, made during the war, had compelled those who owed debts to British subjects to pay them into the treasury of that State. This had been done by Dorsey before the date of the treaty; yet the Judges of the State General Court decided that the treaty not only repealed the law for the future, but for the past also, and decreed that the defendant should pay the money all over again. In Virginia, Mr. Monroe, one of the Senators of that State in Congress and a lawyer of eminence tells us (No. 52) that both Court and counsel there announced the opinion that the treaty would control any law of the State opposed to it. . . . In New York, Mr. Harrison, Attorney for the United States in that District, assures us (No. 45) that the Act of 1782 of that State relative to debts due to persons within the enemy's lines was immediately after the treaty, restrained by the Superior Courts of the State from operating on British creditors, and that he did not know a single instance to the contrary."

[1] *10th Cong., 2d Sess.*, Dec. 3, 1808, p. 675.

CHAPTER NINE

DECISIONS OF THE COURT HOLDING ACTS OF CONGRESS UNCONSTITUTIONAL

The fifty-three decisions of the Court holding Acts of Congress unconstitutional from 1789 to June, 1924, together with the exact citations of the statutes involved, and a brief summary of the grounds of the decisions are as follows.

1. *Marbury* v. *Madison* (1803, Feb. 24.), 1 Cranch 137.
    Act September 24, 1789, c. 20, last subsection of sec. 13; 1 Stat. 81.
    Section 13 (of the original Judiciary Act) authorized the Supreme Court to issue writs of mandamus "in cases warranted by the principles and usages of law, to any courts appointed or persons holding office, under the authority of the United States." On an original motion for a writ of mandamus to the Secretary of State to direct the delivery of a commission as justice of the peace in the District of Columbia, a rule to show cause why the writ should not issue was discharged on the ground that the provisions in Section 13 was unconstitutional, being an attempt to enlarge the original jurisdiction of the Supreme Court as prescribed in Article III, section 2, clause 2, of the Constitution.

2. *Scott* v. *Sandford* (1857, March 6), 19 How. 393.
    Act March 6, 1820, c. 22, sec. 8; 3 Stat. 545, 548.
    Section 8 contained a proviso (the Missouri Compromise) prohibiting the existence of slavery within the Louisiana Territory north of Missouri. One

question involved in the case was its effect on the status of a slave of residence within Wisconsin Territory. Six of the Justices declared the proviso unconstitutional (and therefore without effect to change Scott's status as a slave in Missouri), one did not pass on the question, and two (Justices Curtis and McLean) held it valid. Of the six who held it unconstitutional, four had already in their opinions decided the question of jurisdiction adversely to Scott, which was sufficient to dispose of the case.

The proviso was repealed by the Act of May 30, 1854, c. 59; 10 Stat. 289, about a month after the Dred Scott case was instituted in the United States Circuit Court.

3. *Gordon* v. *United States* (1865, March 10), 2 Wall. 561; 117 U. S. 697, Appendix.

Act March 3, 1863, c. 92; 12 Stat. 765.

An appeal from the Court of Claims, taken under section 5, which authorized appeals in cases involving over $3,000 was dismissed, without written opinion, for want of jurisdiction, since section 14 of the Act cited provided that no judgments of the Court of Claims should be paid until estimated for by the Secretary of the Treasury, and as explained in *United States* v. *Klein* (13 Wall. 128, 144): "This Court being of opinion that the provision (*i.e.*, sec. 14) for an estimate was inconsistent with the finality essential to judicial decisions, Congress repealed that provision in 1866, 14 Stat. 9. Since then, the Court of Claims has exercised all the functions of a court, and this Court has taken full jurisdiction on appeal."

Justices Miller and Field dissented.

4. *Ex parte Garland* (1867, Jan. 14), 4 Wall. 333.

Act January 24, 1865, c. 20; 13 Stat. 424.

The Act required taking of a specified test oath, by persons applying for admission to the bar of the

Supreme Court, and also by attorneys previously admitted, before doing further business. Garland had been admitted before passage of the Act. During the Civil War he served in the Confederate Congress (thereby becoming disqualified to take the oath). Subsequently he was pardoned by the President and applied for permission to practice without taking the test oath. It was held that he was entitled to do so; the Act being, as applied to one previously admitted, *ex post facto* and a bill of attainder and an interference with the pardoning power of the President and therefore unconstitutional.

Chief Justice Chase and Justices Miller, Swyane, and Davis dissented.

5. *Reichart* v. *Felps* (1868, March 16), 6 Wall. 160.
Act February 20, 1812, c. 22; 2 Stat. 677.

A grant of land was duly confirmed under authority of an Act of the Continental Congress of 1788, passed to carry out an agreement with the State of Virginia. It was held that the Act directing a revision of such claims, under which the land in question was again sold and patent issued, was invalid to affect the prior title.

No dissent.

6. *The Alicia* (1869, Jan. 25), 7 Wall. 571.
Act June 30, 1864, c. 174, sec. 13; 13 Stat. 306, 310.

Section 13 authorized the transfer to the Supreme Court of prize cases then pending in the Circuit Courts. This case was brought in the District Court for Southern District of Florida, and decree of condemnation entered. Appeal was then taken to the Circuit Court. On an order for transfer to the Supreme Court under section 13, it was held that the Supreme Court had no jurisdiction; that its jurisdiction in prize cases was, under the Constitution (Art. II, sec. 2), appellate only, and would not include a case of transfer.

No dissent.

7. *Hepburn* v. *Griswold* (1870, Feb. 7), 8 Wall. 603.
   Act of Feb. 25, 1862, c. 33, sec. 1; 12 Stat. 345:
   Act March 3, 1863, c. 73, sec. 3; 12 Stat. 709, 710.

   These sections provided, *inter alia*, that United States notes should be "a legal tender in payment of all debts, public and private, within the United States", with certain specified exceptions. The payee of a promissory note made before, but falling due after passage of the Act, refused tender of United States notes in payment. It was held that he was not obliged to accept such tender; that is, so far as the Act attempted to make the notes legal tender in payment of preëxisting debts, it was unconstitutional, as the power to make a credit currency legal tender is not expressly granted by the Constitution and cannot be upheld as a legitimate implied power under Article I, section 8; it constituted, in fact, an impairment of the obligation of contracts contrary to the spirit of the Constitution (the prohibition in Art. I, sec. 10, is limited to action by the States).

   The Court divided, five to three, there being a vacancy on the Court. The Court having been increased to nine by the resignation of Justice Grier and the appointment of Justices Bradley and Strong, the case was overruled in *Knox* v. *Lee* (12 Wall. 457), decided by a vote of five to four, Justices Field, Clifford, and Nelson, and Chief Justice Chase dissenting.

8. *United States* v. *DeWitt* (1870, Feb. 21), 9 Wall. 41.
   Act March 2, 1867, c. 169, sec. 29; 14 Stat. 471, 484.

   Section 29 (of an Internal Revenue Act) made it a misdemeanor for any person to "offer for sale — oil made from petroleum, for illuminating purposes inflammable at less temperature or fire test than 110° F." Dewitt was indicted under this section in the United States Circuit Court of Michigan. That Court certified the question of constitutionality to the Supreme Court. It was held that except within territory within the exclusive jurisdiction of Congress the Act could have no constitutional operation, being not an exercise of the taxing power or the power over interstate commerce, but an interference with trade within the separate States.

No dissent.

9. *The Justices* v. *Murray* (1870, March 14), 9 Wall. 274.

Act March 3, 1863, c. 81, sec. 5; 12 Stat. 755, 756.

Section 5 provided, *inter alia*, for removal to United States Circuit Courts, after final judgment, of cases brought in State Courts against Federal officers, the Circuit Court to try the facts and the law as though the case had been originally brought there. In an action of assault against a United States marshal, jury trial was had in a New York Court and judgment rendered for plaintiff. The Circuit Court awarded a mandamus for removal of the case under section 5. This judgment was reversed, on the ground that the provision in section 5 was unconstitutional under the Seventh Amendment: "No fact tried by a jury shall be otherwise reëxamined in any court of the United States than according to the common law;" removal not being common-law procedure.

No dissent.

10. *Collector* v. *Day* (1871, April 3), 11 Wall. 113.

Income Tax Acts — Act of June 30, 1864, c. 173, sec. 116; 13 Stat. 223, 281: Act March 3, 1865, c. 78; 13 Stat. 467, 479: Act July 13, 1866, c. 184, sec. 9; 14 Stat. 98, 137: Act March 2, 1867, c. 169, sec. 13; 14 Stat. 471, 477.

Suit by a Massachusetts Probate Judge to recover Federal income tax paid under protest. Judgment for the plaintiff was affirmed; that is, the tax was held unconstitutional in so far as it applied to the salary of the judicial officers of the States as being an interference with the reserved power of the States to maintain a judicial department.

Justice Bradley dissented.

11. *United States* v. *Klein* (1872, Jan. 29), 13 Wall. 128. Act July 12, 1870, c. 251; 16 Stat. 230, 235.

The Act carrying appropriations for the payment of judgments of the Court of Claims contained a proviso that no pardon or act done in pursuance of a pardon should be admissible to establish the standing of any claimant or his right to bring suit, etc., under the Abandoned and Captured Property Acts; and that acceptance by any suitor in the Court of Claims of a pardon which in terms declared that the person had taken part in the Rebellion, etc., should, unless protest of innocence were made at the time, be conclusive evidence of the guilt of the party, and on proof of such acceptance suit should be dismissed for want of jurisdiction. Klein, as administrator, brought suit to recover the value of certain cotton owned by one Wilson and abandoned to the United States. Wilson had subsequently availed himself of the amnesty proclaimed by the President on December 8, 1863, to any who, having taken part in the Rebellion, should take a prescribed oath to uphold the Constitution. The Court of Claims gave judgment for the plaintiff in May, 1869, before passage of the Act of 1870. This judgment was affirmed, on the ground that the proviso was unconstitutional as an attempt to prescribe rules for the decision of cases and as an interference with the pardoning power of the President.

Justices Miller and Bradley, though dissenting from the judgment, held the proviso unconstitutional as an interference with the pardoning power.

DECISIONS OF THE COURT 279

12. *United States* v. *Railroad Co.* (1873, April 7), 17 Wall. 322.

    Internal Revenue Act June 30, 1864, c. 173, sec. 112; 13 Stat. 233, 284, as amended by Act July 13, 1866; c. 184, sec. 7; 14 Stat. 98, 138.

    Section 122 laid a tax of 5 per cent on the interest on indebtedness of railroads, etc., and authorized the railroads to deduct the tax from their interest payments. The city of Baltimore, with the consent of the State, loaned money to the Baltimore & Ohio, taking a mortgage. Upon the refusal of the Baltimore & Ohio to pay the tax, the United States brought suit. It was held that such tax was in effect a tax on the creditor and could not constitutionally be collected in this case, since the city was a part of the sovereign authority of the State.

    Justices Clifford and Miller dissented.

13. *United States* v. *Reese* (1876, March 27), 92 U. S. 214. Act May 31, 1870, c. 114, sec. 3, 4; 16 Stat. 140.

    Section 3 laid a penalty on State election officers, etc., for refusal to receive the vote of "any citizen" who had duly offered to qualify as a voter, and section 3 penalized the obstruction of "any citizen" from qualifying as a voter or from voting. On an indictment against two inspectors of a municipal election in Kentucky for refusal to receive the vote of a negro, the question was limited to whether the Act was appropriate legislation for the enforcement of the Fifteenth Amendment. It was held that a judgment for the defendant, admitting the facts in the case, was correct; that is, the power of Congress to legislate with respect to State elections is, by the Fifteenth Amendment, limited to prevent denial of the right to vote on account of color, etc.; and sections 3 and 4 above are in language broad enough to cover cases outside of this power, and therefore unconstitutional.

These sections, as included in Revised Statutes, sections 2007–2009, 5506, were repealed by Act of Feb. 8, 1894, c. 25; 28 Stat. 36.

Of the two dissenting Justices, Justice Hunt alone expressly passed on the question and held the provision constitutional.

14. *United States* v. *Fox* (1878, Jan. 7), 95 U. S. 670.
R. S. sec. 5132, sub-sec. 9; Act March 2, 1867, c. 176, sec. 44; 14 Stat. 517, 539.

The Bankruptcy Law provided that any person respecting whom bankruptcy proceedings were commenced, who, within three months before their commencement, "under the false color and pretense of carrying on business and dealing in the ordinary course of trade, obtains on credit from any person any goods or chattels with intent to defraud" should be punishable by imprisonment. On an indictment under this section, the question of constitutionality was certified to the Supreme Court. It was held that subdivision 9 was unconstitutional. It was an attempt to render an act, which at the time of commission did not concern the United States, but the State only, an offense against the United States by reason of a subsequent independent act; and, not being limited to acts done in anticipation of bankruptcy was not supportable as incidental to the execution of the bankruptcy power of Congress.

No dissent.

The Bankruptcy Law was repealed entirely by Act of June 7, 1878, c. 160; 20 Stat. 99.

15. *Trade Mark Cases* (1879, Nov. 17), 100 U. S. 82.
R. S. sec. 4937–4947, Act July 8, 1870, c. 230, sec. 77; 16 Stat. 198, 210; Act August 14, 1876, c. 274; 19 Stat. 141.

The R. S. sections were trade-mark regulations, providing that "any person — in the United States

— entitled to the exclusive use of any lawful trademark, or who intend to adopt and use any trademark for exclusive use within the United States, may obtain protection for such lawful trade-mark by complying with the following requirements." The Act of 1876 made fraud, etc., in connection with such trade-marks a criminal offense. On indictment under the latter Act, the question of constitutionality was certified to the Supreme Court which held: the R. S. sections could not be upheld under the power of Congress to regulate interstate commerce, and were unconstitutional; and the later Act fell with them.

No dissent.

In consequence of this decision, Congress passed a new statute, Act of March 3, 1881, c. 138; 21 Stat. 502, confined to foreign commerce which was upheld by the Court in *A. Leschen & Sons Rope Co. v. Broderick Co.* (1906), 201 U. S. 166; *Thaddeus Davies Co. v. Davids* (1914), 233 U. S. 461.

16. *United States v. Harris* (1883, Jan. 15), 106 U. S. 629.

R. S. sec. 5519, Act April 20, 1871, c. 22, sec. 2; 17 Stat. 13, 14.

R. S. 5519 provided a punishment in case of two or more persons in any State or Territory conspiring to deprive "any person . . . of the equal protection of the laws. . . ." The indictment was brought in Tennessee. On demurrer the question of constitutionality was certified to the Supreme Court, which held that the section being directed against individuals, without reference to State action, is not supported by either the Thirteenth, Fourteenth, or Fifteenth Amendments or Article IV, Section 2, of the Constitution.

Justice Harlan dissented on other than constitutional grounds.

17. *Civil Rights Cases* (1883, Oct. 15), 109 U. S. 3.
Act March 1, 1875, c. 114, sec. 1, 2; 18 Stat. 335, 336.

These sections declared all persons within the jurisdiction of the United States entitled to equal enjoyment of facilities of inns, theaters, etc., subject to conditions applicable alike to citizens, of every race and color, with a penalty for violation. Five cases brought under this Act by indictments in Tennessee, Georgia, New York, Kansas, and Missouri, were decided together on the question of constitutionality. Held, that both sections were unconstitutional so far as their operation in the States was concerned, neither the Fourteenth nor the Thirteenth Amendment supporting them, the Fourteenth applying only to State action and the Thirteenth to "slavery or involuntary servitude."

Justice Harlan dissented.

18. *Boyd* v. *United States* (1886), 116 U. S. 616.
Act June 22, 1874, c. 391, sec. 5; 18 Stat. 187.

Section 5 authorized the Court, in proceedings other than criminal arising under the revenue laws, to require production of papers in possession of defendant or claimant, the allegations expected to be proved thereby to be taken as conceded on refusal to make such production. In an action for forfeiture of certain goods for fraud in connection with customs invoices, information was secured from the defendant under this section. Judgment for the United States was reversed by the Supreme Court on the ground that the action for forfeiture was essentially a criminal proceeding, and therefore section 5, as applied to such a case, was unconstitutional under the Fourth and Fifth Amendments (unreasonable search and seizure, and witness against oneself in a criminal case).

Chief Justice Waite and Justice Miller held it unconstitutional under the Fifth Amendment only.

19. *Baldwin* v. *Franks* (1887, Mar. 7), 120 U. S. 678.
R. S. 5519 (see *United States* v. *Harris*).
R. S. 5519 was held invalid as a ground for detaining certain individuals for conspiring to deprive certain Chinese aliens of the equal protection of the laws. Its validity within a Territory was not considered.
Justice Harlan dissented.

20. *Callan* v. *Wilson* (1888, May 14), 127 U. S. 540.
Revised Statutes of District of Columbia, sec. 1064.
Section 1064 dispensed with jury trial in the Police Court of the District of Columbia. Section 773 provided for jury trial in the Supreme Court of the District on appeals from the Police Court. Callan was tried in the Police Court without a jury on a charge of conspiracy and sentenced to pay a fine. On refusal to pay, he was arrested, and the Supreme Court of the District refused to release him on habeas corpus. It was held that he be released — that is, in so far as it covered offenses triable at common law by a jury, section 1064 was unconstitutional under Article III, section 2, requiring that "the trial of all crimes . . . shall be by jury"; and it was not sufficient that jury trial was provided for on appeals.
No dissent.

21. *Counselman* v. *Hitchcock* (1892, Jan. 11), 142 U. S. 547.
R. S. sec. 860, Act Feb. 25, 1868, c. 13, sec. 1; 15 Stat. 37.
Section 860 provided that no evidence, etc., obtained from a party by means of a judicial proceeding should in any manner be used against him in any Court of the United States in any criminal proceeding. During a grand jury investigation of certain railroads under the Interstate Commerce Act, Counselman was called as a witness and refused to answer certain questions on the ground

that they might tend to criminate him. He was adjudged in contempt and arrested. The Circuit Court dismissed a writ of habeas corpus on the ground that section 860 would have afforded him all the protection guaranteed by the Constitution. It was held that he should be discharged from custody; section 860, which only provided that the evidence obtained shall not be used against the party, was not a complete substitute for the prohibition of the Fifth Amendment that no person "shall be compelled in any criminal case to be a witness against himself."

No dissent.

Section 860 was repealed by Act of May 7, 1910, c. 216; 36 Stat. 352.

22. *Monongahela Navigation Co.* v. *United States* (1893, March 29), 148 U. S. 312.

Act August 11, 1888, c. 860; 25 Stat. 400, 411.

A clause of the River and Harbor Appropriation Act provided that, in condemnation proceedings to acquire a certain lock and dam, the franchise of the company to collect tolls should not be considered. Compensation having been fixed and adjudged on this basis, the company appealed to the Supreme Court. It was held that judgment be reversed, as the determination of "just compensation" required by the Fifth Amendment is not a legislative but a judicial matter, and therefore the declaration in the statute was not binding on the Court.

Justices Shiras and Jackson took no part in the decision.

23. *Pollock* v. *Farmers' Loan and Trust Co.* (1895, April 8), 157 U. S. 429.

Act August 27, 1894, c. 349, sec. 27–37; 28 Stat. 509, 553.

Pollock v. *Farmers' Loan and Trust Co.* (1895, May 20), 158 U. S. 601.

Act August 27, 1894, c. 349, sec. 27–37; 28 Stat. 509, 553.

These sections laid a 2 per cent tax on incomes over $4,000, "derived from any kind of property, rents, interest, dividends, or salaries, or from any profession, trade, employment, or vocation, or from any other source whatever"; and made regulations for returns, etc. Suit was brought by a stockholder of a New York trust company to restrain the company from making returns and paying the taxes required on its income from real estate and from certain New York City bounds. On the first hearing, it was held that such taxes were invalid (the tax on rent as being a direct tax not apportioned in compliance with Art. 1, sec. 2, and the tax on bonds as an interference with State functions); and a restraining decree was ordered to be entered.

Justices White and Harlan dissented. The Justices — only eight being present — being equally divided in opinion as to the validity of the remaining provisions nothing was decided as to those provisions. On the rehearing the decision went further and held that taxes on personal property or the income therefrom also were direct taxes and that sections 27–33 entire were invalid.

Justices Harlan, Brown, Jackson, and White dissented.

24. *Wong Wing* v. *United States* (1896, May 18), 163 U. S. 228.

Act May 5, 1892, c. 60, sec. 4; 27 Stat. 25.

Section 4 provided that Chinese persons "convicted and adjudged to be not lawfully entitled to be or remain in the United States shall be imprisoned at hard labor for a period of not exceeding one year and thereafter removed from the United States, as hereinbefore provided." An Act of Sept. 13, 1888 (25 Stat. 479) extended by this

Act, authorized deportation of Chinese after summary hearing before any United States Judge or Commissioner. Wong Wing was sentenced by a Commissioner to serve 60 days and be then deported. Habeas corpus writ was dismissed. On appeal, this judgment was reversed; section 4 was held unconstitutional, in so far as it authorized imprisonment at hard labor, being a violation of the Fifth and Sixth Amendments requiring indictment by grand jury in cases of infamous crimes and trial by jury in all criminal prosecutions.

Justice Brewer took no part in the decision.

25. *Kirby* v. *United States* (1899, April 11), 174 U. S. 47.
Act March 3, 1875, c. 144; 18 Stat. 479.

Section 2 punished embezzlement from the United States, or receipt of stolen property with knowledge, and made a judgment against the embezzler conclusive evidence of the theft or embezzlement in a prosecution for receiving with knowledge. It was held that admission of such a judgment was error and the clause authorizing it unconstitutional under the Sixth Amendment which entitles an accused person to be confronted with the witnesses against him.

Justices Brown and McKenna dissented; Justice Brewer did not sit. The entire Act was repealed by the Criminal Code Act of March 4, 1909, c. 321, sec. 341; 35 Stat. 1088, 1155.

26. *Fairbank* v. *United States* (1901, April 15), 181 U. S. 283.
Act June 13, 1898, c. 448, sec. 25; 30 Stat. 448, 459, 462.

The Act laid stamp taxes "for and in respect of the several bonds . . . and other documents . . . mentioned in Schedule A of this Act, or for or in respect of the vellum, parchment, or paper upon which such instruments . . . shall be written. . . ." Among the taxes was one of 10 cents on bills of lading for goods destined for export. The Act further required railroad companies to issue bills of lading. Fairbank was convicted of issuing a bill of lading without the required stamp. On review of the constitutional question, it was held that the judgment be reversed, that the tax, so far as it is a tax on export bills of lading, was in effect a tax on the exports, and therefore repugnant to Article I, section 9, prohibiting Congress from laying a tax on articles exported from any State.

Justices Harlan, Gray, White, and McKenna dissented.

27. *James* v. *Bowman* (1903, May 4), 190 U. S. 127.

R. S. sec. 5507; Act May 31, 1870, c. 114, sec. 5; 16 Stat. 146, 147.

This section provided for the punishment of "every person who prevents, or intimidates another from exercising, the right of suffrage to whom that right is guaranteed by the Fifteenth Amendment to the Constitution. . . ." Bowman was indicted for bribing certain Negroes to refrain from voting at an election for Representatives in Congress. A writ of habeas corpus was granted by the District Court. It was held that this action was correct. R. S. 5507, upon which the indictment was founded, was unconstitutional, not being supported by the Fifteenth Amendment, which is a restriction on State action only.

R. S. 5507 was repealed by the Criminal Code Act of March 4, 1909, c. 321, sec. 341; 35 Stat. 1088, 1155.

Justices Harlan and Brown dissented; Justice McKenna did not sit.

28. *Matter of Heff* (1905, April 10), 197 U. S. 488.

Act January 30, 1897, c. 109; 29 Stat. 506.

The Act made it unlawful to give or sell, etc., intoxicating liquor to any Indian to whom allotment of land had been made while title was held in trust by the United States, or to any Indian ward of the Government, etc. Petitioner was convicted and imprisoned under this statute for selling liquor to an Indian allottee who had not yet received his final patent in fee. He applied for writ of habeas corpus. It was held that he be discharged; that so far as it applied to Indian allottees, the Act was unconstitutional. By the General Allotment Act of Feb. 8, 1887, c. 119; 24 Stat. 388, every Indian "to whom allotments shall have been made under the provisions of this Act is hereby declared to be a citizen of the United States, and is entitled to all the rights, privileges, and immunities of such citizens." . . . The Indian in this case, being an allottee, was a citizen and the provisions of the Act, being mere police regulations, had no constitutional foundation as applied to citizens.

Justice Harlan dissented.

The decision in this case was reversed and the Act was held constitutional in *United States* v. *Nice* (1916), 241 U. S. 591.

29. *Rasmussen* v. *United States* (1905, April 10), 197 U. S. 516.

Act June 6, 1900, c. 786, sec. 171; 31 Stat. 321, 358.

Section 171 of the Alaska Code provided, in part, that in trials for misdemeanors six persons should constitute a legal jury. Rasmussen being convicted of an offense, punishable by fine or imprisonment for from three months to one year, by such a jury, brought the question of constitutionality to the Supreme Court for review, and it was held that a new trial be granted. Alaska, as shown by the treaty of acquisition and by subsequent legislation, was incorporated into the United States, and therefore the Constitution applied; and under the Sixth Amendment all persons are entitled to a common-law jury in all criminal prosecutions.

No dissent.

30. *Hodges v. United States* (1906, May 28), 203 U. S. 1.
R. S. sec. 1977; Act May 31, 1870, c. 114, sec. 16; 16 Stat. 140, 144.

R. S. 1977 provided that "all persons within the jurisdiction of the United States shall have the same right in every State and Territory to make and enforce contracts . . . as is enjoyed by white citizens." R. S. 5508 makes punishable a conspiracy to injure any citizen in the exercise of rights secured to him by the Constitution and laws of the United States. This case was an indictment against Hodges and others for preventing, by threats and intimidations, certain Negroes from carrying out their contracts of labor, on account of their race and color. The facts were admitted, and the defendants found guilty and sentenced. It was held that the case should have been dismissed for want of jurisdiction; R. S. 1977, which in terms applied to all citizens and purports to guarantee the right of contract, is not supported by the Thirteenth Amendment, interference with the right of contract not being "slavery or involuntary servitude."

Justices Harlan and Day dissented.

31. *The Employers' Liability Cases, Howard v. Illinois Central R. R.* (1908, Jan. 6), 207 U. S. 463.
Act June 11, 1906, c. 3073; 34 Stat. 232.

The Act made all interstate carriers liable to their employees for injuries resulting from negligence of the carriers' agents, officers, etc., or from insufficiency of roadbed, equipment, etc. Two damage suits brought under this Act were dismissed on demurrer and the Act was held unconstitutional, because although within the power of Congress in respect to employees of interstate carriers actually engaged in interstate commerce, it by its terms also applied to employees not so engaged, and as to them was a police regulation not warranted by the Constitution.

Justices Moody, Harlan, McKenna, and Holmes dissented; one ground being that the Act could be read as applying to interstate carriers while engaged in interstate traffic only.

A later Act of April 22, 1908, c. 149; 35 Stat. 65 confined to interstate commerce was held constitutional in *Mondou* v. *N. Y. N. H. & H. R. R.* (1912), 223 U. S. 1.

32. *Adair* v. *United States* (1908, Jan. 27), 208 U. S. 161, Act June 1, 1898, c. 370, sec. 10; 30 Stat. 424, 428.

The Act made it a misdemeanor for any employer subject to the Act — *i.e.*, interstate carriers — to discriminate in certain ways against members of labor organization; *inter alia*, to threaten an employee with loss of employment because of membership in a labor organization. Adair was indicted on a charge of discriminating against one Coppage by discharging him solely because of his membership in a labor union. Judgment in the lower Court was on demurrer. This was reversed, the part of the section on which the indictment was founded being held to be a violation of the Fifth Amendment, as constituting an abridgment of the right of contract and a deprivation of liberty and property.

Justices Holmes and McKenna dissented; Justice Moody took no part in the decision.

The entire Act was repealed by the Act of July 15, 1913, c. 6, sec. 11; 38 Stat. 108.

33. *Keller* v. *United States* (1909, April 5), 213 U. S. 138. Act February 20, 1907, c. 134, sec. 3; 34 Stat. 898, 899.

The section made it a felony for any person to "harbor in any house or other place, for the purpose of prostitution, or for any other immoral purpose, any alien woman or girl, within three years after she shall have entered the United States." Two convictions under this provision were reversed and the indictments quashed on the ground that the Act could not be sustained as incidental to the power of Congress to regulate immigration or by any police power.

Justices Holmes, Harlan, and Moody dissented.

Most of the existing immigration laws, including the section above, were repealed by Act of Feb. 5, 1917, c. 29, sec. 38; 39 Stat. 897.

34. *United States* v. *Evans* (1909, April 19), 213 U. S. 297. Code D. C. sec. 935; 31 Stat. 1345, c. 854.

Section 935 of the District of Columbia Code authorized the Government to bring appeals in criminal prosecutions, but no verdict could be set aside for error found to have occurred during the trial. Evans was tried for murder and found not guilty. The United States appealed to the Court of Appeals, which dismissed the appeal for want of jurisdiction. On certiorari to the Supreme Court, the writ was quashed; *i.e.*, the Act was construed as not applicable in case a jury had given verdict for defendant — the determination of such an appeal not being an exercise of judicial power.

No dissent.

35. *Muskrat* v. *United States* (1011, Jan. 23), 219 U. S. 346. Act March 1, 1907; c. 2285; 34 Stat. 1015, 1028.

The Indian Appropriation Act for 1908 authorized certain Indians to bring suit in the Court of Claims to test the validity of Acts of Congress passed since July 1, 1902, increasing the restrictions on alienation of Cherokee allotments. Right of appeal to the Supreme Court was given. The United States was to be made a party defendant and the Attorney-General to defend the suits, expenses to be paid from the Treasury.

Two separate suits were brought, and the Court of claims in each case sustained the Acts of Congress questioned. On appeal, it was held that these judgments be reversed and the suits dismissed for want of jurisdiction. The Act was an attempt, in guise of judicial proceedings, to obtain from the Court advance opinions as to the validity of certain legislation, whereas under the Constitution, Article III, section 2, the judicial power extends only to "cases" arising under the laws, etc.

No dissent.

36. *Coyle* v. *Oklahoma* (1911, May 29), 221 U. S. 559.

Act June 16, 1906, c. 3355; 34 Stat. 267.

This case affirmed the validity of an Oklahoma statute of December 29, 1910, providing for the immediate removal of the State capital from Guthrie to Oklahoma City. This was contrary to the Enabling Act above cited, which prohibited such removal until 1913. It was held that the power to admit new States, under Article IV, Section 3, did not support a provision which interfered with strictly internal affairs and placed a State, when admitted, on an inequality with other States.

Justices McKenna and Holmes dissented.

37. *Butts* v. *Merchants Trans. Co.* (1913, June 16), 230 U. S. 126.

Act March 1, 1875, c. 114, sec. 1, 2; 18 Stat. 335, 336.

The constitutionality of the Civil Rights Act of March 1, 1875, in its operation outside the States was considered, and it was held that, since it was impossible to separate the provisions which were constitutional (*i.e.*, the application of the act within Territories, etc.) without altering the expressed intent of Congress, the Act was unconstitutional *in toto*.

No dissent.

38. *Choate* v. *Trapp* (1912, May 13), 224 U. S. 665.

Act March 27, 1908, c. 199, sec. 4; 35 Stat. 312, 313.

By the Atoka Agreement of 1898 (30 Stat. 507) with the Choctaw and Chickasaw Indians it was provided that lands allotted thereunder should be non-taxable "while the title remains in the original allottee." The Act of 1908 above cited removed the restriction on alienation contained in the Act of 1898 and in section 4 provided that such land should be "subject to taxation as though it were the property of other persons than allottees." The State of Oklahoma brought suit for taxes on certain of these lands. The Supreme Court of the State held that the State was no party to any contract with the Indians, and that in any case the tax exemption was a gratuity which the United States could withdraw at will. This was reversed on the ground that the exemption constituted a vested right which could not, under the Fifth Amendment, be abrogated by statute, *i.e.*, section 4 is invalid to affect the rights of original allottees.

No dissent.

39. *United States* v. *Hvoslef* (1915, Mar. 22), 237 U. S. 1.
    Act June 13, 1898, c. 448, sec. 25; 30 Stat. 448, 460.

    This case involved a tax on charter parties. Such tax was held, in effect, a tax on the goods carried, and therefore unconstitutional as applied to exports.

    Justice McReynolds took no part in the decision.

40. *Thamoo and Mersey Ins. Co.* v. *United States* (1915, April 5), 237 U. S. 19.
    Act June 13, 1898, c. 448, sec. 25; 30 Stat. 448, 461.

    It was held that marine insurance is so essential to export trade that a tax on marine insurance policies is a tax on exports and unconstitutional.

    Justice McReynolds took no part in the decision.

41. *Hammer* v. *Dagenhart* (1918, June 3), 247 U. S. 251.
    Act September 1, 1916, c. 432; 39 Stat. 675, 676.

    The Act prohibited interstate shipment of the products of factories, etc., "in which within 30 days prior to the removal of such products therefrom children under the age of 14 years have been employed or permitted to work. . . ." In a suit to enjoin the enforcement of the Act, the District Court of the Western District of North Carolina held the Act unconstitutional. On appeal, this judgment was affirmed on the ground that the natural, reasonable effect of the law was an interference with the control by the States over industry within their limits, and thus exceeded the interstate commerce power of Congress.

Justices Holmes, McKenna, Brandeis, and Clarke dissented.

42. *Eisner* v. *Macomber* (1920, March 8), 252 U. S. 189. Act September 8, 1916, c. 463; 39 Stat. 756.

The Revenue Act of 1916, laying income taxes, included in net income stock dividends made out of profits accrued since 1913, "which stock dividend shall be considered income to the amount of its cash value." This action was brought to recover amount of such tax paid under protest. Judgment for taxpayer affirmed; *i.e.*, Congress was held without power under the Sixteenth Amendment to extend the definition of income and a tax on stock dividends being a tax on property and not on income was a direct tax, and hence the Act in question was invalid under the provision of the Constitution, Article I, sections 2, 9, requiring apportionment of direct taxes.

Justices Holmes, Day, Brandeis, and Clarke dissented on the ground that the Sixteenth Amendment was intended to cover everything that could fairly be regarded as income.

The Income Tax of 1916 was repealed by Act of Feb. 24, 1919, c. 18, sec. 1400; 40 Stat. 1057, 1149.

43. *Knickerbocker Ice Co.* v. *Stewart* (1920, May 17), 253 U. S. 149.

Act October 6, 1917, c. 97; 40 Stat. 395.

The Act amended the Judicial Code relating to

admiralty jurisdiction by "saving to claimants the rights and remedies under the workmen's compensation law of any State." An employee of the ice company while engaged in maritime work was drowned. His widow claimed and recovered damages under the New York workmen's compensation law. On appeal this judgment was reversed; *i.e.*, the New York law was inapplicable to employees in maritime work, notwithstanding the saving clause cited. The Constitution adopted and established approved rules of maritime law, and (by Art. I, sec. 8) granted power to Congress to legislate. This power cannot be delegated, and the saving clause, being an attempt to permit the application of State workmen's compensation laws to injuries within the maritime jurisdiction, was held unconstitutional.

Justices Holmes, Pitney, Brandeis, and Clarke dissented.

44. *Evans* v. *Gore* (1920, June 1), 253 U. S. 245.
Act February 24, 1919, c. 18, sec. 213; 40 Stat. 1057, 1065.

The section included in the term "gross income" under the income tax the salaries of Judges of United States Courts. A District Judge paid under protest an income tax computed on his official salary and brought suit to recover it. It was held that he should recover; *i.e.*, the section, so far as it attempted to impose an income tax on the salaries of United States Judges, was unconstitutional. Article III, section 1, of the Constitution, declares that the compensation of Judges shall not be diminished during their continuance in office, and taxing official income amounts to such diminution.

Justices Holmes and Brandeis dissented, on the ground that the constitutional prohibition was not intended to exempt Judges from the ordinary duties of citizenship.

45. *United States* v. *L. Cohen Grocery Co.* (1921, February 28), 255 U. S. 81.

Act August 10, 1917, c. 53, sec. 4; 40 Stat. 276; amended by Act October 22, 1919, c. 80, sec. 2; 41 Stat. 297.

The Act provided in part "that it is hereby made unlawful for any person willfully . . . to make any unjust or unreasonable rate or charge in handling or dealing in or with any necessaries . . ." followed by a penalty. Defendant was indicted, charged with making an unjust and unreasonable rate and charge in handling and dealing in a certain necessary, specifically alleging sale of sugar at $10.07 for 50 pounds and $19.50 for 100 pounds. Demurrer was entered on the ground that the section was so vague that it was unconstitutional. The indictment was quashed, and this judgment was affirmed; *i.e.*, the clause of the section penalizing the making of an "unjust or unreasonable rate or charge" was held unconstitutional under the Sixth Amendment; "the accused . . . shall be informed of the nature and cause of the accusation. . . ."

Justices Pitney and Brandeis concurred in result on the ground that the case did not fall within the clause at all; and therefore the question of constitutionality should not be considered. Justice Day took no part in the decision.

Several cases involving this same provision of section 4 were decided on the strength of the Cohen case, on the same day, as follows: *Tedrow* v. *Lewis & Son Co.*, 255 U. S. 98; *Kennington* v. *Palmer*, 255 U. S. 100; *Kinnane* v. *Detroit Creamery Co.*, 255 U. S. 106; *Oglesby Grocery Co.* v. *United States*, 255 U. S. 108.

In each of these cases Justices Pitney and Brandeis concurred in result only, and Justice Day took no part, as stated above.

DECISIONS OF THE COURT

See also *Weeds (Inc.)* v. *United States*, 255 U. S. 109 (Feb. 28, 1921). This case involved the constitutionality of the clause of section 4 penalizing conspiracy to exact excessive prices for any necessaries. It was held that this clause was unconstitutional, for the same reason, *i.e.*, vagueness as to standard of guilt.

As in the previous cases, Justices Pitney and Brandeis concurred in result only, and Justice Day took no part in the decision.

46. *Newberry* v. *United States* (1921, May 2), 256 U. S. 232.
Act June 25, 1910, c. 392; 36 Stat. 822; amended by Act August 19, 1911, c. 33; 37 Stat. 25.

Section 8, added to the Corrupt Practices Act, limited expenditures by candidates for United States Senator according to the laws of the States, with a maximum of $10,000. A conviction for excessive expenditures at the primary election of 1918 in Michigan was reversed on the ground that the power of Congress over election is drawn solely from Article I, section 4, and that "manner of holding elections" could not be stretched to cover regulation of primaries, popular election of Senators not being provided for until the Seventeenth Amendment in 1913.

Chief Justice White and Justices Pitney, Brandeis, and Clarke dissented on the constitutional question; Justice McKenna reserved judgment as to the power of Congress under the Seventeenth Amendment.

47. *United States* v. *Moreland* (1922, April 17), 258 U. S. 433.
Act March 23, 1906, c. 1131; 34 Stat. 86.

By Act of March 23, 1906, desertion of wife or child was made a misdemeanor in the District of Columbia; by Act of March 19, 1906, c. 960, sec. 13; 34 Stat. 73, a Juvenile Court was established, prosecutions therein to be on information. By the

Act of June 18, 1912, c. 171, sec. 8; 37 Stat. 174, the Juvenile Court was given concurrent jurisdiction of prosecutions for desertion. Moreland was prosecuted upon information and sentenced to six months in the workhouse. Judgment of the Court of Appeals dismissing the complaint was affirmed. It was held that the punishment prescribed was infamous, and therefore prosecution must, under the Fifth Amendment, be on indictment.

Chief Justice Taft and Justices Holmes and Brandeis dissented. Justice Clarke did not sit.

48. *Bailey* v. *Drexel Furniture Co.* (1922, May 15), 259 U. S. 20.

Act February 24, 1919, c. 18, sec. 1200, *et seq.*; 40 Stat. 1057, 1138.

The Act laid a tax of ten per cent on the net profits of any person, etc., operating mines, factories, etc., in which children under 14 years of age were permitted to work, or children between 14 and 16 permitted to work more than eight hours a day. The furniture company paid the tax under protest. Judgment of the District Court in favor of the company was affirmed; *i.e.*, the whole Child Labor Tax Act was held unconstitutional, on the ground that, on its face, it was apparent that it was a penalty rather than a tax and an attempt to interfere with powers reserved to the States under the Tenth Amendment.

Justice Clarke dissented.

49. *Hill* v. *Wallace* (1922, May 15), 259 U. S. 44.

Act August 24, 1921, c. 86; 42 Stat. 187.

The essential feature of the Act was a tax (sec. 4) of 20 cents a bushel on grain involved in contracts of sale for future delivery, except when made through designated Board of Trade, etc. Most of the Act, which comprised 13 sections, made regulations relating to such Boards of Trade. This was a suit by a member of the Chicago Board of Trade to enjoin enforcement of the Act, or compliance with it, by officials of the Board. The District Court dismissed the suit for want of equity. This decree was reversed, with directions to grant the relief asked. The tax was held invalid on the reasoning of the first Child Labor Case. It was held not to be sustainable as an exercise of the commerce power of Congress, not being limited to or leading to obstructions of *interstate* commerce.

Justice Brandeis concurred in holding the Act unconstitutional.

Congress, by Act of Sept. 21, 1922, c. 369; 42 Stat. 998, enacted legislation on the same subject which was held constitutional by the Court in *Board of Trade* v. *Olsen* (1923), 262 U. S. 1.

50. *Lipke* v. *Lederer* (1922, June 5), 259 U. S. 557.

Act Oct. 2, 1919, c. 80, sec. 2; 41 Stat. 277, 298.
Act Oct. 28, 1919, c. 8, sec. 35; 41 Stat. 305, 317.

The section provided in part "upon evidence of such illegal manufacture or sale a tax shall be assessed against, and collected from the person in double the amount now provided by law, with an additional penalty of $500 on retail dealers." Acting under this sanction, the collector of Philadelphia assessed a tax against Lipke and threatened distraint. Lipke sought an injunction, but his bill was dismissed. This decree was reversed in the Supreme Court on the ground that the "tax" laid by section 35 was in fact a penalty, imposed without provision for a hearing as required by the Due Process Clause of the Fifth Amendment.

Justices Brandeis and Pitney dissented without expressing an opinion on the constitutionality of the section.

51. *Adkins* v. *Children's Hospital* (1923, April 9), 261 U. S. 525.

Act September 19, 1918, c. 174; 40 Stat. 960.

The District of Columbia minimum wage law

established a wage board with authority, under regulations to fix standards of minimum wages in any occupation for women, adequate to supply the necessary cost of living to such workers, to maintain them in good health, and to protect their morals and also to determine minimum wages for minors and what wages are unreasonably low. The cases involved only the minimum wage for women. One was brought by an employer, the other by an employee, to enjoin enforcement of the Act. Injunctions issued by the lower Court were confirmed, the Act being held unconstitutional at an interference with the right of freedom of contract guaranteed by the Due Process Clause of the Fifth Amendment.

Chief Justice Taft and Justices Sanford and Holmes dissented; Justice Brandeis took no part in the decision.

52. *Keller* v. *Potomac Electric Power Co.* (1923, April 9), 261 U. S. 428.

Act March 4, 1913, c. 150, sec. 8, par. 64; 37 Stat. 938, 974.

An Act of Congress affecting the District of Columbia vested in the District Supreme Court, power to revise proceedings of the District Public Utilities Commission, with a right to parties to appeal to the Court of Appeals and thence to the Supreme Court of the United States. It was held that this portion of the Act was invalid, as such legislative or administrative jurisdiction could not be conferred by Congress on the Supreme Court of the United States either directly or by appeal.

53. *Washington* v. *Dawson & Co.* (1924, Feb. 25), 264 U. S. 219.

Act June 10, 1922, c. 216; 42 Stat. 634.

It was held that Congress has no power to permit application of the Workmen's Compensation laws

DECISIONS OF THE COURT 301

of the several States to injuries within the admiralty and maritime jurisdiction.

Note. In some lists of cases holding Acts of Congress unconstitutional which have appeared in various publications, the case of *Yale* v. *Todd,* 13 How. 51, note (Act of March 23, 1792, 1 Stat. 243), is included, on the authority of the note in *United States* v. *Ferreira* (1851), 13 How. 40, 51, 53; but such inclusion is a mistake, since the Court did not hold the statute invalid, but construed it as inapplicable; see *The Supreme Court in the United States History* (1922), I, by Charles Warren; *The American Doctrine of Judicial Supremacy* (1914), by Charles G. Haines, p. 159. In some lists, the case of *United States* v. *Ferreira* (1851), 13 How. 40, itself is included; but this also is a mistake, for the Court did not hold the Act of Congress therein concerned invalid, but only held that the Judge of the District Court had wrongly construed the Act.

A Joint Resolution of August 4, 1894 (28 Stat. 1018), was held unconstitutional in *Jones* v. *Meehan* (1899, Oct. 30), 175 U. S. 1.

For the synopses of the decisions given above, I am considerably indebted to an excellent compilation entitled "Unconstitutional Acts", prepared by Representative Charles W. Ramseyer of Iowa and appearing in the *Congressional Record, Appendix,* Feb. 11, 1925; see also *The Supreme Court of the United States and Unconstitutional Legislation,* an address by William Marshall Bullitt, May 6, 1924; and *Judicial Review of Legislation* (1923), by Robert von Moschzisker.

INDEX

ACTS OF CONGRESS, number of, held invalid, 134–136; number of, decided by vote of five to four, 183–184; bill to forbid inferior Federal Courts to hold invalid, 188, 220; affecting Labor, held invalid, 238–240; affecting Labor, held valid, 240–241; involving due process, 244; detailed list of, held invalid, 273–301.
Adair Case, 136, 216, 239, 290.
Adams, John, 7, 14, 15, 18; fears aristocracy, 72.
Adams, Samuel, 14, 15, 22; and Bill of Rights, 82, 91.
Adamson Law, 160.
Adkins v. *Children's Hospital*, 57, 63, 136, 183, 216, 240, 270, 299.
Advisory Opinions, Court refuses to give, 259.
Amendments to Constitution, 16, 33, 34, 83–85, 93–94; views of U. Tracy as to, 128; La Follette's proposed, 138–140; arguments against La Follette's, 141–177.
American Steel Foundries Case, 226, 227.
Appellate Jurisdiction, what is, 213–214.
Attainder, Bills of, 81, 151 152.

BACON, JOHN, and judicial review, 126.
Baldwin, Abraham, and judicial review, 52, 97, 103, 115, 123.
Baldwin, Judge Henry, 263, 268.
Bank of the United States, debate on charter of, 105–110; attacks on, 194, 198, 268.
Barbour, Philip P., proposes in 1829 concurrence of Judges, 219.
Bayard, James A., as to powers of Congress, 42, 156; as to 25th Section of Judiciary Act, 104; as to judicial review, 118; as to power of State Courts to hold Acts of Congress invalid, 138; as to Presidential instructions, 260.
Bayard v. *Singleton*, 45.
Bedford, Gunning, Jr., opposes judicial review, 52.
Berrien, John M., opposes power of Congress over States, 157–158.
Bill of Rights, and George Mason, 6; and Franklin, 6; and John Adams, 7; of the States, 36–37; need for, in Federal Constitution, 79–83; why essential, 86–90; enforcement of, rendered of no avail by La Follette's proposed Amendment, 142–153; violations of, by Congress, 150–152.
Blackstone, Sir William, 25.
Bland, Richard, 14.
Booth Case, 198, 199, 266.
Borah, William E., proposal to require concurrence of seven out of nine Judges, 179–217.
Boudinot, Elias, as to judicial review, 106.
Brandeis, Louis D., 230, 243.
Breckenridge, John, opposes judicial review, 125, 126.
Bryan, George, as to judicial review, 65.
Burke, Edmund, 7.

CALHOUN, JOHN C., 24; as to Madison, 93.
Carriage Tax, debate on, 113; case to test validity of, 114–115.
Charles River Bridge Case, 268.
Chase, Chief Justice Salmon P., 266.
Chase, Judge Samuel, 260.
Checks, on Power. *See* RESTRICTIONS.
Child Labor Law Cases, 136, 183, 215, 239, 244, 293, 298.
Choate v. *Trapp*, 60, 292.

304 INDEX

Clayton Act, decisions construing, affecting Labor, 223–230, 245.
Concord, resolutions of, for a Constitution, 87.
Concurrence of Judges, Borah's proposal for, 178–217; previous proposals for, in Congress, 218–230.
Congress of the Confederation, and judicial review, 48–49.
Congress, limited powers of, 3, 6; curbs on power of, 35–40, 79–85; views of early, as to judicial review, 98–127; powers of, under La Follette's proposed amendment, 139–159; violations of Bill of Rights by, 150–152; and the rights of the States, 154–159; decisions of the Court upholding powers of, 194–202; motives of, not enquired into by Court, 242–243; as a coördinate branch of government, 247–252.
Connolly Case, 216.
Constitution, meaning of the word, 12, 13; American view of, 14–16; unamendable, 16; titles of, in different States, 16; enforcement of prohibitions in, 39–43; who framed, 78; demand for Bill of Rights in, 79–82; contemporaneous views of, 98–99.
Constitution of the United States, not an invention of the Convention, 10, 12; dual system of government in, 17–21; division of powers in, 22–24; representative government in, 25; local self-government in, 25–26; Executive in, 28; Judiciary in, 28–29; copied from State Constitutions, 30–33; framers of, alive in 1803, 127; provisions of, as to Supreme Court, 208–209; coördinate powers under, 247–253. *See* ACTS OF CONGRESS; CONGRESS: SUPREME COURT; JUDICIARY.
Contempt, power of Court in cases of, 209–210, 229, 230; power of President to pardon for, 250.
Coolidge, Calvin, views of President, as to proposed change in powers of the Court, 174.
Coördinate Branches of Government, meaning of, 22–24, 247–252.

Coppage Case, 236.
Coronado Coal Co. Case, 226–228.
Corrigan Case, 237.
Cromwell, Oliver, as to need of a Constitution, 86.

Danbury Hatters Case, 224, 269.
Davie, William R., as to judicial review, 46, 51, 69; as to division of powers, 248.
Davis, Judge David, 264.
Davis, Thomas T., as to power of Judiciary, 62, 123.
Debs Case, 230–231.
Dickinson, John, as to English Constitution, 11; as to judicial review, 52.
Dollard, Patrick, and Bill of Rights, 80.
Drayton, William, as to power of Court, 41.
Dred Scott Case, 135, 216.
Due Process, 37, 60, 74, 83, 242–245.
Duplex Printing Co. Case, 225.

EIGHTEENTH AMENDMENT, 148–149, 200.
Ellsworth, Oliver, as to judicial review, 51, 69.
Employers' Liability Acts, 160, 191; of States held valid, 233.
Employers' Liability Cases, 135, 239, 289–290.
England, powers of Parliament of, 13–15; no power of judicial review in Courts of, 165–167; lack of rights of citizens of, in time of war, 168–173.
English Principles, found chiefly in the first ten Amendments, 22.
Espionage Law, 148, 270.
Executive. *See* PRESIDENT.

FEDERAL CONVENTION, 7–10; members of, favoring judicial review, 50–51; Judiciary Article in, 56–57, 61; weight of views of members of, 67; members of, alive in 1803, 127.
Federalist, The, as authority on Constitution, 64.
Fifth Amendment. *See* DUE PROCESS.
First Amendment, 84, 145, 201.

INDEX 305

Fitzsimmons, Thomas, as to judicial review, 111.
Fourteenth Amendment, 74, 242–244.
Foy Case, 173.
Franklin, Benjamin, and Bill of Rights of Pennsylvania, 6; in Federal Convention, 9, 14; fear of power of President by, 71.
Freedom of the Press, 33, 37.
Freedom of Religion, 35, 37, 83, 145.
Freedom of Speech, 84, 145, 201.
Futures Trading Act, 160.

GALLATIN, ALBERT, as to judicial review, 117, 119, 120.
Gerry, Elbridge, and judicial review, 50, 102, 103.
Gibbons v. *Ogden*, 196, 268.
Giles, William B., as to judicial review, 107, 113, 114.
Gompers, Samuel, 161.
Gompers Case, 225, 227, 233.
Gorham, Nathaniel, fears Constitution not lasting, 72–73.
Griswold, Roger, as to power of Court, 95, 124.

HAMILTON, ALEXANDER, 8, 41, 43, 64, 175, 271.
Harper, Robert G., as to judicial review, 116, 119.
Harrington, James, 13.
Hayburn Case, 108–110.
Hayne, Robert Y., as to judicial review, 75; as to supremacy of Congress, 128.
Henry, Patrick, as to judicial review, 69; and Bill of Rights, 80, 92.
Hitchman Coal Co. Case, 231–232.
Holmes, Oliver Wendell, 77, 89.
Hours of Labor Laws, of States held valid by Court, 234.
Holmes v. *Walton*, 44.
Hutchinson, Thomas, 18.
Hylton v. *United States*, 114–115.

Income Tax Case, 135, 160, 183, 240, 284–285.
Inferior Federal Courts, action of, holding Federal statutes valid, or invalid, 185–188; legislation to prevent, holding Federal statutes invalid, 188–220.
Injunctions, and right of jury trial, 146–147; decisions of Court on, in Labor cases, 224–232.
Insular Cases, 267.

JAY, JOHN, 20.
Jackson, Andrew, views of, as to power of Court, 256.
Jefferson, Thomas, 19; as to Judiciary, 30, 68; and Bill of Rights, 80; enforcement of Bill of Rights by Judiciary, 92; opposes confidence, 153; opposes consolidation, 154–155; attacks Supreme Court for upholding powers of Congress, 195–196; as to power of Court, 254–255.
Johnson, Robert M., proposes in 1823 concurrence of Judges, 218.
Johnson, Judge William, 261.
Judicial Power, differs from jurisdiction, 54–56, 214; what is inherent in, 57–58, 213, 214.
Judicial Review, and State Courts, 43–48; and Congress of the Confederation, 48–49; in Federal Convention, 50–53; in contemporary writings, 65–66; in State Conventions, 67–70; views of early Congresses as to, 95–127; first opposition to, 122–126; in foreign countries, 161–165; reason for no, in England, 165–166.
Judicial Veto, 52–54; wrong use of the term, 132, 253.
Judiciary, appointment of, 28; jurisdiction of, 29; enforcement of Bill of Rights by, 91–93; attack on, for failure to hold Acts of Congress invalid, 121, 193–199; coördinate powers of, 247–251. See ACTS OF CONGRESS; CONSTITUTION; SUPREME COURT.
Judiciary Act, 25th Section of, 104, 195.
Jurisdiction, differs from judicial power, 54–56, 213–214.
Jury, right of trial by, 33, 44–46, 47, 150, 151; requirement of unanimity of, not universal, 206–208.

306 INDEX

Kamper v. *Hawkins*, 58.
Kansas Compulsory Arbitration Case, 238, 270.
Kentucky, Bill of Rights of, 89.
King, Rufus, 19, 30.
Kittera, John W., as to judicial review, 119.

LABOR, and injunctions, 146–147; and compulsory arbitration, 147, 270; cites lack of judicial review in England, 167; cases affecting, decided by Court, 223–241.
La Follette, Robert M., as to usurpation, 96; misleading statements of, 131–134; proposed Constitutional Amendment of, 139–140, 222, 242–245.
Lansing, John, 17, 52.
Laurance, John, as to judicial review, 103, 106.
Lee, Richard Henry, and Federal Convention, 9, 14; and enforcement of Bill of Rights, 92.
Lennon, Ex parte, 224.
Letcher, Robert P., proposes in 1825 concurrence of Judges, 219.
Lincoln, Abraham, Cooper Union speech of, 96; views of, as to power of Court, 257.
Lee Case, 265–266.
Legal Tender Case, 135, 184, 191, 240, 266, 276.
Legal Tender Laws, 37, 191.
Local Self-Government, 25–26, 158–159.
Lochner Case, 236, 269.
Lowell, James Russell, as to Anglo-Saxon institutions, 10.

McCulloch v. *Maryland*, 194, 198, 268.
McCumber, Porter J., 245.
Macon, Nathaniel, as to judicial review, 120.
Madison, James, 8, 11, 17; and dual government, 20, 21; as to Judiciary, 30; explains Virginia Plan, 34; and judicial review, 50; as to *The Federalist*, 64; as to views of members of Federal Convention, 67; as to State Conventions, 68; proposes ten Amendments, 83, 92–93; and minority, 89; as to exposition of Constitution, 98, 112; as to Bank charter, 108, 110; as to division of powers, 24–25, 248.
Majority, despotism of, 90, 149.
Marbury v. *Madison*, 57, 96, 127, 274.
Marshall, John, as to judicial power, 62; as to judicial review, 70.
Martin, Luther, as to judicial review, 50, 70.
Maryland, freedom of religion and provision as to electors in, 28, 33.
Massachusetts, Constitution of, and Federal Constitution, 7, 23, 26, 28, 30–32; demand of Convention in, for Bill of Rights, 82.
Mason, George, and Bill of Rights of Virginia, 6; and dual government, 20; as to Judiciary, 30; fears of Constitution, 71; and Bill of Rights, 88.
Mercer, John F., opposes review, 52; fear of aristocracy, 72.
Metcalfe, Thomas, proposes in 1824 concurrence of Judges, 218.
Michaelson Case, 229.
Miller, Judge Samuel F., 265.
Milligan Case, 168, 252, 264.
Minimum Wage Law Case, 136, 183, 216, 240, 270, 299.
Minority, need of Bill of Rights to protect, 88; rights of, lost under La Follette's proposed Amendment, 149–150; Borah's proposal to vest power of decision in, of the Court, 170–211.
Monongahela Navigation Co. Case, 135, 240, 284.
Montesquieu, 23, 24.
Morris, Gouverneur, and final draft of Constitution, 8, 26, 45; and judicial review, 50; and Judiciary Article, 56–57; fears aristocracy, 72; as to supremacy of Congress, 175.
Munn v. *Illinois*, 269.

Nebraska German Language Case, 238, 270.
New Hampshire, judicial review in, 46.

INDEX 307

New Jersey, judicial review in, 45.
Nicholas, George, as to judicial review, 69, 126.
Nicholas, John, as to judicial review, 117, 118.
Niles, Nathaniel, as to judicial review, 111.
Noell, John W., 253.
North Dakota, Constitution of, requiring concurrence of Judges, 188-190.
Northern Securities Company Case, 268, 270.
Nullify, wrong expression, 62, 253; double use of the word, 132.

OATH, taken by Justices of the United States Supreme Court, 222.
Oceana, 13.
Ohio, Constitution of, requiring concurrence of Judges, 186, 192.
Oregon Private School Law Case, 238.
Otis, James, 14, 15.

Paine Lumber Co. Case, 232.
Pennsylvania, Bill of Rights of, 6; Legislature of, and jury trial, 44; judicial review in, 48; free speech in, 85.
Pinckney, Charles, 8, 19, 21, 26; as to Judiciary, 30, 39; fear of weakness of President, 71; as to Amendments to Constitution, 94; opposes judicial review, 96, 122, 123, 127.
Pittsfield, resolutions of, for a Constitution, 88.
Pope, John, on judicial review, 59-60.
President, popular election of, 28; powers of, 28, 32, 33; fear of powers of, 39-40; as a coördinate branch of government, 247-252; actions of, held void by Court, 251-266.
Presumption of validity of Acts of Congress, 132-133, 203, 242-243.
Prohibitions, in Federal Constitution, 34-36; enforcement of, 37-42; need of, as a balance, 249. *See also* BILL OF RIGHTS; CONGRESS.

QUORUM, power of Congress to fix, of Judges, 210, 213, 214, 220.

RADICALS, need of, 76; and free speech, 84; assaults on Constitution by, 85; right of, to attack Constitution, 130.
Raich Case, 237.
Ralston, Jackson H., 48, 247.
Randolph, Edmund, 8, 34, 71, 72.
Randolph, John, as to Bill of Rights, 75.
Reasonable Doubt, not created by mere difference of opinion among Judges, 204-206.
Removal, debate on power of, 99-103.
Representative Government, 25.
Restrictions on Congress, 34-36, 37-42, 249; on the President, 249-250; on the Court, 250.
Retail Lumber Dealers' Case, 229.
Rhode Island, judicial review in, 44.
Roane, Spencer, on judicial review, 57-58; as to need of a Constitution, 86-87.
Robinson, Ex parte, 209.
Rowan, John, as to power of Judiciary, 62, 195; proposes in 1826 concurrence of Judges, 219.
Rutledge, John, Jr., as to power of Court, 124.

SEARCH AND SEIZURE, 83, 146, 150, 171, 258.
Sedition Act, debate on, 118-121.
Separation of Powers of Government, 22-24, 247-250.
Sherman, Roger, 26, 27.
Sherman Act, decisions construing, affecting Labor, 223-230.
Slaughterhouse Cases, 267, 269.
Smith, William, as to power of Court, 43, 101, 107, 115.
Smith Case, 236.
South Carolina v. United States, 202.
Spaight, Richard D., opposes judicial review, 46, 52.
Stamp Tax Act of 1864, 137, 191.
States, effect of La Follette's proposed Amendment on powers of, 154-159; statutes of, affecting Labor held constitutional, 233-236; statutes of, involving due process, 242-245.
State Constitutions, and Federal Constitution, 23, 24, 30-33.

INDEX

State Conventions, opinions of members of, as to judicial review, 67–70.
State Courts, and judicial review, 43–48; holding Acts of Congress invalid, 136–138, 191–192; decisions of, as to inherent judicial powers, 211–213.
State Legislatures, curbs on, 35–38; fear of power of, 37–39, 43; violate jury trial, 44–46; and Bill of Rights, 79, 81, 82, 89.
Stock Dividend Case, 136, 183, 216, 240, 294.
Story, Judge Joseph, 261–263.
Sutherland, George, and protection of minority, 89.
Supreme Court of the United States, method of appointment of, 28; jurisdiction of, 29; judicial power of, 54–56; power of judicial review of, 57–70; has operated as intended, 70–72; misleading statements as to decisions of, 131–134; number of Acts of Congress held invalid by, 134–136; La Follette's proposal to curb power of, 139–177; Borah's proposal to require concurrence of seven out of nine Judges of, 178–217; inherent judicial power of, 205–215; decisions of, affecting Labor, 222–241; decisions of, holding President's actions void, 251, 266; independence of, 257–272.
Sylvester, Peter, as to judicial review, 103.

TAFT, CHIEF JUSTICE WILLIAM H., 250, 267.
Tannen Case, 237.
Trevett v. *Weeden*, 44.

USURPATION BY COURT, untrue, 96.

VAN BUREN, MARTIN, proposes in 1824 concurrence of Judges, 218.
Veto. *See* JUDICIAL VETO.
Virginia, Bill of Rights of, 6, 23, 248; judicial review in, 45, 47; demand of its Convention, 82.
Volstead Law, 147, 193, 200.

WASHINGTON, GEORGE, and Federal Convention, 9
Webster, Daniel, on the court, 4; as to Madison, 93.
Webster, Noah, 19, 21.
Webster, Pelatiah, 19, 21.
West River Bridge v. *Dix*, 269.
White, Alexander, as to judicial review, 102.
Wickliffe, Charles A., proposes in 1827 concurrence of Judges, 219, 220.
Williams, Thomas, proposes in 1868 concurrence of Judges, 220.
Williamson, Hugh, and judicial review, 50; fear of President's power, 71.
Wilson, James, 14, 50; and judicial veto, 53; as to judicial review, 69–70; fears weakness of President, 71.
Wilson, James F., proposes in 1868 concurrence of Judges, 188, 220.
Women's Employment Laws, of States held valid by Court, 234.
Workmen's Compensation in Admiralty Case, 135, 183, 240, 294–295, 300.
Workmen's Compensation Laws, of States held valid by Court, 233–234.
Wyoming, Bill of Rights of, 89.
Wythe, George, compiles Bill of Rights, 83.

YATES, ROBERT, and judicial review, 52, 65.

Zadig Case, 168–170.